Obama's Odyssey

Obama's Odyssey

The 2008 Race for the White House

by Connie Corcoran Wilson

2015

Obama's Odyssey: The 2008 Race for the White House

© 2015 Connie Corcoran Wilson

Quad City Press

Layout and design by John Teehan

Published in the USA

ISBN—978-0-69252-738-2

Table of Contents

Introduction

I **FOLLOWED THE 2004,** 2008 and 2012 presidential election(s) with press passes. In 2004, the year of Howard Dean's early "Sleepless Summer" surge, I wrote for a blog called "Blog for Iowa" (www.blogforIowa. com). Those articles are still up. They were largely partisan articles from a Deaniac trying to help "take our country back." Howard had not (yet) let out the blood-curdling, campaign-ending "Scream Heard 'Round the World" at the Val-Air Ballroom in West Des Moines, but I was there when he did that, too.

This all began because I was bored in retirement and the Iowa caucuses are right across the I-74 bridge in Iowa—roughly 2 miles away.

At the time, I was also teaching classes at Eastern Iowa Community College. I offered my students the opportunity to score extra "points" for

With then-candidate Howard Dean at Davenport North High School in 2004.

1

attending any political rally by any candidate of any party (*as long as they provided proof of their attendance*). This was in the hope that they would become part of the political process in our democracy, which is dependent on voters believing that they *CAN* make a difference. (*Most of my students expressed the opinion that they wouldn't have any impact on who won, anyway, and were, therefore, indifferent and woefully uninformed about what policies each candidate or party represented.*)

In 2008 and 2012, I covered the conventions for Yahoo, starting with the Iowa caucuses and ending up inside the DNC convention in Denver, the RNC convention in St. Paul, Minnesota at the Excel Center, the Ron Paul Rally for the Republic at the Target Center in Minneapolis, the Belmont Town Hall meeting in Nashville, Tennessee, and Rudy Giuliani's odd campaign in Florida.

My 1,000 articles for Yahoo were "hit" some 3 million times and I was named the Yahoo Content Producer of the Year for Politics. I stuck with the campaign from the beginning in Iowa right up to and through the Inauguration. I even "live blogged" from outside Grant Park in Chicago on November 8, 2008 (*which is near my Chicago "Writer's Lair" condo*)

Fred Thompson at the Thunder Bay Grill in Davenport, Iowa. Horrified onlookers
appear alarmed that a giant fish might attack Fred at any moment. Perhaps the trout is
a dissatisfied reverse mortgage user.

Blue Mustang convertible with GPS. I lost it one night and had to hire a young man from Wisconsin pulling a rickshaw to drive me around for hours. When I asked him how much I owed him, he said, "I don't know, Lady. Usually, I charge by the block, but we've been driving around the same block for hours!"

the night that Obama came out to acknowledge victory in the last of the primary states. (*Somewhere on YouTube there is a very grainy video of the people lined up to enter the park.*)

Meanwhile, I had fun.

The piece I did about Fred Thompson, where I got a picture that looked like a giant trout was about to eat Fred's head was pretty unique.

Attending the Ron Paul Rally for the Republic in Minneapolis, Minnesota with the Libertarians was definitely different. Denver, St. Paul and Nashville were the experience(s) of a lifetime.

Even more remarkable is the fact that I was a retired 63-year-old English teacher (*with Journalism credentials*) hiking 15 miles a day to get anywhere, despite having rented a blue Mustang convertible with GPS (*which I kept losing, because there was nowhere to park it.*) I still remember saying to my then-editor, when he called to ask if I would fly to Denver to cover the DNC, "Heck! I'd pay YOU for that opportunity!"

However, I also noted that he'd have to find me some place less pricey than $500 a night to stay, and that meant rooming with some 20-something staffers and sleeping on an air mattress.

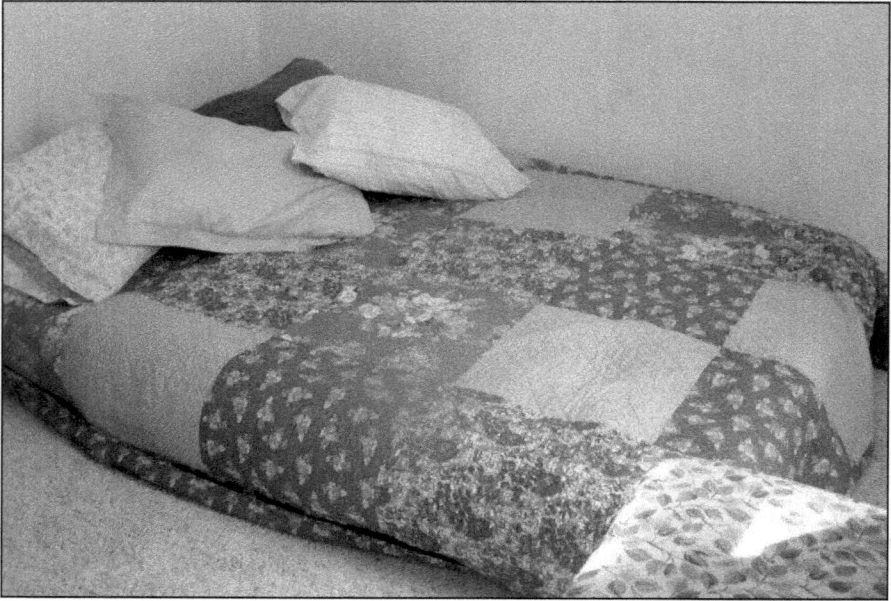

Air Mattress in Denver upstairs bedroom of house of Yahoo writers.

When I attended the Ron Paul Rally for the Republic at the Target Center in Minneapolis, onstage was Jessie Ventura ("My governor can beat up your governor."). Jessie was talking about running for president in 2012. Tucker Carlson was up there, too, wearing his trademark bow tie.

Ron Paul was onstage, looking really old. And Barry Goldwater, Jr., who is a doppelganger for his famous right-wing father…took me back to the days of "In your heart you know he's right—far right." The Ron Paul Rally for the Republic (*$17 a head if you weren't press*) was truly a surreal experience. Did I mention I was surrounded by Germans (*for reasons I have never understood?*)

The Germans around me kept trying to explain Libertarianism to me in heavily accented English, while Ron Paul lobbied for the legalization of hemp and a return to the gold standard. An interesting assignment, which I undertook primarily because my WeeklyWilson.com blog expert, Phil Bennett, told me I had to go to it or he wouldn't help me sort out my problems with posting pictures to my blog.

I noticed that MANY attendees sported badges marking them as participants in the REAL Republican National Convention that was going on across town in St. Paul at the Excel Center. When I asked them why they were here, in Minneapolis, instead of inside the auditorium where

Ron Paul speaking at the Ron Paul Rally for the Republic ($17 a head),
while a young staffer in the background examines his I-phone.

At the Press Table at the Ron Paul Rally for the Republic, Target Center,
Minneapolis, Minnesota.

John McCain was being nominated (*a largely old and white audience*), each one replied, "This is where the REAL action is." In retrospect, I think they were right. Most of them went on to become the Tea Party we now see within the Republican party ranks. I have to admit I was treated royally at the Ron Paul Rally for the Republic (*better than I was within the civic center in St. Paul, where you were given a one-hour hall pass and had to leave the Excel Center after that hour was up*).

Following Rudy Giuiliani around in Florida while he stood on a box and handed out autographed baseballs, (*which seemed to be his entire campaign strategy since he never left Florida*) was another odd moment in my campaign travels.

On my way into a John Edwards rally at the Putnam Museum in Davenport, Iowa, I slipped on the ice and literally slid under his bus. When I got inside the Putnam Museum, I posed with Edwards and said, "Act like you're having fun." (*Who knew then that he already WAS having fun?*) One thing that struck me about the Edwards rally versus the Obama rally I had just left was the much larger turnout of young people at Obama's rally at the Davenport River Center. I also usually count the number of TV tripods to see which candidate is pulling the most television coverage, an old habit that is predictive.

With John Edwards inside the Putnam Museum in Davenport, IA, in 2008.

That night, I covered Hillary, Obama and Edwards, all in Davenport, Iowa, at the same time but appearing in different places. [*Very hard to get to 3 places simultaneously, but, somehow, I managed to make it to the Davenport River Center (Obama), the Figge Art Museum (Hillary) and the Putnam (Edwards).*] Except for slipping on the ice and falling under the bus, it went well. [*Later, Edwards himself fell under his own bus, metaphorically speaking*].

I had a wonderful time in Denver and St. Paul and elsewhere. These on-the-spot pieces represent a picture of that historic run for the White House that should not be totally lost. In July of 2014 Yahoo decided to dissolve the Content Contributors' Network entirely and go entirely to film coverage with names like Katie Couric. Our articles would not be left up on the Internet. We had 2 weeks to get them down.

I hired 3 people and spent those 2 weeks downloading the articles that Yahoo profited from initially, but now felt were not worth maintaining on Internet browsers—historic articles detailing what it was like to be present, in person, during much of the campaign. It was a once-in-a-lifetime campaign, featuring the first successful run of an African American presidential candidate and the first time a female candidate was seriously considered for the top spot on the ticket of a major party. Picking the nominee didn't end with the primaries; it went right through the Democratic National Convention, making it a very exciting race (*unlike the 2012 coronation*).

Towards the end of the caucus season, I predicted, in writing, that Obama would carry Iowa. Some readers and fellow writers on Yahoo told me they'd come back and make me eat those words. They couldn't believe that an upstart young senator from Illinois could beat the Clinton machine. But people liked Obama. They didn't like Hillary as much. (*Or, in some cases, at all.*)

I had been doing my homework. And attending rally after rally while traveling around the state and the nation. I was paying attention.

Obama was on a roll; he was arguably the most charismatic candidate to run for President since Bill Clinton or John Fitzgerald Kennedy. History was being made, folks, as the first African American and the first woman went head-to-head. I think you might enjoy hearing all about it from an average citizen who was *really* involved and in attendance. [*What a thrill to hear Ted Kennedy's last major speech at the Democratic National Convention, or to hear James Leach (R, IA) endorse the Democratic candidate there*).

So, here they are: my articles, salvaged when Yahoo threw all their money at Katie Couric for film coverage instead of analytical reporting from Old School reporters.

Katie Couric, in a "Time" April 6th, 2015, Q&A said, in response to "What makes a good anchor?" "Someone who's experienced and who has credibility...It's a very hard balance, because there are stories that warrant the anchor being there, but you also have to be cognizant that it not be as window dressing. You have reporters out there, day in and day out, covering a story, and then you have an anchor parachute in. You hope whoever that anchor is brings something to the table."

Yes, you do indeed.

I can tell Ms. Couric what she TOOK from the table. That would be the writing jobs of literally thousands of experienced journalists like me (*59 years of writing for pay, 5 newspapers, Ferner/Hearst Journalism Scholarship recipient at the University of Iowa*). When Yahoo decided to dumb down their offerings because the American public would rather watch a video clip with a sound bite than actually read a well-researched, well-written article from thousands of reporters with credentials as good as Ms. Couric's, (reporters who were actually already "in the field" so she wouldn't need to "parachute in" at all), they did not leave our articles up on Internet servers.

If you were Googling the 2008 campaign (*or, if you're Yahoo, Bing-ing the 2008 campaign*) the many great on-the-spot articles from all of us, all over the country, written by the reporters in the Content Contributors' Network could have remained available to the general public. But they were taken down, as it might have cost a small amount to maintain the servers to keep them up.

Because I feel that the articles we wrote represent a slice of history-in-the-making, I'm putting mine in this book (or books). I reported as objectively as I could on the event(s) at hand. But I also had—as my former Editor Bill Wundram used to say—"a nose for news." I tried to find the absurd and amusing anecdote(s) to share with my readers, whether it was a photo or an observation. For purposes of this book, I've added some parenthetical "notes" in italics, reflecting the hindsight of the 8 years of President Obama's two terms.

The night I attended a rally at the Davenport River Center at which Rudy Giuliani spoke, I paid careful attention to the musical selections filling the hall. (Elvis' "A Little Less Conversation" seemed somehow inappropriate for the Republican uber-religious evangelical base.)

One of my favorite funny stories involved the reporter for a London newspaper who was present that night. When I asked what he'd be doing next, he answered with the one word: "Lacrosse."

At that time, our local civic center was sponsoring a lacrosse exhibition, for some strange reason. Therefore, I wrote a piece on my blog about how confused this young man from the UK was going to be about life in the Midwest, when nobody here *really* plays lacrosse all that much.

The next day, I printed a retraction, after the young reporter wrote me and said, "I meant Lacrosse, Wisconsin."

Oh.

I hope the scholars among you find these articles valuable. I hope those with a sense of humor find them enjoyable. I always attended any rally attempting to soak up the flavor of the event and let readers who were far, far away know what the mood in the room and the country was really like. Television networks with agendas ("fair and balanced, my foot") aren't very objective in today's journalistic landscape, so I tried to tell readers what was really going on.

And I always tried to have fun while doing it. (*Otherwise, why bother?*) I don't know many sixty-something retired English teachers (*with journalism credentials*) who would have enjoyed doing this, but I did.

I do thank Yahoo for that opportunity and for the 7 years of writing that preceded it, even if the dissolution of an entire army of seasoned veteran reporters dumped, unceremoniously, so Katie Couric could make comments like this *Time* quote seems unfair: "But right now I'm really excited about the work I'm doing at Yahoo. It's wonderful to feel entrepreneurial…It's great to be part of a place that's expanding optimistically instead of managing decline."

Wellllllll.

Those of us in the Content Contributor Network who gave our best efforts reporting on events all over this great land did not (*and do not*) appreciate having our hard work for 7 to 10 years erased in a heartbeat. Most think that Yahoo would have benefited from keeping us. Or, at the very least, keeping the articles that we wrote for them up and available on the Internet. But that didn't happen.

Here's what I wrote on the final night of the Battle Royal of primaries, with Obama emerging victorious and me blogging "live" all night for Yahoo (*along with other Content Contributors nationwide*) from Grant Park:

DAY AFTER THE PRIMARY SEASON THOUGHTS

(*DNC in Denver & RNC in St. Paul to follow in Volume II of "Obama's Odyssey")

On this "day-after-the-election" (primary season) I wanted to share with you, my readers, some of my thoughts and feelings about the historic journey we have all witnessed, and explain my fascination with the cause.

I began covering the candidates who appeared at the Iowa caucuses the year that (Dr.) Howard Dean ran for president. My long-dormant political passion was ignited when I drifted across the street from teaching classes at the Kahl Building in downtown Davenport, Iowa for Eastern Iowa Community College, and wandered into the downtown Dean headquarters. We were urged to stay and share our thoughts and feelings about the state of America.

Initially, I became completely disillusioned by the assassination of JFK when I was a freshman in college. I was "apolitical" for all those intervening 40 years.

I became hugely disillusioned a second time in the wake of the 2000 election that saw "hanging chads" in Florida and the Supreme Court select George W. Bush as our 43rd president. I found it incomprehensible that one man's brother *(then-Governor Jeb Bush of Florida, who is actually running for president in 2016)* could hand the most important office in our land to someone totally unprepared. The process was broken. I felt betrayed.

I have felt that only once before…when a 1st Ward Alderman race I had labored long and hard in turned out to be rigged. It was proven to have had officials at the top playing fast-and-loose with absentee ballots, but nothing…not one word…was written in the local newspaper, despite the presence of a reporter from same *(Jenny Lee of the Moline, Illinois, Daily Dispatch)*. The recount showed the popular vote announced in the paper the morning after the election was wrong. Things went downhill from there.

It is one thing for candidates to cheat and get caught. That happens every day. My point: where is the retribution? Where is the "gotcha'" moment that restores the true, natural order of the universe? It seemed that the sense of decency and honesty in the election process that I had watched my father maintain in his races for Democratic County Treasurer of Buchanan County (IA) back in the fifties had evaporated, and in its place was corruption at the very heart of the political process…even in small-town America.

If counties like Rock Island County, Illinois, were as dirty as Cook County in Chicago, what was the world coming to? And if proving it, in court, didn't bring at least a slap on the wrist for the perpetrators, could our national election process be far behind in granting complete immunity to those who would steal our democracy from us?

I live in a divided household, an Arnold Schwarzenegger/Maria Shriver split (*Note: now REALLY split, in their case*), with no one but me weighing in as a Democrat or...at times...as an Independent. When one family member admits to glee at hearing that JFK had been shot, the feeling of complete alienation from what is right and what is good becomes pervasive. I have never wished death on a candidate, no matter how corrupt or evil I might perceive that candidate to be. I have the same horror for that kind of thinking as I do for not trying (*at least*) to see the other person's point of view.

Many times, my life partner would tell me that, in expressing my support for a candidate that (*apparently*) did not prove congruent with his own choices, I was or had been "obnoxious." This meant that I had spoken my mind about the lack of preparedness or the general quality of the candidate. I had found the candidate wanting and not kept that information to myself, which he would have preferred. And, no, it was not always a Republican. (*Rod Blagojevich, anyone?*)

At the same time I was accused of being blind to the merits of those of a different political stripe, I hosted a wine-and-cheese party in Rock Island for a Republican neighbor (*Ray LaHood, last representing Peoria and later serving under Obama as Secretary of Transportation*) and contributed to more than one Republican candidate (*Andrea Zinga, Dave Machacek*) so, was I really the blind straight-party voting ticket person that my spouse accused me of being during various discussions that generated more heat than light?

No. I was someone who would weigh the candidates and try my best to select the individual who could best lead our country in troubled times.

No times are more troubled than now. The economy is spiraling downward. We are fighting on two fronts. Our esteem abroad seems irreparably shattered by a pre-emptive war that should never have been started, begun by a man who wanted to show dear old dad that he could do it better. History will judge if junior did a better job or a worse job than his father. As for me, in my semi-retirement, determined to write as I had always planned to do, I became overtly political for the first time in half a century.

Oh, we still observed the political sticker moratorium, after the years of a Republican bumper sticker being applied over a Democratic bumper sticker on the family automobiles, but I was not content to sit idly by and watch my country go down the tubes in the wake of George W. Bush. I became convinced that electing a president in 2008 who was determined to "win at any cost" and a running mate with little or no foreign policy experience and some very esoteric views about the rest of the world, science, and religion spelled certain doom for what remained of this once-great nation. The choice(s) were clear.

And I also decided that the best way for me to contribute to the victory of one *(of many excellent Democratic candidates: Obama, Clinton, Richardson, Edwards, et. al.)* as opposed to the reactionary forces of the Republicans arrayed against them was to throw off the cloak of meek-and-mild indifference and DO SOMETHING. Anything. Even if it was the wrong something, it would be better than another "W" in the White House.

After all, what more could the man ruin? Do we really want to find out if an equally incompetent successor can finish us off totally as a nation?

It was this decision, made during a previous election run in 2004, that led me to "blog for Iowa" (www.blogforiowa), which, no doubt, earned me a place on George W. Bush's enemies list. I took popular song lyrics and turned them into political gems aimed at exposing the Man Who Would be King. With humor, I aimed barbs at "the Decider," reported on Abu Ghraib and all things horrible similar to it. My journey had begun. It would not end until November 4, 2008, in Grant Park in Chicago. And, even then, I would travel beyond the primary season to other political venues (DNC, RNC, etc.) to report for regular readers like me what was really happening.

Through the bitter cold of Iowa's winter, I tracked caucus candidates like Joe Biden and Christopher Dodd and Hillary Clinton and John Edwards and Barack Obama to school gymnasiums and people's living rooms. I listened to their message(s) of change and hope. I contributed cash, but, more importantly, I contributed time and effort, attempting to let others know what I was able to observe, up-close-and-personal. Yes, some of those candidates turned out to have feet of clay (*Edwards, anyone?),* but the eventual winner of this marathon race seems like the right man for the job at the right time in history.

The palpable enthusiasm at last night's gathering was like a city celebrating a World Series or a Super Bowl victory. Just a few moments ago, sitting in my 7th floor condo on Indiana Avenue near Hutchinson Field, a red balloon, no doubt left over from last night's celebration, drifted past my balcony door.

Today, though I am tired, I feel that, somehow, we, as a nation are back on the right track. It is a given that other nations will see Barack Obama as a worthy representative of this nation's highest ideals. After years of a stumbling, incoherent leader who not only could not speak well, but could not lead well, we will have a well-qualified, well-educated, hard-working man who seems to genuinely love his family and his country in ways that do not deliver death and destruction to the rest of the world.

I pray for Barack Obama on this day-after-the-election. I revel in the knowledge that I was "there," inside, at the Pepsi Center in Denver, at the Excel Center in St. Paul, at the Target Center for the Ron Paul Rally in Minneapolis, at the Iowa caucuses, at the Belmont Town Hall Meeting in Nashville, Tennessee, and, last night, in Grant Park where Barack Obama started this nation on a brand new journey that I hope will restore this country's honor and reputation, both abroad and at home.

"Fasten your seatbelts, it's going to be a bumpy ride!"

Picking Obama Over Hillary

Huckaboom or Huckabust?
Republican Debate in Iowa's Heartland

Dec 13, 2007

In what one commentator (Britt Hume of Fox News) pronounced, "One of the weirdest debates I've ever seen," the Iowa Republican Debate from Johnston, Iowa's Maytag Auditorium on Wednesday, December 12th at 1:00 p.m. CDT often was as icy as the weather outside.

Fred Thompson's refusal to raise his hand for moderator Caroline Washburn, (Editor of the sponsoring *Des Moines Register*) to vote "yes" or "no" on the question, "Is global climate change a serious threat?" will be the YouTube News Clip of the Day. The other candidates and the audience onstage applauded Thompson's act of rebellion against the school ma'arm ways of Ms. Washburn, the moderator.

Audience members polled by Fox News after the debate, when asked to give a one-word description of Ms. Washburn's performance as moderator, called her "rigid," "boring" and "inflexible." One on-air commentator compared her to the teacher in the comic strip "Peanuts." The result of the restrictions imposed by Ms. Washburn? A boring debate with nothing new from any of the candidates. No real engagement between candidates was allowed by the Washburn Rules of Engagement and the moderator intentionally chose questions that would primarily be of local interest (eg., Ethanol over Iraq).

Front-runner Huckabee came out of the debate somewhat bloodied but unbowed. In a ten-minute solo segment on Fox following the debate, (which gives some credibility to Thompson's recent claims that Fox is being unfair in not apportioning equal time to the candidates), Mike Huckabee said, "I was glad to come out of it (the debate) with all the blood left in my body."

Aside from the "raise-your-hand-to-vote" fiasco that elicited Thompson's "I'm not doin' a show of hands today" retort, Allan Keyes seemed the most aggravated participant. Keyes was one of Reagan's National Security team and Ambassador to the United Nations Economic and Social Council. He was peeved by the moderator's attempt to move on and ask a question of Ron Paul, rather than allowing him to comment on an education question. Ms. Washburn eventually conceded to Keyes demands, saying that Keyes could have 30 seconds for his follow-up. Keyes retort? "They had a minute (to comment). Why do I only get thirty seconds?" Thompson, as well, railed at the restrictions that kept candidates from any real debate, saying to Washburn after the "Not-Gonna'-Raise-My-Hand" comment, "Do you want to give me a minute to answer that?" (Answer: no). It all played out like a Bad Day in the One-room Schoolhouse. (Any minute you expected to hear, "No recess for any of you today!").

The big winner of the debate, according to Iowans in the audience was Romney, who struck those present as better-prepared and more fact-based. The winner of the debate according to Fox News official commentators Fred Baines of "The Weekly Standard" and Nina Easton of "Fortune" magazine was former Arkansas Governor Mike Huckabee. A divide between Iowa and the rest of the nation on who won or *if* anyone won seems a fair statement.

The twenty-eight Republican Iowa caucus-goers hooked up to a device to measure their response(s), question-by-question, weighed in. This cross-section of moderate and conservative Republican voters felt Romney carried the day, citing more facts and figures and appearing Presidential and "electable", while Huckabee quoted platitudes and Bible verses, attempting to carry the day with his quick wit while striving to remain in first place in Iowa. According to the latest polls, Huckabee, entering the debate, was at 32.4% in Iowa to Romney's 22% with 22 days until the caucuses on January 3rd in Iowa. Since Romney has spent $5 million on television spots in Iowa, including the first negative attack ad against Huckabee, while Huckabee has only fourteen workers on the ground, the man from Hope, Arkansas reminds many of Howard Dean in 2004 at this point in the race: outfront and targeted by everyone. (*Note: Bill Clinton was the first presidential candidate from the small town of Hope, Arkansas, preceding Huckabee.*)

Of the 13 Giuiliani supporters (out of 28) who entered the room, only 3 remained firm in their commitment to the former New York Mayor after his onstage response(s). However, Romney picked up traction for his command of facts and figures, as well as his "Thank you to the people of Iowa," and his statement that he had visited 67 Iowa counties, while his son Josh has visited all 99. (Ninety-two family members helped work the straw poll on the ground in Ames, which Romney won.)

Another humorous moment occurred when, after some debate on taxes and who is most burdened by them, former Senator Fred Thompson said that he would like to become a member of Mitt Romney's tax bracket, drawing laughter from all. Duncan Hunter...another candidate that no one knew...also earned a chuckle when he asked, "Could you repeat the question? I was lost in Governor Romney's answer, which I thought was quite good." Attempts to attack Romney on the issue of Bain Capital, which he established in 1984, were largely deflected and did not damage him.

Giuiliani was asked a question about the spending records that have recently resurfaced, expenses incurred while in office for security and transportation to escort him to destinations such as the Hamptons while he was courting his current wife. Giuilani's defense: "Everyone knew exactly what I did almost the minute I did it. I can't think of a public figure who has had a more transparent life than I have."

One big surprise was that Allan Keyes was onstage as a Republican Presidential candidate at all, especially since the *Des Moines Register* (which establishes the criteria for invitation and co-sponsored the debate with Iowa Public Television) excluded Dennis Kucinich from the upcoming Democratic debate. Keyes came across as strident and angry. He suggested, regarding global warming, that one way to solve the problem might be to cut down on the hot air of politicians who don't deliver on their promises. (When asked to comment, Fred Thompson said, with a chuckle, "I agree with Ambassador Keyes' position on global warming.") At the very end of the debate, the moderator asked each candidate to make a New Year's Resolution *for someone else* onstage. Huckabee said, "I would vow to be a lot more careful in what I say." The moderator repeated that the resolution was to be *for someone else* onstage, which caused the quick-witted Huckabee to respond, "I'd like to make that resolution for them, too."

(*Huckabee would ultimately carry Iowa's caucuses as the Republican winner, primarily because McCain did not campaign in the state, but it would be John McCain who would win the Republican nomination to run against the Democratic candidate—yet to be chosen when these pages were written)*

Fred Thompson Trots Towards White House

Dec 10, 2007

A small but attentive group of about 120 Republican faithful listened to Fred Thompson, (*better known from television's "Law and Order" series and a variety of movie roles*), praise federalism and right-to-lifers ("When we stray, we pay.")

In his opening remarks at the Thunder Bay Grille in Davenport, Iowa, at 2:30 p.m. on Friday afternoon, December 7th (Pearl Harbor Day), Thompson identified liberal judges as a clear and present danger, saying, "You don't have to tell me the good kind of judges from the bad ones. I can tell the liberal judges from the conservative judges." Apparently, a "liberal" judge, to candidate Thompson, is synonymous with a "bad" judge, although progress very often comes only from those who tend to rock the boat, and who are (sometimes) liberals.

Regarding the endorsement of his campaign by the Pro-lifers, he commented, "I'm very proud of that fact." A woman stood nearby passing out flyers for the anti-abortion cause.

Regarding the war in Iraq, familiar often-heard phrases like "turning the corner" and "I think it's going to be successful" were used, as well as much talk about "being on the right track." To this reporter all were very reminiscent of a 2004 Davenport rally, at which Cheney, Bush and Rudy Giuliani appeared and pronounced the U.S. to be "on the right track" in Iraq. Going further back, it reminded of Secretary of Defense Robert McNamara's "light at the end of the tunnel" pronouncements during the Vietnam War.

Thompson, in his folksy Tennessee drawl, declared that Iraq is "Nothin' that we can't handle and nothin' that we haven't done before.

People have always rallied and done the right thing." (How, exactly, he would "do the right thing" in Iraq Thompson did not say.)

Another point in Thompson's presentation to the potential January 3rd Iowa caucus goers focused on illegal immigration and the need to secure our borders. "A nation that does not secure its borders is asking for trouble. We must secure out borders." Does he favor the fence? Didn't say. (*The fence proposed by some Republican lawmakers would definitely cut down on fishing in the waters that separate this country from Mexico.*)

Thompson also articulated the idea that "we must quit spending our children's birthright," and commented that "we can't tax our way out of it; it'll shut the economy down." He pronounced Social Security and Medicare to be in imminent danger (*although a recent poll showed that the estimated date at which Social Security will not be able to pay out full amounts is 2041.*) He also shared the information that Tennessee has no state income tax; the connection to the Iowa caucus-goers was not clear.

By far the biggest cheer of the night came when an audience member erupted in response to Thompson's comment, "Who do we want to have sitting on our side of the table during international negotiations?" The bystander shouted, "Not Hillary!" Thompson said, "I think that's a very good place to leave it right there" and then fielded questions from the audience. (**Note: Interesting that Hillary Clinton has since this rally served a full term as a successful Secretary of State, sitting on our side of the table during international negotiations.*)

Thompson took the first question from a man in a cowboy hat, because, he said, "Everybody in Nashville wears a hat like that." Although Thompson offered few, if any, specifics of what he would do if elected President, and seemed mainly to agree with his questioners ("You're exactly right," he responded to the cowboy of the first question) he was affable and the crowd was kind in return.

Some have faulted Thompson for not being hard-working while holding elected office, with little or no legislation sponsored. Critics say he isn't so much "running" for the White House as he is "ambling" towards it. Thompson used phrases and concepts about how important it is to safeguard our children's security and praised communication, saying, "Do it often. Do it truthfully. Do it with some credibility."

It was not clear if his comments about communication were a slap-in-the-face for the incumbent team of Bush and Cheney, which has been less than truthful and, as a result, are now considered by many to be less than credible. The way the homespun Thompson put it, "I'm trying to establish myself as someone who tells the truth. We don't want to go into the woods looking for the b'ar (bear), but sometimes the bear visits you." Thompson made this comment while a huge fish directly behind his head seemed ready to impale him.

Mrs. Thompson, traveling with the candidate, a very pretty and slim blonde in a beret, was most gracious. I came away from the rally feeling that the entire campaign is, indeed, very low-key, and that Thompson might, indeed, enjoy fishing for the tremendous trout behind his head, as much as trying to stomp out the liberal judges he claims are the root of all evil and the source of all the nation's woes.

Democratic Candidates Debate in Iowa as Caucus Day Nears

Dec 14, 2007

The Democratic candidates, in a debate from Des Moines on Thursday, December 13th, broadcast by Iowa Public Television and sponsored by the Des Moines, Iowa *Des Moines Register* newspaper gave *Register* Editor Carolyn Washburn an easier time than the previous day's Republican participants. While the Republican candidates refused Washburn a "show of hands" vote on global warming, Hillary Clinton offered, unbidden, a show of hands from all onstage (on the global warming issue), eliciting a chuckle from the moderator. Ms. Washburn seemed more at ease and looser than in the previous day's widely criticized appearance questioning the Republican candidates.

The positions that the Democratic candidates took, (while in stark contrast to those articulated by the Republican candidates), were seldom that divergent, and the debate was not contentious.

A CNN poll after the debate aired showed that 39% of potential caucus goers present said that, if they had to vote today, they would vote for Edwards. Surprisingly and somewhat contrarily, they also said that Obama had "won" the debate. Obama trailed Edwards with 26% and Hillary was third with 23% in these very recent CNN standings, coming a mere three weeks before caucus night.

One thing is for sure: the caucus race is far from over. It will be a horse race to the wire. As Christopher Dodd characterized the debate, "Iowans make up their own minds and that's a good thing for America." Candidate Joe Biden (Delaware) added, "People in Iowa take it seriously, and they always treat you with respect." Hillary Clinton, thanking Iowans,

Candidate Christopher Dodd and me in Davenport, Iowa.

said, "I will never forget the people of Iowa." Long-shot Bill Richardson of New Mexico mentioned the fact that Iowans "like the underdogs. You're tough. You're knowledgeable."

This veritable love-fest of the six candidates left standing (*Dennis Kucinich, surprisingly, was not invited*) was held at 1:00 p.m. CDT Thursday afternoon. It revealed no new schism amongst the contending candidates. Indeed, some spent time atoning for their remarks, apologizing to each other, or, as in the case of Joe Biden, being defended by the very candidate Biden was accused of inadvertently defaming earlier (with an off-the-cuff remark that Obama was "clean and articulate.")

Obama shrugged off the premise of the question lobbed at Biden by Washburn ("Are you uncomfortable talking about race, or are people just too sensitive?"), which implied that Biden had defamed a variety of ethnic groups with insensitive remarks, saying of Biden, "Joe is on the right side of the issues, in his heart."

The breaking news that Clinton's national co-chairman, Bill Shaheen, a prominent New Hampshire political figure, has resigned in the wake of an interview with the *Washington Post* after suggesting that Obama's teenaged drug experimentation (detailed in Obama's own biography) might pose an electability issue, left Hillary apologizing for this tactic to Obama on the tarmac of Washington's Reagan Airport, as both headed to the debate site in Iowa. (Shaheen's wife, Jeanne, is a former New Hampshire Governor who is running for the United States Senate next year).

All the candidates did well in the debate, from the perspective of seeming well-informed, articulate and sounding "Presidential." Biden, in a one-on-one interview on television's "The Situation Room" after the debate was over, suggested that he was the best-equipped to deal with foreign policy, after 35 years in the Senate. When asked how important one's faith should be (Biden is a devout Roman Catholic), Senator Biden said that he "thought it was a shame that he (Romney) had to make that speech. I don't think it should be important to anyone but him or her." He also defended Barack Obama's youthful indiscretions with the comment(s), "What Barack did or didn't do as a teen-ager shouldn't affect his electability."

Dodd touted his 26 years in the Senate, as well as his time as a Peace Corps volunteer and the fact that he is the only veteran in the race. Said Dodd: "This election is not about wealth or celebrity."

New Mexico Governor Richardson, at Invesco Stadium.

Richardson of New Mexico, who was Energy Secretary, wants 50 mpg cars to be the goal, not 30 mpg ("I think that's pathetic," he commented) and agreed with all others that education was one of the defining issues of this election. All were critical of the No Child Left Behind Act, with Richardson saying "I'd scrap it. It's gotta' go. It's an unfunded mandate."

Senator Christopher Dodd drew laughter when Richardson ran long on an answer about what he could be expected to do in his first year in office, saying, "It's gonna' be a long year." The remark prompted Moderator Washburn to say, "That was longer than Senator Biden's answer!" (Biden has been criticized as overly verbose.)

All of the Democratic candidates seemed to have concrete policy action in mind, rather than pie-in-the-sky promises that they perhaps cannot deliver. None came off as merely angry, or overly fond of folksy sayings or Biblical quotations. Faith was mentioned only by Biden in "The Situation Room" and in his quotation from a well-known hymn. Instead, the character and integrity of the candidate(s) was often mentioned. (*Note: character and integrity certainly became huge issues for Edwards later in his race.)

Said Edwards, "I will make absolutely certain that our three branches of government are co-equal. The White House, the Oval Office and the Presidency does not belong to one person. George W. Bush may think he is King, but the office of President belongs to the American people..We have to take back our country, starting right here and now."

The group of candidates had obviously spent a great deal of time proposing nuts-and-bolts solutions and approaches to complex problems and issues. All had done their homework and none seemed to be poorly prepared or "winging" it.

The agreement(s) on issues amongst the candidates were these:

1. The War in Iraq must end.
2. The US has to get on a path of sustained growth to dig out of the deep legacy of fiscal debt that any new President will inherit from the current administration.
3. Education is a top priority.
4. Energy independence is a top priority.
5. Health care is a top priority.
6. Revising NAFTA is a top priority.
7. The environment is a top priority.
8. Losing the tax gap that lets the rich get richer (while the poor get poorer) is a top priority. (*Note: hasn't happened yet, a full 7 years later.)

It is fair to say that the candidates similarities were stronger than their differences, but the presentations ranged from sprinkling remarks with facts (like the cost of the war in Iraq, currently $10 to $12 billion a month) to eloquent pronouncements, some of the best of which I will condense and attribute here, in alphabetical order:

Joe Biden: "It's about priorities. I'll start by ending the war in Iraq." At this point, Biden quoted from the hymn, "I Will Lift You Up on Eagles' Wings."

Hillary Clinton: "Enlist the American people. (Ask them for) a new form of American patriotism… Everyone on this stage wants change. Some say we should get it by demanding it. Some say we should get it by hoping for it. I say we will get it by working hard for it."

Christopher Dodd: "There are 37 million people in this country in poverty. Twelve or thirteen million of them are children. We must lift people up, invest in growth." He cited his 26 years in the Senate, his veteran status, and his Peace Corps work as reasons to caucus for him.

John Edwards: "Corporate power and greed have literally taken over the government. We need a President who will take these powers on… We need a President who tells the American people to be patriotic about something other than war… If you want a fighter, you are looking at someone 54 years old who has been fighting and winning (against power brokers) his whole life."

(*Dennis Kucinich's comments would have appeared here, if candidate Kucinich had been invited to the debate.)

Barack Obama: "Dr. King spoke of 'the fierce urgency of now.' The planet is in peril..Let's send a message to the world that we will restore the traditions that made this country great and made us admired around the world."

Bill Richardson: Richardson pledged to restore the Constitution and said, "China is America's banker, with $9 trillion in American debt in Chinese banks. I would take a harder line against China, banning defective toys and contaminated food and being stronger on human rights…There should be trade sanctions, such as those against Burma and Sudan, when a country violates human rights. There should be no child or slave labor and the workers should have the right to unionize. We have to transmit our Democratic qualities."

Richardson also earned one of the few laughs of the night when he said he wanted to "thank the people of Iowa for putting us through this… (pause) good (laughter)… debate."

Vice-president Joseph Biden and me at the "Red, White & Blue" Banquet in Davenport, Iowa.

Democats at Iowa "Red, White & Blue" Banquet Hear Christopher Dodd and Joe Biden

Dec 15, 2007

Presidential candidates Joe Biden and Christopher Dodd spoke to approximately 500 Scott County (Iowa) Democrats on Friday, December 14, at their "Red, White & Blue Banquet" fundraiser, hoping to make their way into the Winner's Circle on caucus night, January 3.

Senator Biden pointed out the importance of the Iowa caucuses this way: "The rest of the country is somewhat envious that you have so much control. If you do not send someone out of here with a ticket, that person does not get a chance nationally. You and New Hampshire are the only thing between money being the only thing picking the candidate. You take the process really seriously. Otherwise, the regular guy without $10 million-plus to spend on a campaign couldn't do it. Absent you, there is no gate whatsoever. Nothing like this takes place anywhere else in the world. Don't let them take it from you."

That last statement was a veiled reference to the many states, including Michigan, that have made attempts to wrest the "first-in-the-nation" title away from the Hawkeye state.

Biden noted that at least three Democratic candidates have spent $20 million on their campaigns in Iowa. He said at least four of the candidates have spent between $5 and $11 million in Iowa on TV ads alone.

Biden called the 2008 election "the single most important election of my lifetime. There is so much at stake. It is not political hyperbole. The American people are ready to stand up. When have the American people ever let their country down? We believe that our tomorrows will be better than our yesterdays."

Telling the crowd that he has been to Iraq "more times than all of the other candidates combined," Biden lamented the burden of the war on its young soldiers. "If we brought all of the soldiers home right now...if it ended tomorrow...14,500 of those who returned would be so seriously injured that, over the average life-span of 38 years that they will have left, they will need $600 billion in support." He based this on the well-reported facts that MASH units are saving more soldiers than in any previous conflict. He then added, "This conflict is producing more amputees than the Civil War."

Christopher Dodd led off the speeches, calling Joe Biden "one of my best friends in politics and in life" and repeated, as his introduction, what he called "the best introduction I've ever heard."

The favorite Dodd introduction was of William Howard Taft, by Chauncey DePeuw, at the Waldorf Astoria, when Taft—the country's largest President—was running for office. Taft, who (according to Dodd) stood 6' 8" and went 400 lbs., came to the stage, he was introduced by DePeuw as "A man who is pregnant with courage and integrity." Reaching the dais, Taft responded, "If it is a girl, I shall call her Integrity. If it is a boy, I shall call him Courage. However, if it is, as I suspect, just gas, I shall call it Chauncey DePeuw."

Former Vice President Mondale Endorses Hillary Clinton in Davenport, Iowa

Dec 15, 2007

Walter "Fritz" Mondale, Democratic Vice President under Jimmy Carter, came to Davenport, Iowa's, Scott County fund-raising dinner on Friday night and delivered a less-than-five-minute endorsement of former First Lady Hillary Clinton in her run for President. Clinton was not present in person, but sent Mondale as her spokesman. Other candidates (Obama, Richardson) also sent emissaries, albeit not ones who were as well-known as the former Vice President.

Mondale chose, as his own Vice Presidential running mate in his 1984 ill-fated campaign for the Presidency, Geraldine Ferraro. This was the first time that a woman was given the opportunity to run for one of the two highest offices in the land.

Calling Hillary "one of the finest people I've ever known" and "brilliant," Mondale said, "She's had unbelievable experience(s) in the White House." *(An audible gasp was heard from a table next to me.)*

Mondale quickly went on to add, "You need to know how to operate that office from the beginning," commenting that Hillary Clinton could hit the ground running because she had been First Lady during her husband's Presidency and knew the lay of the land. *(*Note: possible gasp #2).*

Mondale also commented, in admonishing the current Republican administration, that, while serving as Carter's Democratic Vice-President, the pair might have had some setbacks, but they accomplished three things: "We told the truth We obeyed the law. We kept the peace."

Finnegan Biden, granddaughter of then-Senator (soon-to-be Vice President) Joe Biden.

The Families of Candidates Biden and Dodd Discuss Living in Iowa, (or)

Will Santa Claus Be Able to Find Me in Iowa, If Daddy's Running for President?

Dec 16, 2007

While waiting for the Chris Dodd/Joe Biden remarks to begin at the Scott County Democratic Party "Red White and Blue" annual fund-raising dinner on Friday, December 14th, I had the great pleasure of talking at length with Joe Biden's granddaughter, Finnegan Biden.

Finnegan is nine years old and in the third grade at the Sidwell Friends School in Washington, D.C., where her best friend, Sophie, "is taller than me." Finnegan's dad is Joe Biden's Washington, D.C. attorney son, Hunter, who was also present with wife Kathleen. Finnegan's mother, Kathleen, originally hails from Chicago. Finnegan has a sister, Naomi, age 14, and another sister, Maizie, age 7. (Finnegan did not express a desire for brothers…and I did ask.)

Finnegan told me that her unusual first name is a family surname, and I told Finnegan that she could "be a model," but she mentioned that both of her grandmothers are teachers, so perhaps Finnegan will follow in their footsteps after she graduates from third grade.

Or maybe Finnegan will follow her father into the practice of law? Finnegan, literally, can do anything she wants in life, it would appear, and has the world by the proverbial tail, a tribute to what has made America great for all the Finnegans who have gone before.

Finnegan resembled a small china doll as she skipped around the Mississippi Valley Fairgrounds venue in Iowa, long blonde hair bouncing, happily unself-conscious in blue jeans, wheras all the Bidens (and the Dodds) were "suited up" elegantly on this cold snowy evening, in prepara-

Finnegan Biden's father, Hunter Biden, son of VP Joseph Biden at a rally at Iowa Senator Joe Seng's house in Davenport, Iowa, during the 2008 caucus season.

tion for Dad's (and Granddad's) remarks. The Dodds and the Bidens all "clean up real nice," as Iowans might say. Both sets of families could not have been more cordial to the rural crowd, where the dress code ran from "glitter and lots of it" to blue jeans basic.

I asked Finnegan if she had to take a bus across the state (John Edwards has been using a Main Street Bus Tour and will arrive in Davenport, Iowa in the bus on Monday, December 17th for a rally.) Finnegan shook her head no. *(Lucky girl)*.

The Biden family has taken up temporary residence in Iowa, and Chris Dodd's family rented a temporary "home" in Des Moines during the campaign. However, Finnegan told me that she was only missing Thursday, Friday and Monday at her Washington, D.C., Sidwell Friends school and was not traveling with a tutor. Finnegan struck me as a bright student who could easily miss a couple of school days without too much backlash. The veteran teacher in me was glad to hear she was going back to her regular school after a very brief absence. No doubt Finnegan will get an education of its own that is unique while participating in her grandfather's campaign, (as will the entire family.) The Edwards family has opted for taking their children, Emma Kate and Jack, and tutoring them as they travel together across the state.

Later, Joe Biden, in his remarks, spoke of flying across Iowa from campaign stop to campaign stop in a twin engine Navajo, observing the green land below. (Not so green in December, but Biden's been here through the dog days of summer, too.) Senator Biden commented on the beauty of the state, especially of the northern portions of the state (northeast Iowa—Independence— is my home town area). "The people I know from 23 years ago in Iowa are still my close, close friends," said Senator Biden, and he singled out some to particularly thank, including State Senator and veterinarian (Dr.) Joe Seng, who hosted a gathering on his front lawn earlier in the year that also attracted Senator Edwards. (*Note: In 2015, Dr. Seng is battling brain cancer.)*

"I look down there and see those lights twinkling and I think of the parents sitting down at the kitchen table after the kids are in bed, and the questions they are asking each other are as profound as they are ordinary. We have to let them know we understand and sympathize," said Biden.

Biden went on to say that the middle class in Iowa worries about the price of gas and whether Dad will still have a job, just like ordinary families in Brooklyn or Watts or Appalachia, and that he can remember when his own father had to temporarily move to Wilmington (Delaware) because of a lack of work. In earlier remarks, Biden had commented on his very first trips to Iowa, years ago, with Senator Culver (the current Governor's father) and bemoaned the apparent disappearance of the family farmer. Biden was Jimmy Carter's National Campaign Chairman, so he knows a thing or two about campaigning in Iowa from way back. Biden has served during the tenure of 7 Presidents.

When Senator Christopher Dodd of Connecticut took the podium, he told a humorous story about his two young daughters, Christina and Grace, ages 6 and 2 and ½. Senator Dodd was accompanied by his wife, Jackie, and other family members, including his brother, Thomas, a former Ambassador to Uruguay from 1993 to 1997 and Ambassador to Costa Rica from 1997 to 2001, who has also taught law courses in Poland.

Because the Dodds have taken a temporary home in Des Moines during the campaign, daughters Christina and Grace were worried.

"Daddy…will Santa Claus be able to find me in Iowa? How will Santa find me if we're not at home in Connecticut?" the girls wondered.

Dodd said, "I went outside right then and there and planted a sign on the family lawn in Connecticut so Santa could find the kids in Iowa."

That's nice to know. Even if Senator Dodd doesn't get *his* Christmas present (a win in the Iowa caucuses) Christina and Grace won't miss out on a visit from the guy in red.

John Edwards Endorsed by Iowa's First Lady

Dec 18, 2007

At a rally attended by about 200 Democratic caucus-goers, many of them steelworkers and other union members, John and Elizabeth Edwards were joined by Mari Culver, the wife of Iowa's Governor Chet Culver and Roxanne (Barton) Conlin. Mari Culver, an attorney, has endorsed Edwards, while her husband has decided to remain officially neutral.

Roxanne (Barton) Conlin, who was one of three people who introduced Edwards, is a Drake graduate (at the age of 21, with honors, after entering college at age 16 in 1961). She has, among other "firsts," been the first woman to run for Governor of Iowa. She narrowly lost, but was one of the first two women to become a United States Attorney and also be elected President of the Federal Executive Council. In 1975, she was named one of 44 Women Who Could Save America and declared "Cabinet-worthy." She was the first woman President of the Association of Trial Lawyers of America, a 60,000-member organization to which Edwards also belonged during his law career.

In introducing Edwards, Conlin, whose remarks followed those of Citizen-Activist Caroline Vernon, said she had known John Edwards for twenty years, both as a friend and as a colleague. "If you care about these issues, he's your guy. When they come at John Edwards, he will fight back. If you want change, he's your guy!" Conlin stressed Edwards' electability.

Conlin also exulted that the Edwards camp "can feel the momentum. It feels a little like 2004, when Edwards was running only 5% in the polls and came in second only to Kerry at the caucuses."

Conlin said that the Democrats, this year, have "an embarrassment of riches" in terms of qualified Democratic candidates. Of the Republican

candidates, she said, "They've got an embarrassment, but not of riches." She added, "We can't stand four more years of Republican leadership. It is our country. We want it back. We want an end to the ignorance, greed and corruption."

Elizabeth Edwards was present, campaigning alongside her husband and, of the couple, Mari Culver, First Lady of Iowa commented, "They are a solid team, and I know something about solid political teams. John Edwards is right on the issues. I like a winner, and I know John Edwards can win. He's ready. He's battle-tested. In a recent CNN Poll, only John Edwards was shown to beat each and every Republican candidate in a head-to-head contest. He inspires people. He is optimistic. He lifts people up. He is a class act all the way." (*Note: Well, maybe he does go all the way. Class comment deserves scrutiny.)

Ms. (Caroline) Vernon declared that Edwards was absolutely the best candidate in the field, especially on the issues of health care and labor. Physically disabled, she used a cane to gain access to the podium where she commented, "No one's physical well-being should be held hostage to the dollar" to enthusiastic crowd applause.

On the issue of corporate greed in America, Vernon said, "When we bring corporate America to the table, they eat all the food." She followed that remark with: "Be the change you want to see. Think globally; act locally," and remarked that, of all the candidates running, Edwards was the one who most "walked the walk" as he "talked the talk."

Vernon shared a quote with the crowd from the local newspaper that her daughter read to her as they left the house for the rally, in urging those Iowans present to exercise their right to caucus. The quote by Pericles (c. 495-429 BC, the first citizen of Athens, Greece) was: "Just because you don't pay attention to politics doesn't mean that politics won't pay attention to you!"

When Edwards took the stage, to tumultuous applause, he said, "It is time for us to rise up and take this democracy back," a message echoing Dr. Howard Dean's slogan from 2004. Bruce Springsteen's "The Rising" played as Edwards departed, and Jon Bon Jovi's "It's my life" entertained the crowd as they waited for the rally to begin, which began over 40 minutes late.

After some stories of his family's hardscrabble roots in a mill town in North Carolina and about the "virtue of hard work" Edwards said, "America doesn't belong to the power brokers and the corporations. It belongs to us. I want to make this promise that I have lived available to all. Rise up. You're gonna' start a rising that cannot be stopped. We are going to meet our responsibility to our children but we have a huge epic fight in front of us."

Said Edwards, "Do you think that the current Powers That Be are simply going to hand over their power to us? Not in my world. They'll give their power away when we take their power away. If we walk over to the bargaining table and say, 'Just give us what we want. It's the right thing to do,' do you think that is going to work?" Answering his own question, he said, "We need someone ready to lead the fight. I was born for the fight. Something monumental and historic is going to happen in Iowa at the caucuses on January 3rd."

Iowa Caucus Goers: Do They Vote like the Rest of Us?

Comments by Romney, Iowa Caucus-goers, and a First-time Voter at an Iowa Caucus

Dec 20, 2007

Iowa Caucus-Goers: Do They Vote Like the Rest of Us?

With the Iowa caucuses almost here (January 3rd) and only 2 weeks left of Iowa caucus chaos, this question can legitimately be asked: "Are Iowa caucus voters just like you and me? How do they make a decision on who they'll vote for?" The rest of the country does not get to see the candidates, up-close-and-personal, warts and all.

Iowa does.

After all, Iowans live in a predominantly rural, white state with almost no large cities, no professional sports teams, and some pretty horrible weather. On the plus side, Iowans are well-educated and prepared to vote on the issues. Iowa is a state that has scored consistently well on all meaningful literacy measures.

Iowans gather in small folksy town-hall-like meetings at their local schoolhouses on caucus night and argue, loudly and vocally, for their favorite candidates. These small focus groups (i.e., caucus meetings) are the exact opposite of the sound bite strategy that voters-at-large will eventually be subjected to during the national campaign.

Most voters in the nation at large will have only sound bites to use as their basis for making up their collective minds on the candidate(s) that come out of Iowa with "the Golden Ticket." Either listen to regular folk from Iowa (*and New Hampshire, et. al.*) or you're left only with a collection of national talking heads on television and radio news shows, who seem increasingly "out of touch" with the average voter. (*Seemingly the sound bite option is what Yahoo now favors, with the hiring of Katie Couric and the loss of on-the-ground locals writing about these rallies.*)

In Davenport, Iowa, the major paper, the *Quad City Times*, approached first-time voters, asking them to follow the candidates and submit stories for publication. One of the young first-time voters selected by the *Times* was St. Ambrose University student Miles Chiotti, who turned out for a December 7th Fred Thompson rally decked out in Thompson gear. (He stood out because he was the *only* young voter present, fully decked out in Thompson gear.)

Chiotti's story eventually appeared in the *Quad City Times*— a full 10 days after the candidate's appearance at the Thunder Bay Grille. (*No need to rush a Thompson story into print, I guess.*)

Chiotti asked candidate Thompson this question, "Would you call yourself a Federalist…and through Federalism, how do we once and for all give power back to the states?"

[Holy Ballot-Box, Batman! That was some question from a young person who didn't look old enough to drink! Good going!]

Thompson gave a rambling response to Chiotti's question, commenting that "the Founding Fathers were Federalists" (*without any explanation of that term for the majority of the audience present*), reminiscent of a later response he would give during the televised Johnson, Iowa, Republican debates on December 12th when, asked about NAFTA he said, "I have nothing in particular to point out."

It's fair to say that Chiotti's Federalist question is not one that Joe Blow from Kokomo, given the opportunity, might pluck, ready-made, from his (or her) brain-pan. When I asked him later, Chiotti identified himself as a student at St. Ambrose University in Davenport, Iowa, who hails from Peoria, Illinois ("from Ray LaHood's district"), so perhaps we shouldn't identify him as an Iowan, although, (like Obama supporters that are pandering to youth who live in one state but attend college in Iowa), Chiotti announced that he "intends to caucus" as a registered Iowa voter on January 3rd.

So, what have some of the legitimate average potential caucus-going Iowa residents been saying about the candidates turning up in their backyard?

Iowa House Minority Leader Christopher Rants (R - Sioux City), quoted December 20th in Davenport (Iowa's) *Quad City Times*, said of the *Des Moines Register's* endorsed Republican candidate, John McCain, "He's (McCain's) trying to sell stuff that people don't want to buy. I just don't see how the coalition comes together for him." Rants is supporting Romney.

When the Richardson campaign tried to make a claim that a hedge fund that Edwards once had money invested in somehow made him guilty of closing down the Newton, Iowa Maytag plant and shipping the jobs to Mexico and overseas, Max Tipton, an Edwards supporter from Newton and retired UAW representative said, "I think it's asinine for any candidate to suggest that John Edwards in any shape or form had anything to do with the closing of Maytag."

During a brief appearance on December 20th outside the Boat House Restaurant in Davenport, Iowa, Republican candidate Mitt Romney, a Mormon, commented, "Iowans are not going to make a decision based on what church they go to." Romney went on to attack Arkansas Governor Huckabee's positions on a variety of issues, saying, "I was not impressed with his (Huckabee's) assessment that Iran was in the posture of being a friend. I was not impressed with Huckabee's perspective on foreign policy." (*Some of the rest of us aren't impressed with his knowledge of science, especially in relation to evolution and global warming, and he's running right now, in 2016.*)

Romney attack ads targeting Huckabee, running on local television stations, take Huckabee to task, point-by-point, on a variety of issues where their views differ. What has Huckabee countered with? A "Christmas-y" television spot urging everyone to have a lovely religious holiday season. (*Strategically-speaking, Iowans tend to frown on negative attack ads and negativity, in general; we'll have to wait till January 3rd to see which strategy worked best.*)

Mary Ellen Evans of Davenport, quoted in the *Quad City Times* after Romney's brief appearance at the Boat House rally said, "He (Romney) appears very… well,… very Presidential, and I think he doesn't talk about the other candidates in an unkind way, and we like his whole attitude about people and family. And I think (he's) the one that we think would be the logical candidate." (**Note: Romney WAS the Republican candidate in 2012, and we know how well that worked out for him.*)

Pat Schmidt, owner of Fulton's Landing Bed and Breakfast in the area, added her two cents' worth, saying, "Oh, I think he's the most Presidential of anyone. I just wanted to hear him in person, and I haven't changed my impression at all. I think he'd make a great President."

True to the last-minute-decision-making that Iowa caucus-goers are famous for, however, Ms. Schmidt added, "I think he'd make a great President, but I haven't made up my mind for sure yet."

These regular Iowans had better get crackin' on their final decision-making caucus vote. As of today, Iowans—including Peoria, Illinois, residents like Miles Chiotti— have about 14 days to decide, once and for all who(m) they will send out of Iowa with a crucial win here, with New Hampshire, South Carolina, Florida and others hot on Iowa's heels.

After January 3rd, it'll be Sound Bite City for the rest of the nation, so let's hope that Iowans take their task seriously and perform it well.

Joe Biden Rallies Supporters in Iowa Appearance

Dec 23, 2007

Senator Joseph Biden (D, Delaware), running fourth in the Iowa caucus race and gaining momentum, spoke to a crowd of about 150 potential caucus-goers in the Davenport, Iowa, home of Iowa State Senator (Dr.) Joe Seng on Saturday, December 22nd at noon. The two "Joe(s)" have been personal friends for years, and Seng, a local veterinarian and long-time Iowa pol, has actively supported Biden since the beginning of the caucus race. Seng also hosted an outdoor gathering at his large home on Tremont Street in Davenport during nicer weather at which both Biden and Edwards appeared, Edwards arriving aboard his Main Street Express bus.

Biden workers passed out literature citing the Senator's work as a strong advocate for women. Television spots now airing in Iowa also play up the Biden Exit Strategy for withdrawal from Iraq, which garnered 75 votes in the Senate and, according to Biden, "overwhelming support" in the House of Representatives. Biden was quite clear about one point, saying, "The military did NOT recommend going into Iraq."

Presidential candidates have spent more than $7 million on radio and television time in the Quad Cities market, according to an article in the Moline, Illinois *Daily Dispatch* that appeared today (12/22/2007). Romney began running his ads in March; Romney and Obama have been the biggest spenders, although Thompson, Richardson, Biden, Edwards and Huckabee have been spending till it hurts, as well.

Biden, whose son Beau is serving in Iraq, said, "These kids (soldiers) are incredible. They're brave as hell" and told a story about being asked to accompany a family to claim their son's casket, as it was flown into

Senator Joe Biden at the Davenport, Iowa, Radisson Hotel during the 2008 campaign, his brother behind him on the left.

Dover, Delaware. The current administration has tried very hard to keep the public from becoming more aware of the tragic toll of the conflict in terms of soldiers killed.

When the family of a fallen soldier, with Senator Biden accompanying them at their request, reached the air force base in Dover, there was an attempt to keep the Chairman of the House Judiciary Committee from setting foot on the base. This outraged Senator Biden. He presented it to the receptive crowd as an outrageous act by the Republican administration. (Biden was…finally and very reluctantly…granted permission to join the family in claiming the dead body of their son, but not until after a heated discussion with the authorities.)

Biden touched on many of the topics he has previously addressed: health care; the eroding status of United States' reputation in the world-at-large; Bin Laden; the Saudi, Arabian problem. Biden shared an encounter that occurred when he was speaking in Davos, Switzerland at a plenary session and said, to the Crown Prince of Saudi, Arabia, "You have become my country's problem." This remark was in reference to the suppression of democracy in Saudi, Arabia that became the original impetus for the rise of groups such as Al Qaeda and leaders like Bin Laden. Said Biden, "Bin Laden wanted to take down the Royal Family, which was depicted as flying around in 747s with gold faucets and European prostitutes."

When explaining his Biden Health Care plan (and how it differs from those of other front-runners in the Democratic race), a questioner from the audience asked, "How about Giuliani's plan?" Biden responded, with a chuckle, to much applause, "I've got a plan for Giuliani."

Decrying the current administration's spending habits, Biden said, "I call Bush Houdini. How do you take a $5.7 trillion surplus and turn it into a $3.5 billion deficit, unless you're Houdini?" He added, "My father used to say, 'Don't tell what you value. Show me your budget and I will *show* you what you value.' "

Family members accompanying Biden (Brother James, son Hunter and family, et. al.) left the crowded residence to fly home for the holidays, but the beat will go on after December 25.

The Fear Factor:

How Does Fear Affect Voters?

Dec 21, 2007

An interesting article by Sharon Begley in the December 24 *Newsweek* magazine poses the question: "Have ham-fisted scare tactics lost their power at the polls?" New York University researcher LeDoux says, "We've gone from 'vote for me or you'll end up poor' to 'vote for me or you'll end up dead.'" Researchers found that subliminal reminders of death increased support for George W. Bush in 2004 and decreased support for John Kerry.

Begley reminds the reader of a number of "scare tactic" ads that have run throughout the years. Remember the television spot that kayo-ed Barry Goldwater in 1964 when he ran against LBJ? It only ran once, but the picture of the little girl pulling the petals off a daisy, while, in the background, we heard a boom and saw a mushroom cloud with a voice-over saying: "These are the stakes... Vote for President Johnson" did the trick. Goldwater had suggested that, if President, he might authorize the use of low-level nuclear weapons in Viet Nam. And th-th-th-th-that was the ballgame, Folks! Goldwater's goose was cooked after the mushroom cloud ballooned on television screens nationwide. (Sample slogan used against this conservative Republican from Arizona: "In your heart you know he's right... dead right!")

If you're too young to remember 1964, a more recent example of a "scare tactic" ad is the wolf pack ad that Bush and Cheney used against Kerry and Edwards, suggesting that a weak President would draw predators. A pack of hungry-looking wolves are gathering, getting ready to attack in a dark forest. A female voice is heard saying, "John Kerry and the liberals in Congress voted to slash America's intelligence operations. By $6 billion. Cuts so deep they would have weakened America's defenses.

And weakness attracts those who are waiting to do America harm." Primal fear. Weakness. Flip-flopper. Scary carnivores with big white teeth and lolling hungry tongues. (Yikes!)

Or perhaps you remember the Willie Horton ad that derailed Michael Dukakis and helped George Herbert Bush win twelve years before Junior retooled the tactic? The primitive nature of fear is best triggered not by wordy arguments but by images that stimulate the brain's emotional centers. Willie Horton was a black man serving a life sentence for murder in Massachusetts (Governor Dukakis' home state) when Michael Dukakis was the opponent of George Herbert Bush ("W's" father). Given a weekend pass from prison, Horton stabbed a man and raped a woman.

If I remember the ad correctly, there was also the imagery of a revolving door connected to it. Of course, Dukakis later surfaced riding in a tank, wearing a ridiculous helmet that made him look like Mighty Mouse. This just proves that Howard Dean's Des Moines ValAir Ballroom debacle in 2004 was not the only political gaffe committed by someone running for President.

Indeed, there have been candidates who cried in public (Edmund Muskie in Maine, for one) and were condemned for their sensitivity, and Jimmy Carter had a memorable battle involving a rabbit and an oar, in a canoe, as I recall. I still own a campaign button that says "Kennedy/Eagleton." History buffs may remember that Senator Eagleton from Missouri was hounded from the national ticket and replaced by Sargent Schriver after he admitted he had had shock treatments for depression. With Kennedy's Chappaquiddick incident in the news then, wags proclaimed the ticket "Shock Proof and Water Proof." Eagleton was gone in sixty seconds.

Here's a really frightening, albeit fascinating, bit of information contained in the *Newsweek* article: Brain-scanning techniques (MRIs) show that when whites—even those who claim they are not racist—are shown black faces, the more Afrocentric the face (the darker the skin, the broader the nose, the more Afro the haircut), the more the amygdala pulses into activity on an MRI. Showing Willie Horton's face in the anti-Dukakis ad mentioned above, was much more powerful in drumming up fear in the electorate than just talking about Horton would have been.

This factoid (p. 39 of the Dec. 24, 2007 *Newsweek*), raises an interesting question about current Democratic front-runner, Barack Obama, whose ethnicity will surely be targeted in some fashion by the opposition should he ultimately win the Democratic nomination. It's a sad bit of MRI information for Democrats. A charismatic, articulate, honorable, well-qualified candidate, but how do you short-circuit or circumvent human brain chemistry? The article would suggest, "It's all in the (human) wiring." (I'm not even going to discuss the deep-seated anti-feminist bias that might be trotted out against another well-qualified, experienced frontrunner, should she prevail.)

When Bush was beating the war drums in 2003, making his case for invading Iraq using flawed Intel, he raised the specter of the mushroom cloud (again) and asked America to "imagine with me this new fear." Says Republican pollster Frank Luntz, "The key to emotional language is simplicity and clarity... If it requires you to think, it's less powerful. If it requires you to explain, it's less powerful."

The goal for politicians is to appeal to the amygdala, not the cortex.

Why do these ads "work?"

"Elementary, my dear Watson": the amygdala. The amygdala overrides the work of the more thoughtful cortex of our brains. It is a vestigial organ that testifies to the superior nature of the brain's fear circuitry. Neurons only carry traffic one way from the cortex to the amygdala, which allows it to override the more logical and thoughtful cortex; it doesn't work the other way around. You might be able to "think" yourself out of an unreasonable or irrational fear, but, usually, the amygdala hobbles logic and reasoning, making fear "far, far more powerful than reason," according to neurobiologist Michael Fanselow of the University of California at Los Angeles, whom Ms. Begley quoted in her article this way, "It (the amygdala) evolved as a mechanism to protect us from life-threatening situations, and, from an evolutionary standpoint, there's nothing more important than that."

Even as far back as the 18th century the theorist Edmund Burke said, "No passion so effectually robs the mind of all its powers of acting and reasoning as fear." It's no wonder, then, that the electorate since 9/11 has been constantly manipulated with "orange" and "red" alerts and color-coded systems of assessing threats of terrorist attack. (Duct tape, anyone?) After 9/11, few of us doubt that there are terrorists who threaten our country, but constantly invoking that threat for political purposes has become Plan "A" for this Republican administration. And it seems to be getting a great deal of play on the caucus stump, as well, especially from Republican hopefuls.

Here is one interesting example of fear trumping reason. Flight insurance was offered that would cover "death by any cause" or "death by terrorism." The specificity of the word "terrorism," combined with the responses that it triggered, caused more people to spend money on "terrorism" insurance than they spent for "death by any cause" insurance, even though "terrorism" insurance is merely a small part of the "death by any cause."

Harvard University psychology researcher Daniel Gilbert is quoted in the article: "Negative emotions such as fear, hatred and disgust tend to provoke behavior more than positive emotions, such as hope and happiness do." Gilbert speculates that an important issue like global warming suffers because it does not have the ability to trigger *immediate* fear in the populace. The melting ice caps just seem too far away to pose an imminent threat." My own dear husband is a good example of this logic. His take on global warming? "I'll be dead by then." (*Please direct all negative comments about social responsibility to him, not me.*).

Warnings about Medicare or Social Security faltering fail to mobilize voters (or my husband) because they're too far in the future, but if it looks like illegal immigrants might move in next door? Panic! (And now that Tancredo is out of the race, the Fence Guy won't be around to protect us.)

Is there any good news (in this article) for discerning voters this election year?

In a word, yes. The fact is, says Begley, if you keep crying wolf, pretty soon people wise up and start ignoring you. (Notice how the "Iran threat" drumbeat for war was derailed a bit by the recent news releases of the intelligence agencies that contradicted the Administration's claims?)

Also, continually evoking fears without saying what you're going to do about fixing the situation (i.e., raising hope) "is rarely a winning strategy," in Begley's words. Says Matthew Dowd, former political strategist for Bush and now a contributor to ABC News, "Successful candidates understand voters' fears and anxieties and speak to it…" But, adds Dowd, "Politicians who speak only to the fear and anxiety part, without transitioning to something more optimistic, don't win."

In other words, the power of fear can dissipate.

Rudy Giuliani has been sinking in the polls recently, as a variety of bad news stories (check out "Vanity Fair's" most recent issue!) follow him. Joe Biden commented of Giuliani's strategy (during a televised debate), "Giuliani's every sentence consists of a noun, a verb, and 9/11." Just invoking fear isn't working so well for Giuliani. There may be issues with the expense accounts, the alienated children, and the multiple wives in this equation.

So the good news is that heavy-duty scare tactics may no longer be the best way to win an election, but any candidate who comes through the fire in Iowa should not ignore "the fear factor," because it's part of human nature.

Barack Obama: Fired Up and Ready to Go

Barack Obama Rallies Iowa Caucus-goers at Davenport, Iowa, River Center on December 28th, 2007

Dec 29, 2007

Barack Obama's bid for the Democratic nomination for President in the Iowa caucuses came to the Davenport, Iowa, River Center on December 28th, 2007, with supporters chanting "Fired up and ready to go!" during a wait of over an hour for the Senator from neighboring Illinois to arrive on this snowy winter evening.

Lots of up-tempo music ("I'll Take You There," Aretha Franklin's "Think") entertained the crowd during their 75 minute wait, as Field

President-to-be Barack Obama at the
Davenport River Center Rally.

Organizer Adam Hoyer, originally from LeClaire, Iowa, but now from Tampa, Florida, assured the crowd of voters and the media that the man trying to become the first African-American to run for President on a major party ticket, was, indeed, on the way. "Change We Can Believe In" was the slogan projected on the walls of the auditorium and emblazoned on the posters waved by the enthusiastic crowd.

Introduced by newly-elected Davenport Mayor Bill Gluba, whose daughter Stephanie also is a Field Organizer, and by former four-star general Tony McPeak, one of Obama's national Co-Chairmen for his campaign, the crowd warmed to the Senator from across the I-74 bridge in Illinois, just as he warmed to the crowd.

The eloquent freshman Illinois Senator with the rock-star charisma was introduced by no less a dignitary than former four-star General Merrill Anthony "Tony" McPeak. McPeak was appointed Air Force Chief of Staff in 1990, after a distinguished career in the Air Force that saw him fly solo and lead pilot for the Thunderbirds in over 200 air shows between 1966 and1968. After that, McPeak (who Obama said "looks like Clint Eastwood") flew 269 combat missions in Vietnam.

Even more remarkable is the fact that McPeak, who lives in Lake Oswego, Oregon, and is retired from the Air Force, served as Co-Chairman of (Republican) Bob Dole's failed Presidential bid in Oregon and, in 2000, endorsed George W. Bush for President and served as co-chairman of Oregon Veterans for Bush.

McPeak referred to Iowa as "the banana belt" at one point, until corrected by the crowd on this cold December night with murmurs of "the corn belt." Said McPeak in introducing Obama, "A lot of change is required in this country," adding that what was needed in the Oval Office was a man with intelligence, leadership and judgment. McPeak began by praising the Harvard-educated Obama's intellect, "It's as though we've had a 7-year experiment in this country to find out if it makes much difference if the guy in the White House is not-too-bright. No matter who wins, there's gonna' be a big jump in the I.Q. in the White House."

Laughter followed that remark.

McPeak lauded Obama as a man who is the same man in the campaign, day after day. Of Obama's leadership skills, McPeak said, "The guy is just electric. He is incandescent." Adopting an "Aw, shucks" demeanor and pronouncing himself "just a 71-year-old beat-up fighter pilot with scar tissue on scar tissue," the General told the crowd of approximately 350 potential Iowa caucus-goers that Obama was "Right about Iraq from the beginning. Right for the right reasons. He's got the right plan." He went on to say that Obama will have spent 83 days in Iowa campaigning (Edwards can claim many more, having visited all 99 counties at least twice) and said of Obama's honesty, "He plows a straight furrow," noting, "The gap there gets pretty wide between him and the rest of the field."

Explaining why he was not at home with his family during this holiday season, McPeak answered his own question," Nothing too important is happening right now in Portland, but what you do here in Iowa (in helping select a President): that's gonna' be pretty important. Oregon needs your help. America needs your help."

When Obama emerged, following these remarks, to lively applause, he apologized for a recently canceled rally appearance in the area, noting, however, that 200 potential caucus voters still signed up to vote for him and said, with a smile, "I'm more likely to get support if I don't show up."

The candidate greeted the crowd by asking how many had committed to a candidate already and how many voters remained undecided. When a show of hands revealed a few uncommitted folks, Obama said, "I see we've got some live ones here tonight." He also drew a laugh with his comment that he had not yearned to be President all his life, despite the fact that "I know people have been going through my Kindergarten papers" (this a reference to a tactic employed by the Clinton camp in releasing news of a paper written by Obama when he was in kindergarten, in which he said he wanted to be President some day.)

Another laugh came when Obama said, "The name of my cousin Dick Cheney will not be on the ballot this time" (in 2008). [Recent news stories have said that a genealogical survey of Cheney's ancestors revealed that Cheney and Obama were 8th cousins. Said Cheney, "Why couldn't I be related to Willie Mays or somebody like that?"]

Obama decried the past 7 years of the Bush administration, citing "Scooter Libby justice, Karl Rove dirty tricks, and Brownie incompetence," but also cautioned the crowd that "It's easy to be against something and that's been easy the past 7 years," reminding the crowd that he wants to work for better education for all, health care for all, good jobs for all, and lower gas prices at the pump. Of the health care situation, Obama said, "Congress won't let Medicare negotiate for the lowest price(s). Maytag workers who were thrown out of work when their jobs were shipped overseas are now competing with teenagers for jobs at Walmart for $7 and $8 an hour with no benefits."

Obama told the story of a woman in Cedar Rapids, Iowa, who, while trying to care for a sibling with cerebral palsy, had to work two jobs and still attend college. She was able to get only 3 hours of sleep nightly. He described the woman as representative of Americans who are "proud, independent and self-reliant" and who just want to find a decent job when they graduate. "They lost faith that their government can or will do anything about it." He repeated his belief that, "I believe we are a good and generous and decent people, and not as divided as some people say."

Saying that "Longevity in Washington is not the only criteria (to be President)," Obama used a line he has used on the stump before, declaring that Iowans have "earned the distinction (of being first in the nation to help select Presidential candidates) because you take your politics seriously." He used the analogy of Iowans "lifting the hood and kicking the tires" of the candidates for the nomination, including his own candidacy.

Check, Please! What's It Cost To Run in the Iowa Caucus?

Dec 23, 2007

When Senator Joe Biden (D, Delaware) commented, at the December 14th, 2007, Scott County (Iowa) Democratic Fund-Raising dinner in Davenport, Iowa, "Absent you, there is no gate whatsoever," he was talking about hard cold cash spent on campaigning in Iowa. Examining just the cost of television and radio in one small section of the state, the Iowa/Illinois Quad Cities, makes you realize how expensive a run for the Presidency is these days. As Biden said on December 14th, at least 4 of the candidates running in the Iowa caucuses had spent between $5 and $11 million on television and radio spots. Biden was National Chairman of Jimmy Carter's Presidential run, but said the days when you could run a national campaign on $10 million are long gone.

The actual tab for media buys, alone, in the Quad Cities of Iowa/Illinois (Davenport, Iowa) is in the neighborhood of $7 million, at this point, with (approximately) 10 days remaining till the January 3rd caucuses. (This information is courtesy of the Saturday, December 22, Moline (Illinois) *Daily Dispatch*.)

The leading TV station in the area is the NBC affiliate, KWQC, in Davenport, Iowa. Channel 6. The station has long been the ratings leader in the area, which is comprised of approximately 350,000 residents of Iowa and Illinois who live on the Mississippi border with Illinois in towns with names like Davenport (IA), Bettendorf (IA), Moline (IL) and Rock Island (IL). The "bend-in-the-river" location (in this area, the river runs east/west, not north south) is the second most-populated Iowa spot, after the state capitol of Des Moines. If the Iowa communities, alone, are totaled,

Cedar Rapids (IA) comes out on top, population-wise (after Des Moines), but when the Illinois communities of the Quad Cities are included, the area's slogan ("joined by a river") adds up to more live voters in the state living anywhere outside of Des Moines… although Illinois residents are not eligible caucus voters and have to wait for the Illinois action to commence in February.

No one is quite sure why the area is called "the Quad Cities," when the actual number of cities tallied includes Davenport, Bettendorf, Eldridge, Pleasant Valley and LeClaire (in Iowa) and Moline, East Moline, Rock Island, Silvis, Carbon Cliff, Green Rock and Milan, in Illinois. (Apparently, there is no catchy term for an area made up of at least 12 separate communities. Cartographers: take note.)

The Quad Cities has raked in about $5 million in political advertising on radio and television, so far, according to Channel 6's (KWQC) national sales manager, Allen Wiese. Republican Mitt Romney began running ads in March. Romney also was first in line, checkbook at the ready, at the ABC affiliate across the river, Channel 8 in Moline, Illinois. (Stories abound about how much Romney spent to win the Iowa Republican Straw Poll in Ames, which many Republican candidates totally ignored.)

Across the river in Illinois, Moline ABC affiliate, Channel 8 has taken in about $1.2 million for political spots, according to Trent Poindexter, Vice President and General Sales Manager. Second in line with funds spent, beginning in June, was Barack Obama, who "has been on consistently." Mr. Poindexter placed the biggest spenders in this order: Romney, Obama, Clinton and Richardson.

The CBS affiliate in the area, WHBF, Channel 4, in Rock Island, Illinois, has had 9 candidates spend a total of $785,000, according to Vice President and General Manager Martha Huggins. Included in the group were Biden, Edwards, Obama, Richardson, Huckabee, Paul, Thompson and Romney. Said Huggins, the television spots began as early as January of 2007, a full year ago, on Channel 4 (CBS) and then were "inconsistent" until August, when they picked up in frequency.

The Fox affiliates in the area, KLJB and KGCW, according to local sales assistant Faith Sturgill, have banked more than $180,000 in ad money from Barack Obama, with Hillary Clinton spending $45,825 starting in August. Romney started his spots in June on the Fox stations, spending just under $91,000. Others who have placed spots on the stations include Thompson, Richardson, Biden, Edwards and Huckabee.

Radio sales, too, have spiraled, with Scott Lindahl, Vice President for Cumulus Broadcasting in the area, saying that $26,841 had been spent by just two candidates: Barack Obama and Ron Paul, on five local radio stations owned and operated by Cumulus.

Who hasn't spent any media money in Iowa? Aside from the obvious underdogs like Dennis Kucinech and Allan Keyes (who even knew Keyes was a candidate?), Tancredo (who has already withdrawn from the race) and long-shot Duncan Hunter, one notable "no spend" candidate among the early front-runners was Rudy Giuiliani.

Poindexter said that he expects ad money for political spots to keep rolling in, since the Illinois primary was moved from March to February. He stated: "I would imagine they (the candidates) are going to continue to run (ads) up until February 5 and be fairly consistent. They may change their message after the caucus, but I expect they'll still be on."

The figures above do not reflect other charges incurred in campaigning, such as newspaper advertisements, campaign staff, rental of arenas for rallies, transportation to and from the venue for candidates and staff, figures for Clear Channel radio stations in the area (information unavailable), or money spent on signs, banners, buttons, food or lodging.

John Edwards addresses caucus voters in Davenport, Iowa rally.

Edwards Rising in Polls in Iowa:

Addresses Caucus-goers in Davenport

Dec 29, 2007

John Edwards, accompanied by wife Elizabeth and daughter Cate, came to Davenport, Iowa's Putnam Museum and IMAX Theater on Friday, December 28th, 2007, to rally caucus troops and, hopefully, sway a few more undecided Iowa caucus voters to cast their votes for him. Using Bruce Springsteen's "The Rising" (appropriately) as his closing campaign song, Edwards had some good news to share with 200 likely Iowa voters.

A poll taken by the Lee Enterprises newspapers (publishers of the Davenport, Iowa, *Quad City Times*, among other papers), released to supporters at 8:10 p.m. on the 28th, with six days left until the January 3rd Iowa caucuses, showed Edwards moving into the lead, jumping 5 points in 2 weeks. Edwards and Obama— (who was appearing at nearly the same time across town in Davenport's River Center)—hold 29% tied leads in the race, with Hillary Clinton at 28%, and 19% of Democratic caucus-goers still undecided.

Two other polls appearing on the NPR News Blog are also good news for Edwards. One poll conducted of 600 likely Iowa voters by Strategic Vision, on December 26 and 27, gave Obama the lead with 30%, Clinton hanging in with 29% and Edwards 28%. A Los Angeles *Times*/Bloomberg poll showed Clinton at 29%, Obama and Edwards both at 26%. The Big News, however, was whom voters would pick for their second choice. According to the NPR polls, Edwards would pick up Biden and Richardson people and was "second choice" for 23% of caucus-goers. Dodd supporters were split between Edwards and Clinton. [In the Iowa caucus process, if a candidate's supporters do not have 15% of the vote, those voters must join another standard-bearer's group, and it appears that Edwards is in the best position to benefit.]

These "dead heat on a merry-go-round" caucus polls were the backdrop for the discussion of the issues that Edwards has been addressing in repeated town hall meetings for the past year or more. A new twist was added to Edwards' rally remarks, however, by the December 27th assassination of Benazir Bhutto in Pakistan after an election rally in Rowalpindi.

Asked about the tragic death of the former Pakistani leader in a suicide bomber attack, Edwards told the crowd, "I spoke to the Pakistani Ambassador and told him, 'I want to speak to President Musharaff. I talked to Musharaff on the 27th. I told him (Musharaff), 'You have got to continue the process of democraticization.' Musharaff told me that he would (continue leading the way towards democratic elections). But we have to hold his feet to the fire and take his word with a grain of salt. There needs to be an independent investigation of Bhutto's death that is open, fair and verifiable. When I told Musharaff this, he gave me no assurances on that."

Edwards added that Benazir Bhutto was a very courageous woman who knew that returning to her homeland after exile in London would be very dangerous for her, or, as she said earlier, "I may be baptized in blood."

Edwards maintained that, since $10 million in U.S. aid goes to Pakistan, such an independent investigation could be insisted upon, with receipt of these moneys, contingent upon Pakistan's cooperation. He added, "The power to manage the volatility (in that area) is multilateral," stating that other persuasive measures could be taken to convince Pakistani President Pervez Musharraf to do the right thing(s). (*Note: In 2015, reports say Pakistan authorities knew all along that Bin Laden was hiding in plain sight in Pakistan, where he was eventually tracked down and killed.)*

On foreign policy, in general, Edwards said, "I will not lead belligerently."

Other favorite themes that Edwards addressed were health care, education ("College for everyone. That's my ideal. The kids have to work to earn it.") and—after a question from an audience member—the candidate spoke about the pressing problem of global warming (just as Obama was doing, across town, with his recurring " planet in peril" phrase.)

The global warming questioner tried to interrupt the candidate as he began to speak of a pledge to reduce carbon emissions to 80% by 2005. Edwards retorted, in reclaiming the floor, "I let you talk; now I'm gonna' talk." The former Senator from North Carolina went on to say that he does not favor more nuclear power plants, because they are dangerous, it is difficult to dispose of spent fuel rods, and the plants are expensive to bring online. Edwards does, however, advocate "people willing to be patriotic in this crisis facing America."

Edwards also reiterated his pledge to bring all troops home from Iraq within his first year in office, with no permanent bases left in Iraq and promised, among other things, "I intend to lead aggressively," and, "You deserve to have the truth from me." *(*Note: Interesting words, in light of subsequent revelations.)*

Barack Obama Counters Attacks and Says He and Wife Michelle Are "Normal," in Comparison to Wealth of Other Candidates

BARACK OBAMA ADDRESSES NEWTON, IOWA, CROWD ON DECEMBER 3, 2007

Dec 30, 2007

Democratic Presidential candidate Barack Obama (D, IL) traveled to Newton, Iowa, 30 miles east of Des Moines (former home of Maytag) and addressed a crowd of approximately 300 would-be caucus-goers assembled in the Newton Senior High School at 3:49 p.m. (CDT).

Introduced by Senator Kent Conrad from North Dakota, Obama joked that Conrad considers visiting snowy Newton, Iowa "coming South for the winter." Obama mentioned that Conrad still talks about a basketball game he played in Newton and added, wryly, "It was probably the only game where he made more than one basket."

Citing his own background as a campaign organizer for $12,000 a year (plus car expenses), Obama introduced Jasper County organizers Tim Anderson and John Ahull to applause, thanking them for their efforts on his behalf.

Then he got down to business, skillfully spinning the same stump speech he has spread across the Hawkeye state for months. Obama utilized soaring rhetoric: "There is no problem we can't solve; no destiny we cannot fulfill. Iowa, you have vindicated my hope(s)."

Obama used the same "check under the hood" mantra he has employed in many other campaign appearances across the state and told some of the same stories.

So what was new this time?

To this reporter the "new" part(s) of Obama's campaign appearance in Newton involved obliquely countering attacks on him by the two other front-runners. Obama mentioned that Bill Clinton had said of him that electing someone so young and inexperienced would be "a roll of the dice…a gamble." Countering this, Obama proclaimed, "The real gamble is having the same old folks doing the same old things and expecting it to turn out any differently." Obama mentioned that Bill Clinton, when running in '91-'92, was criticized for having no international experience. He countered that statement with, "Bill Clinton was right then and I am right now." Obama used, as proof, his vote to oppose the war in Iraq from the start, saying, "My judgment is informed by the decision to oppose the war in Iraq from the start."

Countering the criticism that he is "too nice," Obama said, "I have to say that I don't need instruction on how to bring about change, because I've spent my entire life doing it." He said, "We can disagree without being disagreeable. There is no shortage of anger and bitter partisanship in Washington. We don't need more heat; we need more light." He said that he attracts Independents and disgruntled Republican voters in this campaign.

One funny anecdote involved a Republican voter coming up to Obama and whispering in his ear, "I'm a Republican, but I support you." Obama's response? *(in a whisper)*, "Thank you. Why are we whispering?"

Obama said, "I don't want to lead the red states or the blue states of America. I want to lead the United States of America." He commented that the latest polls show him as the only candidate beating all of the leading Republican candidates (although it should be noted that some polls showed Edwards holding that position at that time).

Before taking questions from the audience, Obama said, "Let me wrap up by saying this: there seems to be an argument about the meaning of hope. I could not have achieved what I have achieved without hope. They say, 'Oh, he's talking about hope again. He's a hope-monger. He's so naïve.' They seem to think that I don't understand how hard it will be. Hope isn't blind optimism. It isn't ignoring the hard tasks and hurdles ahead of us. Hope is a clear idea of how hard it will be and being willing to try, anyway."

Decrying a country "led into war by fear and falsehood," Obama continued, "Every bit of progress in this country was fed by hope." He added, "The others in the race are saying, "He's gonna' have to do a Tonya

Harding on her and give her a whack." (*Chuckles here*). Obama disagreed that dirty politicking was the way to go.

He went on to say, "There are millions of dollars pouring in from undisclosed groups (a reference to groups which may be running ads for Edwards and/or others). There are distortions. We've seen this movie before, and it won't work this time. When the American people believe it's time for a change, the American people cannot be stopped…That's what hope is…Be willing to work hard on behalf of things that seem improbable, but are possible."

Obama said, "There is a moment in every generation's life. This is our moment. This is our time." Obama concluded his remarks by saying he would take three questions, and he wanted the questions to be from undecided voters.

The first question came from a young woman who began the question sounding like a Valley Girl. She ended up asking a highly intelligent, insightful and worthwhile question.

Her question? "I really, really like your, um, campaign, but I'm concerned about your position on nuclear power."

Obama answered the young woman's question by saying that he would like to establish an Apollo Project to study and research exactly which fuel source would most emphasize clean energy. Obama's opinion is that "nuclear energy is not optimal." He noted that his home state of Illinois has more nuclear plants than any other state in the Union. He mentioned his desire to put taxes on greenhouse gases, which would provide the funding for such an Apollo project. He lauded solar, wind and bio-diesel as alternative energy sources. Obama said that he wanted to use any source of power, including coal, if that source provided clean energy. (*This nuclear power position is in stark contrast to Edwards' opposition to nuclear power plants, articulated at his December 28th, 2007, Davenport rally*). Obama specifically mentioned as a risk the dumping of nuclear waste in Yucca Mountain, Nevada, which, he said, sits on an earthquake fault.

The second question from an audience member addressed the penal system and the United States' position as Number One in incarcerated prisoners. Obama said that he would like to see low-level drug offenders handled more on the local level, but wanted to "keep our streets safe." He decried a penal system that incarcerates a prisoner and gives him no training but releases him into society with an advanced degree in crime. Obama said that the local approach would be "a smarter way of approaching crime" and that the money saved in building prisons could be used to educate prisoners and/or teach them a trade, in the hope of cutting down the high rate of prisoner recidivism.

The third question was "How are you going to better the Special Education program?" The question brought forth a pledge to fund Government mandates and a reference to (Illinois Senator) Paul Simon, who set up a plan that would have had the federal government fund 40% of special education. Obama noted that the federal government currently pays for only 18% of that mandate, putting schools in desperate financial situations.

A fourth and final question was: "All candidates are talking about the middle class. How am I really going to be helped?" Obama, after laying out the details of his health plan, said, "I was talking to my wife the other day, and she said, 'We're not doing this again.' She told me, 'You know. We're not that far away from being normal. (*laughter here*) Five or six years ago we were still struggling with all of our bills for law school. We still remember what it's like. Maybe 8 or 10 years from now, we won't remember. I think we'd still be good people, but you lose track of how hard it is to make ends meet for the average citizen." [*NOTE: *check out the story below "What are the Top-Tier Caucus Candidates Worth?"*]

Ending his remarks with, "I will always tell you what I think. I will always tell you where we stand. I will always listen. I will wake up each day trying to figure out how to make your life better," Obama exited the hall to the strains of "I'll Take You There."

What Are the Top-Tier Candidates Worth?

How Much Money Do the Presidential Candidates Really Have?

Dec 30, 2007

Courtesy of *Money* magazine's January, 2008 issue (pp.88 - 95), we find out how we regular Americans stack up against 7 of the top candidates running in the Iowa Presidential caucus race:

Who's Number One?

1. If you guessed Mitt Romney, you win. Mitt is worth at least $202 million. Although the magazine picked the "mid-range" of reported income(s) from federal financial disclosure forms, Romney still has (at least) a net worth of $202 million. He started with the Boston Consulting Group and moved on to Bain & Company, another consulting firm, where he became vice president in 1978. He then founded Bain Capital, a private equity spin-off with stakes in Domino's Pizza, Staples, etc. With a combination MBA and law degree from Harvard, the Boston version of Wall Street has been "berry, berry good" to the Romneys.

2. John Edwards with $54.7 million comes in second. In addition to practicing mostly medical malpractice and personal-injury law, Edwards worked for Fortress Investment Group, a manager of hedge funds and private equity, as a part-time consultant for an annual salary of $480,000, after his 2004 VP run.

3. Rudy Giuiliani is worth $52.2 million. Giuiliani's wealth, as one wag has termed it, is "all 9/11 all the time." Although some reports say he had only $7,000 in his bank account at the time of his di-

vorce from his ex- wife, he has become a publishing, consulting, speech-giving dynamo and a partner at Bracewell & Giuilani, a Houston-based law firm with close ties to the energy industry. He gave a speech every 3 days in 2006, taking in $11.4 million by delivering 124 of them for up to $200,000 apiece. His influence has given some penny stock (ers) entrée to power, according to a recent *Vanity Fair* article, and there is little doubt that "security" is not only his campaign slogan but also the lynchpin of his personal fortune.

4. John McCain is estimated to be worth $40.4 million, as long as he stays married to wife Cindy, since most of the money is in her name. Cindy is chairman of Hensley & Company, the Anheuser-Bush beer distribution business she inherited from her father. McCain also earns $165,200 a year as a Senator and has a $54,000 Navy pension, plus his book ("Faith of My Fathers") was on the best-seller lists for 24 weeks in 1999. But it is Cindy who wears the pants, money-wise, in the McCain household.

5. Hillary Clinton is worth $34.9 million. She and husband Bill will take a capital gains hit this year of between $500,000 and $1.8 million in taxes, as a result of her need to divest of certain holdings that might signal potential conflicts as she runs for the White House herself. Bill earned $35,000 a year as Governor of Arkansas, but he's earned $41 million speaking to groups in the first 6 years since leaving office. Standard speaking fee: $150,000.

6. Fred Thompson comes in sixth with $8.1 million, most of it from his acting career on such fare as television's "Law & Order." He's been a senator, a lawyer and a lobbyist, but he took in $3.6 million for his acting roles and another $3.6 million as a commentator for ABC radio, plus $1.6 million making speeches.

7. Barack Obama is seventh on the list, with net worth of $1.3 million. Obama's wife, Michelle, quit her $317,000 a year job as Vice President for Community Affairs at the University of Chicago Hospitals in May. Barack's writing has helped boost the family coffers, with *Dreams of My Father* and *TheAudacity of Hope* doing well at bookstores (*Audacity* sold 1,080,000 copies). Obama

earned $60,000 as an Illinois State Senator and another $32,000 as a lecturer in Constitutional Law at the University of Chicago. His first job out of Harvard Law School, however, was leading a voter registration drive and then working for a Chicago law firm that specialized in civil rights and employment discrimination lawsuits. At a December 30th rally in Newton, Iowa, Obama characterized he and wife, Michelle, as "not that far from normal," saying, "5 or 6 years ago we were still struggling with all of our bills from law school."

Mitt Romney Visits Iowa Wooing Caucus Voters:

Four Days and Counting (2007)
Romney Thanks Bush for "Keeping Us Safe" and Asks for Caucus Votes

Dec 31, 2007

Running second in the polls for much of the past few weeks, despite spending more than $15.7 million on television ads this year, $11.9 million of it in Iowa, Mitt Romney is running hard in the stretch towards the January 3rd, 2008, Iowa caucuses. A poll taken tonight showed him gaining on first-place Republican candidate, Arkansas Governor Mike Huckabee. Romney, clad in a casual sweater in an overheated room, spoke in the Mozart room of Jumer's Lodge in Bettendorf, Iowa, on Sunday night, December 30th, 2007, at 7:00 p.m. (CDT) to a crowd that exceeded expectations, numbering perhaps 300 or 400.

Ironically, in a year when Campaign Media Analysis Group (an organization that tracks such things) says that campaign and issue ads nationwide have cost more than $715 million to date, and with the "first-in-the-nation" Iowa caucuses just 4 days away, one of Romney's refrains was, "We're spending too much money."

He meant the nation, of course, and he was right, of course. Quoting his wife, Anne, Romney declared that the financial crisis in this country was like two people in a canoe, arguing rather than paddling, while the canoe heads for a waterfall. He concluded, "It's time to get something done in this country."

Romney said "I'm optimistic about our future because of Moms, Dads and Grandparents," and also said, "It's people who believe in God" who would help save the nation from the abyss. "The key to our future is to strengthen families, strengthen the economy, strengthen schools. I'm the only guy...Democrat or Republican...who actually understand how the economy works."

Romney quoted comic P.J. O'Rourke in regard(s) to the health care system in this country, saying, "If you think health care is expensive now, just wait till it's free." This was an obvious jab at front-running Democratic candidates (take your pick) advocating health care for all Americans.

Declaring that we owe our troops "a special debt of gratitude" at this holiday season (a remark greeted by a "Hear! Hear!" from an audience member), Mitt said that he "believes in our military and supports our troops and I support what they're doing," and followed this with the kicker, "I respect our President and thank him for keeping us safe."

Any number of analysts and books by insiders within the Republican administration ("The Price of Loyalty" by Paul O'Neill, former Secretary of the Treasury, being one; "In Defense of Liberty" another) believe that the ill-advised march into Iraq has made America less safe in that it created a fertile breeding ground for AlQaeda. Bungling by the Administration, a la its Katrina response, gave us a disbanded Republican Guard armed to the teeth, and de-Baath-ification only added to the mess Bush made. These former Administration insiders would take issue with Romney on the concept that George W. Bush has "made us safe," but, rather, feel that he has given the next President a far-bigger international headache to contend with, upon taking office.

Romney told a long story about the 2002 Olympics in Utah, an Olympics with which he was involved. It was a patriotic story about the flag that flew over the World Trade Center on 9/11 and a Los Angeles-born rollerblade skater-turned-ice skater who medaled at that Olympics and who, for his troubles, ended up having to sit with Dick Cheney in his box.

Then came the critter cracks. This time, a story about a nest of baby birds and how his sons saved the small birds by hand-feeding them strips of dog food when worms could not be found. To me, it seemed like Romney was really reaching. He was trying to be a "regular guy" and humanize himself. Surely the very hot and uncomfortable sweater he wore in the near-80 degree heat was part of that effort, and the bird story just did not fly (pun intended).

One thing you can be certain of at a Republican rally: there will be a critter involved in the rhetoric somewhere. It will either be Fred Thompson's b'ar ("Sometimes you go into the woods lookin' for the b'ar, and sometimes the b'ar (i.e., bear) comes lookin' for you.") or a snake (as with

Huckabee) or, apparently, baby birds, which were "saved" by the dedication and compassion of the Romney children back in Belmont, Massachusetts.

What about the issues while the animals are on parade?

The usual: illegal immigration, bad. Army and war: good. Faith and God: good. Romney quoted Yogi Berra: "I don't like forecasting, especially if it involves telling the future." He said, "I don't think we vote for the past; I think we vote for tomorrow." He asked that Iowans vote for him on caucus night and said that, if not the gold, the silver or the bronze medal would satisfy the Romney camp.

Do Polls Reflect the Sentiment on the Ground in Iowa?

Dec 31, 2007

The latest polls for the Democratic candidates for the caucus race in Iowa are all over the map. According to the website RealClearPolitics, Clinton is leading in the Zogby, American Res. Group, and Strategic Vision polls, while the Mason-Dixon poll shows Edwards ahead (by 1%) and the *Quad City Times* (Davenport, Iowa) poll of 500 likely voters showed Obama and Edwards deadlocked at 29%, with Clinton at 28%. All of the margins of error were slight. Clinton did not have a commanding lead in any of the polls in Iowa. In other words, this is still very much anyone's ball game on caucus night, January 3rd, 2008, especially amongst the Democrats.

The Iowa Republican candidates shake out with Romney ahead in the American Res. Group poll, the Mason-Dixon poll and just 1% behind in the Zogby poll. The *Quad CityTimes* poll shows Huckabee at 34%, with Romney at 27%— the largest lead for the Arkansas governor. The Strategic Vision poll places the race between the two men at 27% for Romney and 29% for Huckabee.

Average(s) given for all five of the polls for Democratic candidates were: 28.4% for Clinton; 26.4% for Obama and 25.8% for Edwards. The pollsters asked 934 likely voters for Zogby; 600 for American Res. Group; 400 for Mason-Dixon; 600 for Strategic Vision; and 500 for the *Quad City Times* poll.

When the averages for the Republicans were computed, Romney had an average of 28.2% to Huckabee's 27.6%, with McCain...who has barely campaigned in the state... at a distant 11.4% and Thompson (*who has campaigned in the state, albeit half-heartedly*) at 11.0%.

A born-and-bred Iowan (educated at the University of Iowa), who owned and operated 2 businesses in the state for close to 20 years, and who has attended rallies for candidates on both sides of the aisle this election year *and* in 2004, the feeling that I get, on the ground here (at least in the Quad Cities of Iowa/Illinois) is that people just do not "like" Hillary Clinton, although they respect her intelligence and her experience.

If having intelligence and experience were the sole requirement for the Democratic standard-bearer, however, Joe Biden would be doing better. Right now, Senator Biden is running fifth behind Richardson with 5.2% to Richardson's 6.2% average on these polls. On the Republican side, the experience factor surely should go to McCain, who is running a distant third in Iowa and barely campaigned here. (*Note: McCain did, however, pull out the national Republican nomination, despite Huckabee's win on January 3, 2008).*

The people with whom I speak, personally, at Democratic AND Republican rallies voice several refrains:

1. "I won't vote for Hillary, no matter what." "Why?" I ask them. The voters tell me they don't "like" her. This is something networks have dubbed the "Q" factor. Hillary doesn't have it; Bill (apparently) can't give it to her by simply showing up at her side and holding her hand. In watching an Obama rally from Newton, Iowa on December 30th (on C-Span Live), immediately followed by a Clinton rally from Maquoketa, Iowa, the interest level(s) in the rooms could only be described as dropping drastically from his speech to hers. The Clinton crowd…(which was also noticeably smaller)…was polite. They did not seem very enthusiastic. In fairness, the Newton crowd (for Obama) was not as rowdy as the one in Davenport, Iowa, when he spoke to them on the 28th, but Obama was head-and-shoulders above the former First Lady when you watched the expression(s) of interest on the faces of the audience members.

2. Obama has an eloquent inspiring, upbeat message of hope and has assembled a team of heavy-hitter advisors that most resemble JFK's brain trust team. A reporting team from Rockford (IL), whom I asked, said that, of all the rallies they had attended, Obama's were the most enthusiastic and crowded. They also commented on the youth and the ethnic mix of his gatherings. In a state with 3 million people, of whom 95% are Caucasian,

the ethnic mix might not seem important on caucus night, but, if the youth who are involved in the campaigns follow through and vote in the caucuses, it could get very interesting very fast on January 3rd.

3. I went from an Obama rally to an Edwards rally in the same night. I simply counted the television tripods set up: the Tripod Test. It was undeniable that Obama won the tripod race that night, although the crowds were not that different, in terms of size and enthusiasm. There were more African-American audience members at Obama's rally, but the youth at the Edwards rally were just as prominent and just as committed and enthusiastic. Iowans have had a much longer time to get to know John Edwards, after all, after his ill-fated pairing with John Kerry as Democratic standard-bearers in 2004. And John Edwards has given Iowans some very specific answers to their very specific questions. Perhaps the potential caucus-goers are reserving their final moments before the vote for the candidate from Illinois who will have spent only 83 days in the state, rather than the one who has run, almost non-stop, since the last election and has visited every single county (of 99) twice?

4. Edwards and Romney, respectively, have the "Presidential" look that both parties would like their standard-bearers to present to the public.

5. "Trust" is an issue, for many, with the voters expressing distrust of several of the front-runners (Clinton, Romney, Giuliani, et. al.)

Can I make any predictions about this race simply from covering it primarily in this river corridor of the state?

Not today. Not with Biden and Dodd on my schedule (again) in the next two days, and the Television Tripod Test for Romney just completed (7…which is good, but not as good as Obama, in Davenport).

I'd go so far as to say that the two front-running Democratic men (Edwards and Obama) are in very good shape in Iowa and that Romney—who, let's face it, has spent huge dollars here—is going to do well, despite the early-on Huckaboom predictions. If you're a political junkie, it's going to be a horse race right down to the wire, and the second-place finishers here will be just as important as the winners.

Candidate Christopher Dodd on Tuesday, January 1, 2008 at Kilkenny's Restaurant & Bar in Davenport, Iowa.

Christoper Dodd, Bill Richardson, Joe Biden and Other Democratic Underdogs Rally in Iowa

Jan. 2, 2008

Among the Iowa Caucus Candidates, Stopping by to Say "Howdy"… a Lot…and Throwing Support to Other Candidates: Part of the Game

Can lightning strike these underdogs? Or will the role of the underdogs in the race be that of selecting the ultimate winner amongst the three front-runners by releasing loyal supporters to caucus for _____ (fill in the blank yourself.)

Senator Christopher Dodd (D-Conn.) has been doing some serious statewide sprinting in the closing moments of the Iowa caucus race. An underdog in the race, he's made 28 stops in 26 cities in 5 days and actually moved his immediate family members to a home in Des Moines. Dodd spent time in Davenport, Iowa, at Kilkenney's Restaurant and Bar on West 3rd Street at 1:30 p.m. (CDT) on Tuesday, January 1st.

Dodd is not alone in his last-minute rallies. Senator Joseph Biden (D, Delaware) will hold a rally at 1:30 p.m. at Mojo's Coffee House in Davenport *the very day of the caucuses* (Thursday, January 3rd.) You can almost imagine a candidate speaking to a busload of supporters driving to the 6:30 p.m. start time of the Iowa caucuses. ("My fellow Americans,… errr, Iowans. When you get off the bus, remain firm. Don't let those other sweet talkers in that gym dissuade you.").

Dodd, Biden and Richardson (not to mention Kucinich, although we should) are underdogs in the Democratic caucus race, at this point. But they can still be King…or Queen…makers. The Republicans have their Ron Pauls, successful at fund-raising, anyway, and their Huckabees, schlepping around the state with only a handful of campaign workers (14, one source said) while Romney had 92 *family members*, alone, working the Iowa straw poll in Ames.

If money talks, certainly Romney's spending over $11.9 million on TV spots in Iowa, alone, must echo loudly. The other half of that saying (about "Money talks") might be the non-candidacy of Alan Keyes on the Republican side. Nobody even knew Keyes *was* a candidate until he (somehow) found his way onto the stage of the *Des Moines Register* televised Republican debate from Johnston, Iowa. (And an angrier candidate, in either party, you cannot find.)

The way the Iowa caucuses work, a candidate must have 15% of the vote or his (or her) supporters must throw their support to another candidate. Biden, Dodd and Richardson are currently at the bottom of most independent polls. They do not have the financial clout of Obama, Clinton or Edwards. Both Biden and Dodd are good solid candidates with much international experience, but, surprisingly, that hasn't seemed to help. Maybe the "change" motif chanted by Obama and Edwards is drowning out the voice of experience?

The Quad Cities (of Iowa/Illinois) has been a political hot spot during this caucus season, with most candidates making between 6 and 7 visits. John Edwards has been here 9 times himself since January of 2007; others in his campaign visited at least another 12 times, for a total of 21 visits for Edwards.

"Can lightning strike an underdog?"

Edwards Rally at Davenport North High School featuring Jackson Browne and Bonnie Raitt.

Edwards also brought Jackson Browne and Bonnie Raitt to Davenport North High School in November. Edwards has visited all 99 Iowa counties 2 times in pursuit of the nomination, making Mitt Romney's claim to have visited 67 counties once seem paltry (although Romney sent his son Josh and family to all 99 counties in a Winnebago.)

Hillary Clinton came 7 times, starting in January of 2006. Hillary, herself, visited 3 times in December, alone. She has been hitting the campaign trail regularly since January 28th, 2007. Factoring in Bill's visits and those of others, Hillary supporters have hit the area 38 times.

Although Chelsea (Clinton) came, she wouldn't talk, not even to a fourth-grade reporter from Cedar Rapids. Not talking to reporters at all maybe isn't much of an "appearance" for a candidate. In fact, it may have left behind a bad impression. Likewise, the Oprah appearances for Obama in Des Moines, with faint strains of "black vs. white" in her introductions have been debated as perhaps not-as-helpful as divisive, in a state where "playing dirty" and being divisive is frowned upon. Huckabee even pulled a negative attack television spot he was going to launch against Romney (although not before letting the press get a good look at it.)

Barack Obama made 6 visits to the Quad Cities, one of them canceled due to inclement weather. Obama's wife (Michelle) made 2, and Obama sent in U.S. Senator Dick Durbin, former Senate Majority Leader Tom Daschle, U.S. Representative Jesse Jackson, Jr., retired Four-Star Air Force General Merrill "Tony" McPeak, and actors Jasmine Guy, Hill Harper, Sheryl Lee Ralph and Alfre Woodard. Oprah, of course, was the draw in Des Moines.

Mitt Romney came to the Quad Cities 6 times, starting in April.

And the beat goes on. Certainly Huckabee, Thompson and Richardson have made repeated visits; their camps could not be reached during the final moments of this chaotic campaign, to secure a countdown.

One interesting question we can ask ourselves as we observe is, "Can lightning strike an underdog?"

Huckabee may be asking himself that one right now. (*In Iowa, the question was answered with a "yes" for Huckabee on caucus night, but McCain took it, nationally).

Joe Biden Rallies Supporters in Davenport, Iowa, on January 1st, 2008

Biden Cites Experience and Electability in Closing Hours of the Caucus Race

1/1/2008

Senator Joseph Biden (D-Dela.) spoke to a crowd of nearly 200 supporters at the Quad City Radisson Hotel in Davenport, Iowa, on Tuesday night, bringing with him many family members. He spoke of his 90-year-old mother, who insisted on helping him campaign, saying, "Joe, when you hit Newton, I'm leavin' " but added, "You only have 8 days left and you need me." Son Hunter and brother Jimmy were onstage as Biden delivered the message that his experience in the field trumps all others.

The Television Tripod Test, sadly, showed only 2 Television Tripods: one was the CBS affiliate, Channel 4. One was Cliff Day, who posts on YouTube and who often posts on www.blogforiowa.com. Biden's message is a good one, but if a tree falls in the forest and no one is there to hear it, does anyone recognize that fact?

Many of the themes of Biden's stump speech dealt with his extensive experience in foreign affairs. As he noted, "I've been a Senator since I was 29. There are only 27 in history that have served longer than me."

Introduced by long-time friend and Iowa State Senator Joe Seng, Biden said, "Finally, the national press is noticing that we're drawing crowds as big as the top tier," citing a 500- to 600-person turn-out at 10 a.m. in an Irish bar in Des Moines the day after New Year's Eve.

Said Biden, "My Grandpa Finnegan would not believe this. Iowa is the last level playing field in American politics. You can't do this anywhere but here. We owe you. The whole process owes you. Win, lose, or draw, I'll always be indebted to you," which echoed his words to the Scott County

Biden at the Radisson Hotel in downtown Davenport on January 1, 2008.

Democratic "Red, White & Blue" Banquet when he said, "Absent you (and New Hampshire), it's all about (the) money."

Biden said, "I look forward to a country that is proud of its great heritage," and followed that up by saying that the United States does not torture and does not condone torture.

"The world is not stable," said Biden, and, he added, "George Bush's done more than mess up. He's been the worst president in history… at least the worst in the 21st Century."

Following on the heels of that indictment of the current occupant of the Oval Office, Biden repeated, "The next president has to know what they're about," and remarked that he was "the only person with a specific, concrete plan to end the war." (The Biden Exit Strategy creating a Federal State of Iraq).

Biden bemoaned the current status of Afghanistan, saying that he receives phone calls almost daily from an operative on the ground there and that "Afghanistan is collapsing. Five years ago, when I visited, you could walk down the street. You can't do that now. You have to stay in the Green Zone. We may be in the midst of losing Afghanistan."

Biden also mentioned that he, alone, among the candidates debating onstage recently, singled out Pakistan as a bigger threat than Iran or Iraq or Afghanistan. "You have the most dangerous and complicated nation in the region in Pakistan, armed with nuclear weapons. Their population is larger than Russia's. It's the place where Bin Laden lives, where the Taliban reside. Imagine a Pakistan taken over by the 15% of Muslim zealots. My God, the lack of focus we have! My God, what hath this president wrought?"

He then commented with incredulity on another candidate's suggestion that (Vice President) Dick Cheney be sent there to negotiate, moving on to the theme of this election's significance. "This is the single most consequential election of your lifetimes. If it's about experience, well, heck, I win!" This remark drew applause.

Addressing the concept of change, which many (Obama, Edwards, Clinton, et. al.) have trumpeted, Biden said, "There's good change and there's bad change. It's not about change or experience. It's about pragmatic action. Inaction is a decision (in itself)."

Biden also asserted his credentials as a proponent of laws to stop violence against women, noting that he wrote the Violence Against Women Act "back in the '80s" working alone and that it took him six years to get it passed. He repeated: "Initiating change is about taking action."

Mentioning his status as "the fourth most liberal Senator in the Senate," he cited his Crime Bill that helped put 100,000 more policemen in the streets with $10 billion allocated for that task.

"I've gotten it done in the past, and I believe I can do it again. We cannot sustain four more years of drift towards international anarchy. What other country has the capacity to lead this world?" asked Biden.

Biden also quoted his own line that, he said, had recently been co-opted by another candidate, namely: "The American people should be told not what they want to hear, but what they need to hear." He followed that up by saying that he had, indeed, voted for funding for troops, but did not feel that was an act that made him unelectable in Iowa. "The American people aren't stupid. They know that some things are worth losing elections over. Otherwise, it's just about ambition. We can't send troops over there for up to five years and not give them proper equipment to keep them safe."

Biden—like many others—thought back to the day of 9/11 and, shaking his head, said, "We had the world in the palm of our hands. 40,000 Iranians showed up at the closed embassy in Iran and left flowers and condolences. All of Europe was with us. All the president had to do was to convene a conference of the many countries who wanted to stand with us against terrorism," but, said Biden, George W. Bush blew it. Biden's most vivid memory of the 9/11 tragedy: lines of people standing 6, 7 and 8 hours to donate blood. "It was a silent scream on the part of all Americans. Everyone wanted to help. What did Bush tell us to do? Fly and go to the mall."

Biden followed that comment by saying, "Unless we nominate someone who is prepared and understands what lives in the hearts of the American public," we face more of the same.

Biden was asked in Council Bluffs, Iowa, what his closing argument (Biden holds a juris doctorate from Syracuse Law School) to the caucus voters of Iowa would be? He said "You're kind of like a jury. You're about to adjourn and, in some cases, spend up to 3 hours deciding on a candidate. Close your eyes and ask yourself if this person is capable today of dealing with the crisis in Pakistan or of dealing with how to rejuvenate this economy. In order to govern, you have to win in November. Who can take on Rudy Giuiliani on terrorism? Are you confident that your choice can stand in the ring with John McCain and have more credibility than he does on terrorism and on keeping our country safe?" Smiling, Biden added, "I've forgotten more about how to fight terror than Rudy Giuiliani will ever learn." The remark drew applause.

In stark contrast to the evening before, when Mitt Romney thanked George W. Bush for "keeping us safe," Biden brought up the recent study by 16 agencies, the National Intelligence Estimate, that showed that "this administration has created more terrorists than we had before it came to power." (For 30 years Joe Biden has served on the Senate Foreign Relations Committee and became its chairman last January.)

Biden also seemed feisty when he said, "I have had it up to here with the moralizing on the part of the Republican party. Ask Romney, whom I have never met, 'Where in the Bible does it say torture is good?' Ask Huckabee, 'How can a tax cut for the rich, while millions have no health care coverage and millions more live in poverty, be good or fair?' "

Repeating a phrase he had used at the Scott County Democratic fund-raiser, Biden, seemingly relishing the task, said, "I can hardly wait to debate any of these Republican candidates." He repeated, with enthusiasm, "I can hardly wait." (*Note: And then it turned out to be Sarah Palin and Joe took it easy on her.*)

Thanking the people of Iowa for their hospitality and support, he urged them to caucus for him on Thursday night and said, "I'm not hearin' it much, any more that I can't win the caucuses." Joe Biden eloquence served him well this night, even if the tree fell silently, unreported and unremarked by others. His closing argument for caucus-goers' votes?

"The test for the Democratic candidate for the Presidency is crystal clear. Who can take these guys on and win? Who can turn this nation around? Thank you."

John Edwards, John Mellencamp Rock the ValAir Ballroom on January 2nd, 2008

1/2/2008

Democratic presidential candidate John Edwards brought Indianapolis rocker John Mellencamp to the ValAir Ballroom in Des Moines, Iowa, for a rally on Wednesday that provided the finale to a non-stop, 36-hour round of appearances across the state. Mellencamp performed 4 songs and told the packed crowd of 3,000, "You people better get ready to take over this country, because it's gonna' be yours after this election. But we people over 30 aren't done yet."

With signs overhead that trumpeted, "Iowa Loves John + John," the populist rock star sang "I Was Born in a Small Town," "Little Pink Houses" and "This Is Our Country" to an appreciative audience that had come to hear Edwards talk about taking back the country for the common man.

Introduced by his wife, Elizabeth, Edwards also brought along actresses Madeline Stowe and Jean Smart and actor James Denton ("Desperate Housewives"). Even his parents, Bobby and Wallace Edwards were onstage Wednesday night as Edwards voiced many of the same stump themes he has articulated all over the state for months, if not years.

Edwards talked about health care; he talked about NAFTA and CAFTA; he talked about the Medicare Bill. He proudly proclaimed that he had "never taken a dime from a PAC or a lobbyist" and said that, after watching his father work in a steel mill for 36 years, "I take it very personally when CEO's of large corporations make obscene salaries. I will not stand by and watch corporate greed rob our children of the promise of America."

Edwards told the story he has told many times before, about not starting a fight, but not walking away from one, and said, "You can't nice these people to death. They will drive through you like a freight train…

We must fight relentlessly and never give up until all of your kids and grandkids have a chance… These people have an iron-fisted grip on your democracy. Do what's right. That's what this election is about… We want to leave America better than we found it. Show your courage. Show your character. Go to the caucuses tomorrow night and let's change America together." (*Note: "Do what's right…Show your character" lines seem hypocritical, in hindsight.)*

Who Will Win the Iowa Caucuses?

1/03/2008

Who will win the Iowa caucuses? Tonight's the night! It's now-or-never time for the Democratic and Republican candidates for the Presidency, as they face-off against each other in the Iowa caucuses on January 3rd, tonight, doors opening at 6:30 p.m. (CDT).

As someone who has followed the candidates around the state, met most of them, had photo ops with at least 4 of them, I'm going to venture far out on the proverbial limb and "pick" the winners AND tell you why I feel this way.

The fact that NO ONE feels secure in picking this year should tell you something about how foolhardy this act may be, but here are my picks and why I am picking the race this way.

First, for the Democrats: Obama will win but Edwards will be an extremely close second, so close that it could (literally) go either way. Obama is banking on a high turnout from young voters, first-time voters, disaffected Republicans and Independents. Information from the Center for Information & Research in Civic Learning & Engagement says there will be a high turnout (*the weather is good*) and that there will be record numbers of Independents and Republicans voting Democratic in the caucuses.

The *Des Moines Register* has predicted that as many as 72% of voters may be first-time voters this year. Do you see a trend here? And, if you do, who(m) would it favor?

A high voter turn-out of voters under 34 for Obama will help him capture first place tonight. Many of those voters will be Independents who have registered as Democrats in protest of the current Administration, and there will be disaffected Republican voters present in the Democratic ranks, as well. After all, look at the choices that their own party has put before them. Where, in years of yore and in the last caucuses, in particular, the average voter's age was over 50, tonight the torch will be passed to a new generation.

But, as John Mellencamp said in the rally at the ValAir Ballroom in Des Moines for John Edwards on January 2nd at which 3,000 would-be voters turned out, "We people over 30 aren't done yet." Older voters are often more reliable and more available (there is no absentee-voting in a caucus). If the youth end up not showing up (or at work during the time the caucuses take place), then the established adults rule, and I think they'll go more for Edwards…plus Hillary will pick up some voters, if young people stay home.

The fact that voters over 30 "aren't done yet" and are often more reliable in turning out to vote will help John Edwards capture an extremely close second place. You want percentages? Let's say 29% apiece, with Hillary in third, trailing in the 25 to 28% range. The polls may show Hillary winning everywhere else in the nation. The polls (sometimes maybe not-so-objective polls run by friends of the Clintons?) may say she is everyone's Top Choice. The polls will be wrong. Hillary is not everyone's top choice in Iowa.

In fact, it seems like she's almost no one's top choice in Iowa, but I do realize that money talks and Bill (Clinton), who has helped draw crowds for Hillary, is a charismatic character even on his worst day. But talk of "change" from an insider and dry speeches on health care and Republican pundits targeting her "cackle" and a generally low "Q" factor have not helped Hillary, and Hillary has not helped herself with some of her tactics and in some of her lackluster appearances. You want to talk excitement at a rally? Then you talk Obama or Edwards; you don't talk Hillary. Even Dodd and Biden "rev up" the crowd(s) better as speakers, and seem more genuine and less "scripted."

Unless there is horrific cheating (Florida, anyone?) Hillary will not win first place in Iowa tonight. She will have a respectable showing, but she will not win. That doesn't mean she's "down and out," as there will be "three golden tickets" out of Iowa to New Hampshire this year. It's been debated in the press, and it's true. Neither Obama, Edwards, nor Clinton is "done" after Iowa if they show strength such as I have predicted above. Candidates are only "done" if they are underfunded and have a horrible showing. The Money Train will start loading up after tonight's winnowing process, and candidates who were close to losing the farm will suddenly find new Johnny-come-lately backers if they do well in Iowa tonight.

Why do I think that Obama and Edwards will beat Hillary tonight? Edwards has been unparalleled in building a grass-roots organization in Iowa and then working it on a personal level (2 visits to every one of Iowa's 99 counties) time after time after time. He's an attractive, articulate candidate, who even set up a special website (www.askjohn.com) to answer every voter's questions before the caucuses, whereas Hillary wouldn't even allow her daughter to talk to a fourth grade press representative and has been evasive in answering some questions, herself, during appearances. Obama, too, spends many minutes answering questions from the floor in an open, transparent, Democratic fashion at each rally. Hillary's appearances come off as much more "scripted" and "polite" and "planned." I'd have to compare her most to Romney, who also discreetly left the stage after a brief rally, no questions asked, no questions answered.

Edwards' final 36 hours was spent hitting 16 cities aboard the Main Street Express, and he still found the energy and charisma to come out and captivate the crowd of 3,000 at the ValAir Ballroom, home of the infamous "Scream Heard 'Round the World' (Howard Dean's) in 2004.

Edwards is solid in Iowa…at least solid enough for second, if not a first, place finish. Mrs. Clinton of the planted questions? Not so much. Here in Des Moines, where I am writing this, my college roommate, a local doctor's wife, commented, "Even my (female) friends in my book club don't want Hillary to win."

What are the explanations for the longstanding poll predictions regarding Hillary Clinton's First Place standing, then?

First would be Bill and the Clinton campaign machine and money.

Second would be the question: are the polls really legitimate?

Third would be the argument that polls taken during the holidays, when many are away from home traveling, are not valid. Many independent voters may even see the light and anoint Senator Joseph Biden (D, Delaware) higher than he has been running in the polls. He has been fifth, behind Richardson, but his foreign policy experience put him in a new light after Benazir Bhutto's assassination. Biden is a stronger threat to the top three than many realize. I'm picking Obama and Edwards in a virtual dead heat, Hillary dropping to (probably) third, and Biden upstaging Richardson at the moment of truth. Dodd may drop out, but at least his wealth of experience and great good humor will continue to serve Americans well as the Senator from Connecticut. Any other year, Dodd might have done better. This year: too many are playing the game.

What about the Republican candidates?

I've felt for some time now that the Huckabee candidacy was doomed in terms of the nation as a whole. Too big a reliance on a cobbled-together evangelical framework of church workers, not enough money, not enough field workers (only 14 in Iowa, it's said), some bad stories out of Arkansas (*gift registries as I leave office, please?*) Not much substance, but lots of folksy stories.

The clear choice that the Republicans have to make Thursday night is whether to go with the Presidential-looking Romney or the Hawkish (and elderly) McCain. For those who don't like either of those candidates, citing age or flip-flopping (in Romney's case) or "they're selling what I don't want to buy" (more war, in McCain's case), Republicans can look to Ron Paul, the only candidate who wants to bring home the troops, or Thompson, the only candidate who has been trotting, rather than outright running, for the nomination, banking on his celebrity and good old boy status to get him some votes while the wheels fall off the others' wagons.

Since McCain did so little campaigning in the state (or, otherwise, might well be leading as a bona fide war hero), I think that Romney will take first place. After that, Huckabee may, indeed, take second for Iowa, but, as the campaign moves to New Hampshire, McCain will pick up steam, as he *has* actively campaigned there… The polls have been showing Huckabee up by 3 and Romney at 1.6, as reported by the website www. RealClearPolitics.com today. I'm bucking the trend in reporting Romney first. (**Note: In this case, the RealClearPolitics poll was right and Huckabee did, indeed, beat Romney. Romney's subsequent run at the top of the ticket in 2012 was not successful and the Republican party might have paid more attention to the disconnect that showed itself in Iowa four years earlier.*) Ron Paul will register, but not with enough strength to matter, and this may well spell the end of his campaign, as well as that of many other also-rans.

After this, New Hampshire residents will not be able to snidely say, "In New Hampshire we pick Presidents; in Iowa, they pick corn." Iowa will have winnowed the field tonight and will have definitely made a difference in who goes on to be President. New Hampshire can start cutting the corn off the cobs that Iowa sends them.

Voters in Iowa Caucus for Change: Hillary Clinton, Mitt Romney Take Hits

1/4/2008

As I rode down in the elevator of the Renaissance Savery Hotel in Des Moines, Iowa, with Bobby and Wallace Edwards (parents of John Edwards) near midnight on January 3rd, I asked them, "Are you glad to be going back to warmer weather in North Carolina, now that the Iowa caucuses are over?"

"Oh, no!" Bobby said. "Now we're going on to New Hampshire."

Of course they are. The Edwards campaign did exactly as I predicted in besting Hillary Clinton in the Iowa caucuses on January 3rd. Barack Obama did even better against her on Thursday night. Results showed 914 for Obama, 727 for Edwards and 716 for Clinton, which translates to 38% Obama, 30% for Edwards and 29% for Clinton. After the three front-runners, it dropped off to 51 for Richardson, or 2%. (Figures reflect 97% of the polls reporting, and could change slightly before you read this.) It spelled the end of the road for Dodd, Biden and Kucinich, who never really seemed to gain traction.

On the Republican side, Huckabee received 35,257 votes to Romney's 25,995. (With 97% of precincts reporting). It dropped off to 13,786 for Thompson, 13,473 for McCain, 9,992 for Ron Paul and 3,571 for Giuliani. Duncan Hunter barely showed with 452 votes. Percentage-wise, it was 34% Huckabee to 25% Romney with Thompson at 14% and McCain at 13% with 85% of the precincts reporting.

What does this all mean?

All political analysts said the age of the voters would be a crucial factor. Obama prevailed amongst the young, with 57% of voters aged 17 to 29 favoring Obama, 42% of voters 30 to 44 favoring Obama, 27% of those aged 45 to 64 and only 18% of those over age 65 in the Obama camp. With women, Obama prevailed as well, getting 35% of the votes to Clinton's 30% and Edwards' 23%. Older women placed Hillary Clinton third behind both Obama and Edwards. (These facts and figures all courtesy of CNN.)

All political analysts said that the turnout would be a factor. The weather was good, if cold, and a record turnout showed 220,000 Democrats voting this night, versus 124,000 in 2004 and 140,000 Republicans, versus only 88,000 in 2004. I bet another Content Producer from New Jersey $5 that there would be a record turnout. I hope she pays up. Maybe, if you're in New Jersey, you don't really know how serious Iowans take their politics.

If you've read my analysis of why and how Hillary might lose in Iowa (predictions made before she *did* lose in Iowa), you know that I referenced her "lackluster" speeches, her failure to take many questions, her aloof demeanor at times, and her plasticity on the stump. As James Stockdale (VP candidate with Ross Perot in 1992) once was put down by his opponent when he referenced JFK (and I paraphrase roughly to fit this candidate): "I knew Bill Clinton, and, Madam, you're no Bill Clinton."

John McCain on the stump at the Cedar Rapids airport during the campaign.

On the Republican side, 60% of voters felt that Huckabee's born-again religious values coincided with their own. I think they also had trouble identifying with a candidate (Romney) worth over $200 million.

Fifty-six percent of the Huckabee voters said that religion "mattered a great deal." Thirty percent said religion mattered "somewhat." Fifteen percent answered that religion did not matter much. The take-away for Huckabee for New Hampshire is that what worked in Iowa may *not* work in New Hampshire. Huckabee will have to broaden his appeal. Massachusetts is quite nearby, so who knows if Mitt's money and proximity can put him back in the race? I'm feeling confident that McCain will rise from the (relatively) dead.

All analysts said that disaffected Republicans and Independents would flock to the Democratic caucuses and "declare" themselves Democrats this year, creating unpredictability and volatility. They sure did.

True personal anecdote: about 5:00 p.m. Thursday night, before the doors opened for voters at 6:30 p.m. (CDT) here in Des Moines, I received a cell phone call from a long-time (female) friend in Buchanan County, Iowa, age 67. I had not heard from her in 2 years, since she relocated from Denver to our long-ago hometown of Independence, Iowa. Our parents had been lifelong friends and her mother (Arlene Raymond) was a long-time Republican lobbyist in Des Moines. Sue Ann is an ordained Episcopalian minister.

"Connie," she said, "I'm going to do something tonight that I never thought I'd do in my lifetime and something that may have my mother spinning in her grave. I'm going to go caucus Democratic. Who should I vote for? I don't want Hillary to get in."

Two of the trends pointed out in this piece played out with that statement: women over 65 did not like Hillary, and disaffected Republicans (which she confessed to being, this election year) caucused Democratic.

Sue Ann… [who was nearly arrested with me while photographing a Bush rally in the Coors Amphitheater in Denver, Colorado—her former hometown— during the last election]…knew I would be following both parties' candidates, but following the Democrats more closely, as my father had been four-time Democratic County Treasurer of Buchanan County (IA).. (Let's face it: the Democratic rallies have better music, which is enough of a reason to prefer attending them. And, this year, it seems, the Democrats have better candidates.)

I referred Reverend Raymond to my previous articles for the verbatim words of most of the candidates. I hung up the phone and whispered to myself, "The sky is falling. Sue Ann Raymond is voting Democratic!"

I'm going to be interested to find out for whom she finally caucused. I offer her story as representative of the degree of disillusionment that staunch Republicans are feeling this election cycle.

True Tales from the Iowa Caucuses

1/04/2008

I attended my second set of caucuses as an "observer" tonight in Iowa's state capitol of Des Moines (IA). I accompanied my college roommate and her 24-year-old daughter, a first-time voter, to Merrill Middle School on Grand Avenue, home of the Merill Mustangs, as the sign proudly proclaims. First time I attended as an Illinois resident, they learned I once taught junior high school and gave me the unenviable task of trying to control a passel of children set loose without supervision on a stage in the auditorium; this was something even a veteran 33-year educator did not want to undertake.

We were late, so I pulled in (going the wrong way, as it turned out, in a one-way circular drive) and dropped them off. It was 4 minutes to 7 p.m. The doors to the polling place for precincts 69 through 72 had been open since 6:30 p.m. After the polite policeman told me to try driving the RIGHT way out of the circular driveway, I had to drive 2 miles to find a parking spot. They lock the doors to the polling places at 7:00 p.m., but my friend stood sentinel at the door, staunchly demanding that I be admitted, so I was.

For her troubles, she was told that they had run out of ballots and she couldn't caucus. That turned out to be incorrect. The ballots were for the Republicans, who met in the gymnasium. The Democrats met in the cafeteria, and Democrats don't have actual "ballots." They have hand counts and 2-minute speech-giving opportunities and unorchestrated chaos.

I sidled up next to a gentleman with an impressive-looking camera who turned out to be (Washington, D.C.) correspondent John Hultgren from Norway, who was reporting for Aftenposten.

"What do you think of the caucus process?" I asked him. "Pretty small-town, huh?"

He smiled and replied, "It's absolutely fascinating." (www.aftenposten.no)

There were 372 people in our cafeteria meeting room, one television reporter from CNN blocking the door, and a lot of overhead boom microphones. (Television Tripod count: 3). Precinct Chairman Mark Cooper stood on a raised platform, his waist-length ponytail singling him out, and instructed each group to start the first count, which was done solely by a show of hands. One woman said, "What about the pregnant woman who was sitting here? She just left for the bathroom."

Arrangements were made to wait for the pregnant woman to answer nature's call; the vote went on.

To be "viable," a candidate had to get 54 votes, or 15% of those present. After the first vote, a cheer went up from the Edwards camp, as they had secured 65 votes. The Obama camp, however, had 155 and needed only 15 more votes to get a third delegate. Hillary Clinton had 77 votes, Richardson had 47 and Biden had 34 in Precinct 70.

Confabs could be overheard, especially from the Biden camp, "We don't have a shot. If they (Clinton's group) send us 15, we're viable. We can hold Obama to 2 delegates. We'll move to Hillary to keep Obama at 2, not 3. We will help Joe if we even out the race versus Obama. As much as I like Richardson," (said the organizer to a Richardson supporter) "Joe is my first choice." Joe was also the first choice of my friend, so we hovered near the doomed Biden band. (At least until they were forced to DISband, due to "viability.")

At some point, while 2 minute speeches were going on to convince voters to "switch allegiance" if their candidate was not viable. A woman in the Richardson camp was reading a letter from the candidate in a very boring monotone. I left the cafeteria and traveled to the gymnasium *No Man's Land* where the Republicans present were caucusing.

Hostage Negotiations Seem "Civil" Compared to New Hampshire Debates

The Republicans and the Democrats Square Off—"Live"—in New Hampshire on Saturday, January 5th

1/06/2008

Governor Bill Richardson (D, NM) got the best line (and the biggest laugh) when he exclaimed, in the middle of the live Democratic debate on January 5th from New Hampshire's Dana Humanities Center at St. Anselm College: "I've been in hostage negotiations that are a lot more civil than this. There'll be plenty of time to get hostile versus the Republicans. You just heard them." Richardson went on to ask if experience had now become some sort of "leper," with the comment "We want to change this country, but you have to know how to do it."

I'm making no predictions for New Hampshire. That is best left to those "on the ground" in New Hampshire. Maybe when I get to Florida January 10th through the end of the month, I'll get a "feeling" from the grass roots people in Florida who are likely voters and can weigh in on their contest, firsthand.

What I can say without fear of contradiction is that polls are often misleading. Sometimes, it is to a candidate's advantage to have the polls sway the voters, the tail wagging the dog, by making sure the polls report something that really has no basis in fact. Therefore, the 200 people (a relatively small sampling) in New Hampshire that were sampled for 3 nights just before the debate should probably not be taken as the "last word" on anything. The poll, conducted by McClatchy/MSNBC taken before, during and after the Iowa caucuses showed Clinton dropping from 30% to Obama's 27%, and reported an Obama surge to 39%, with Clinton at 32%.

Let's not forget how inaccurate the polls were in Iowa, reporting Hillary Clinton leading at almost all junctures, only to see her finish third.

During the live debate, with Charles Gibson moderating and "Facebook" users weighing in (and, don't forget: "Facebook" users skew young), the issue of "likeability" was raised with Hillary, as Gibson came right out and said, "They seem to like Barack Obama more." It was Hillary's best—and possibly only— good moment in the debate, as she said, "Well, that hurts my feelings, but I'm going to go on." Hillary has modified her appearance(s) in New Hampshire to take questions from the audience more. I'd like to think my blog article(s) influenced that, but I'm too rational to take credit for what a lot of people pointed out: her plasticity, her "prepared" stump speech, the stiffing of the fourth-grade reporter by daughter Chelsea (and where was Bill during this debate? No crowd shots of our last Democratic President and the current candidate's husband.)

To this viewer, Hillary looked (to use a colloquialism of my mother's), "Mad enough to spit" at several junctures. She took shots at Edwards. She took shots at Obama. She seemed irritable, out-of-sorts and semi-desperate in trying to make her points.

George Stephanopoulus and Diane Sawyer, commenting on the fatigue factor that showed on everyone's faces during the debate, praised Edwards' fiery rhetoric, but I wondered if Edwards, too, was a tad desperate and trying to hitch his wagon to Obama's rising star (to mix a few metaphors)?

Hillary expressed the opinion that the two male front-runners after Iowa were "tag-teaming" her during the debate. This was apparent when Edwards leaped to Obama's defense after Hillary attacked Obama's health care positions. Edwards retorted, "Every time we speak out for change, the forces of the status quo are gonna' attack. I didn't hear these kinds of attacks (from Hillary) when Senator Clinton was ahead, but I hear them now." So the seating was serendipity: Edwards and Obama were (physically) seated on the left and represented the most change; Richardson and Hillary were seated on the right and represented experience and the Old Guard.

Another good moment for Bill Richardson—one of the night's bigger winners if you tally personal appeal—came when he was given the opportunity to "take back" anything he might have said in earlier debates (just as the rest of the candidates were given that opportunity). He specifically mentioned an earlier debate when he had been asked to select his favorite Supreme Court Justice. His initial response to the question had been "Living or dead?" (This brought a small chuckle from the crowd).

Richardson then explained that he had selected Byron "Whizzer" White, because he was a JFK pick for the Court and Richardson had idolized John Fitzgerald Kennedy. Later, he discovered that White was against civil rights, wanted to roll back Roe v. Wade, and, said Richardson with a laugh, "That wasn't a good one." (Edwards could be seen laughing heartily down on the left end.)

Most of the other candidates simply chose to point out the fact that the Democrats were at least *trying* to discuss the issues that concern the American people. They weren't (and aren't) completely hung up on fences or critters, but are talking about the economy, the war in Iraq, energy conservation, alternative sources of energy, universal health care, and global warming.

Not so the Republicans, who were hung up on illegal immigration a disproportionate amount of time, moving on to Iraq and oil, but only touching upon those issues briefly. No talk of the housing crisis. Not much talk of the national debt, except from (former Libertarian) Ron Paul. Some talk of the war, which all but Paul support. Economy issues? Find that discussion elsewhere on your dial.

As Obama put it, "The stark contrast between us and the Republicans (who had just debated prior to the Democrats taking the same stage) is that we are ending the politics of fear. We are trying to bring the American people together."

I had just watched the Republican segment, with six participants, and a more discordant group you couldn't find outside an elementary school playground at recess. Romney seemed to be the Big Target for all of the participants. Somebody should just make him a shirt with a target on the back. He did not seem to be on "good" terms with anyone. He got into it with Huckabee. He got into it with Giuiliani and Paul. Perhaps the biggest gap was between himself and (Republican front-runner) Senator John McCain (R, AZ), who, in my opinion and that of many experts, is the likely Republican winner in New Hampshire. (Question to follow: Is McCain selling what the American public wants to buy, i.e., more war?)

Iowa's big winner, Mike Huckabee, got in a clean shot when he threw out the comment "Which one?" as Romney complained that his opinions on the issues were being misquoted. [Ouch!] McCain chimed in, "When you (Romney) change your positions from time to time, you will get misquoted." McCain, discussing the illegal immigrant issue, said, "Ronald

Reagan had amnesty. I think he'd be in one of Mitt's negative commercials." McCain added, "You can spend your entire fortune on attack ads (attacking McCain's positions on issues), and it still won't be true."

Holy Cow, Batman! I think Mitt has hit several nerves!

Keep in mind that 3 out of 10 likely voters in each party in New Hampshire said they could still change their minds and nearly 1 of 10 Independents (the state is 40% Independent) said that they still hadn't decided in which primary to vote! While the immigration issue may have been McCain's Achilles heel in the past, is it really the nation's "most pressing" issue, with the Iraq War raging, a recession threatening, the economy faltering, housing in crisis, and energy, global warming and education "hot button" issues that the Republicans barely touch upon? [Face-book voters (who weighed in by computer in real time) didn't think so, and neither do I.]

Someone said of McCain, "He was the adult in the room." Others (in the aftermath) thought that Thompson had come out looking better than his previous leisurely trot towards the White House, but the question is whether Thompson's Federalist conservative views have been expressed too little, too late.

I came away with some impressions… and I defer to the New Hampshire residents here. I'm still watching with great interest as things play out in the cold New Hampshire winter. Let's face it: being "on the ground" in New Hampshire is the way to get an accurate "read" when polls and national media may (or may not) be corrupt. (Who knows? I often try the foreign press to get my information these days.)

Later this month, I'll be in Florida, and I will also have that "on-the-ground" advantage in Illinois, but I don't claim to know more than the New Hampshire residents about how things are actually shaping up out there on the East coast. When I was taken to task for predicting an Obama win in Iowa by people in New Jersey and California, I thought, "Time will tell." And it did.

That said, I do have a few comments on the "live" televised debate of January 5th as an outsider, (and, as you faithful readers know, by now, I take my politics seriously, Iowan-at-heart that I am):

1. The boys on the Republican team don't like Mitt. (Mitt, for his part, said, "If they're ignoring you, they're not worried about you.") Let's not forget that Mitt just picked up Wyoming in its primary, but let's not forget this, either: the Republican National

Committee has slashed half of Wyoming's 28 national convention delegates because they moved up the dates of their nomination contest. Similarly, the national party leaders penalized Florida, Michigan, New Hampshire and South Carolina, for the same reason. Food for thought.

2. The front-runners (i.e., Obama and Edwards) on the Democratic side don't like Hillary much, and, as I have said in many articles from Iowa, neither do a lot of other people. Hillary is like the Terminator. She just keeps coming, angrier and more lethal than before. But she is NOT "liked" and Democrats better do some real soul-searching before they pick their ultimate nominee, to make sure that that person can take on a Republican candidate in the national election and win. Nominating the person voted "least likely to succeed nationally" is not a smart move. Democrats have often shot themselves in the proverbial foot with their nominee (*Kerry, anyone?*).

3. The Republicans aren't discussing the issues that really matter the very most to American voters.

4. Obama is on a roll.

5. Hillary is on a slide.

6. McCain is probably holding his own (i.e, the Republican leader in New Hampshire.)

7. Edwards is hanging on.

8. Huckabee will probably go Huckabust in New Hampshire, where evangelical Christians do not have a stranglehold on the Republican process.

That's the way I see it from way out here in the snowy Heartland, and I welcome comments from New Hampshire residents who are "there" and can tell the rest of the nation what is *really* going on! When I hit Florida for a month and/or when the primary is held in Illinois, I'll be among the "on the ground" numbers, but, for now, it's just me and my trusty TV, trying to make sense of this fascinating game called politics.

In New Hampshire, John Edwards Says He'll Fight On

1/07/2008
Working feverishly up until the final moments before the primary vote in New Hampshire, Democratic Presidential contender John Edwards, introduced by wife Elizabeth, appeared with movie stars Susan Sarandon and Tim Robbins.

The crowd was small in the cold outdoor weather as Edwards' Main Street Express pulled up for him to deliver his remarks, but he seemed as fired-up as ever, despite a grueling schedule and little sleep (and being outspent 6-to-1). When Edwards was asked by a reporter about Hillary Clinton's much-reported "Edward Muskie moment," where she appeared close to tearing up at a rally, Edwards (and Obama before him) refused to comment on same, saying, "Running for President is a tough process."

Edwards delivered his usual "stump" messages, but, this time, he was asked if he was going to quit the race if he didn't do well in New Hampshire. His response? "We have no intention of walking away (from the issues). Yes, we are in it to stay." The same questioner then asked if the Edwards campaign had enough money to continue the fight, and the former Senator from North Carolina (1999-2005) said, "This is not an auction; it is an election. Yes, we have the money and we have budgeted for the entire process."

"What if you don't win any primaries?" the questioner persisted.

"I cannot accept that premise," responded Edwards, with a smile. "I will win primaries."

Another new question came from a person in the back of the crowd who expressed the opinion that, if a draft were in force, there would be more pressure from the public to end the war in Iraq. Edwards did not equivocate. He said, "I don't favor the draft for a variety of reasons," and referenced his military advisers who advise him on such issues.

Some other interesting insights into the race in New Hampshire and beyond came from CQ Politics.com contributor Craig Crawford, who phoned into CNN (from Orlando, Florida) and said, "I think that Florida is being set up as a test, sort of like Off-Broadway."

That was good news for me, as I will be there by Thursday and staying there until the eve of their primary. Crawford, who broke his ankle and, therefore, "covered" the Iowa caucuses and the New Hampshire primary totally from afar by watching C-Span, is holed up in Orlando, Florida, right now with a broken ankle.

Kevin Landrigan, political analyst for the Nashua *Telegraph*, reporting on CNN, said that there had been, "A lot of surprises and shock for what's happened to Hillary Clinton" in New Hampshire. He went on to say, "She's got to define Barack Obama and not let him define himself." As for Obama, he cautioned his enthusiastic supporters that, "It is very important for us all to be clear that we have not won anything yet."

On the Republican side, John McCain may be the front-runner, but his adviser Mark McKinnon said that finances had forced the McCain campaign to stop doing their own polling. "We just realized we were going to have to jump out of the plane without a parachute," said McKinnon.

Never fear: there are plenty of other people out there doing the polling. One poll showed Obama up by 9 points over Hillary (whereas Obama and Hillary were tied on Saturday), with Edwards holding at 16%, Richardson at 7% and Kucinech dropping from 2 to 1%. Of the 40% of voters who were still undecided, as reported by Adam Sexton of WMUR-TV in Manchester, Independent voters were still making up their minds at the midnight hour. Only 26% of those who lean Democrat had decided on their guy (or gal) and only 28% of those who normally lean Republican had made their final choice. That means there were still 21% undecideds (who normally lean Democratic) and 27% who were undecided who normally lean Republican.

John Edwards was doing yet another 36-hour non-stop round of appearances, as he did in Iowa, ending with the Red Arrow Diner. When asked about fatigue, Edwards said, "There is no sleep. I get a few minutes here and a few minutes there. But I'm doing okay." Richardson, too, said he was "exhausted, but exhilarated." John McCain made 7 rally stops on Monday, versus only 3 stops for Rudy Giuliani. Mike Huckabee was playing bass guitar with local bands to drum up support for his candidacy.

Fred Thompson up and left for South Carolina, pinning his hopes on that Southern state (Thompson was a Senator from Tennessee) and Ron Paul and Mike Huckabee, like Mitt Romney, are using television to get their message(s) across. Using his considerable war chest, Romney has had a TV spot running on television every 8 and one-half minutes. Meanwhile, Mike Huckabee will appear on Jay Leno while Ron Paul will appear on David Letterman tonight, the night before the Tuesday voting.

Andy Smith of the UNH (University of New Hampshire) Survey Center reported that the difficult-to-predict Independent voters were appearing to primarily plan to vote Democratic, to the tune of 60%. The weather is good and, if the turnout is heavy (and it is expected to be as high as half a million, up from 396,000 in 2000)...Obama and McCain will benefit. Therefore, Smith predicted a 10-point lead for Obama over Clinton on January 8th.

Dixville Notch, New Hampshire, Voters "Diss" Hillary Clinton

1/08/2008

The first voting of the New Hampshire primary took place in Dixville Notch, New Hampshire, at precisely midnight, as its 17 residents weighed in, seriously "dissing" former front-runner Hillary Clinton by giving her a big fat goose egg. Zero votes for Hillary.

For the Republicans, John McCain received 4 votes, Mitt Romney 2, and Rudy Giuliani 1.

For the Democrats, Barack Obama prevailed with 7 votes, the most of anyone, John Edwards got 2, and Bill Richardson got 1.

The ranks of those who actually call themselves "Democrats" had swelled by 100% in Dixville Notch recently with the addition of 1 new voter, because, previously, there had only been one declared Democrat; now there are two. Most in Dixville Notch are independents, not affiliated with either the Democrats or the Republicans. Emerging the biggest vote getter, overall, of either party, has to be viewed as good news for the Obama campaign, still riding the crest of popularity demonstrated in the Iowa caucuses just 5 days ago.

Hillary Clinton and Barack Obama both spent about $5 million in TV spots, with Barack spending slightly more than Hillary. In the state as a whole, reports from TNS Media Intelligence/CMAG say that $26 million plus was spent in New Hampshire (some reports placed it easily at $30 million). $40 million was spent on ads in Iowa, according to the ad-tracking firm TNS Media Intelligence/CMAG.

Can Hillary Cry Her Way to the White House?

1/10/2008

Can Hillary cry her way to the White House? In the wake of the record-setting New Hampshire vote, which was estimated to be near 500,000 (up from 396,385 ballots in 2000, according to New Hampshire Secretary of State William Gardner), there were many surprises and signs that the Presidential nomination race is going to be a fight to the finish for candidates of both parties.

Maureen Dowd wondered, in print, whether Hillary could "cry her way to the White House," citing the now-famous "Muskie moment" of yesteryear, replayed in a diner in 2008 with Hillary in the starring role. It's interesting to see how that teary nano-second with Hillary played out in the media.

Mo Rocca's blog called it the moment that she LOST the Presidency, and many others joined him in that assumption. (*Note: Mo Rocca was across the aisle from me inside Invesco Field in Denver during the acceptance speech following the DNC nomination of Obama.*) As it turns out, in retrospect, it may have "humanized" the Robo-candidate just enough to help her win New Hampshire (along with a Clinton-friendly state and lots of money thrown at it).

I would also mention the male hecklers in Salem, who barged into one of Hillary's press appearances and shouted, "Iron my shirt!" before being shown the door. Incidents like these a political campaign doth make. Following these incidents, New Hampshire women turned to Hillary, which Iowa women did not...especially Iowa women over sixty-five, according to surveys. And let's not forget that New Hampshire has some experience at placing women in office on a state level, while Iowa has not (yet) elected a woman Governor, despite a valiant effort by Roxanne Conlin one year.

I want to reprint what I wrote on the eve of the New Hampshire contest.

I'm making no predictions for New Hampshire. That is best left to those "on the ground" in New Hampshire. Maybe when I get to Florida January 10th through the end of the month, I'll get a feeling from the grass roots people in Florida who are likely voters and can weigh in on their contest, firsthand.

What I can say without fear of contradiction is that polls are often misleading. Sometimes, it is to a candidate's advantage to have the polls sway the voters, the tail wagging the dog, by making sure the polls report something that really has no basis in fact.

Therefore, the 200 people (a relatively small sampling) in New Hampshire that were sampled for 3 nights just before the debate should probably not be taken as the "last word" on anything. The poll, conducted by McClatchy/MSNBC taken before, during and after the Iowa caucuses showed Clinton dropping from 30% to Obama's 27%, and reported an Obama surge to 39%, with Clinton at 32%.

Let's not forget how inaccurate the polls were in Iowa, reporting Hillary Clinton leading at almost all junctures, only to see her finish third.

1. The boys on the Republican team don't like Mitt. (Mitt, for his part, said, "If they're ignoring you, they're not worried about you.") Let's not forget that Mitt just picked up Wyoming in its primary, but let's not forget this, either: the Republican National Committee has slashed half of Wyoming's 28 national convention delegates because they moved up the dates of their nomination contest. Similarly, the national party leaders penalized Florida, Michigan, New Hampshire and South Carolina, for the same reason. Food for thought.

2. The front-runners (i.e., Obama and Edwards) on the Democratic side don't like Hillary much. I have said in many articles from Iowa, neither do a lot of other people. Hillary is like the Terminator. She just keeps coming, angrier and more lethal than before. But she is NOT "liked" and Democrats better do some real soul-searching before they pick their ultimate nominee, to make sure that that person can take on a Republican candidate in the national election (*looking more and more as though it will

be John McCain) and win. Nominating the person voted "least likely to succeed nationally" is not a smart move, and Democrats have often shot themselves in the proverbial foot with their nominee (John Kerry, anyone?).

3. The Republicans aren't discussing the issues that really matter the very most to American voters.
4. Obama is on a roll.
5. Hillary is on a slide.
6. McCain is probably holding his own and will be the Republican leader in New Hampshire.)

Those were my words the day before New Hampshire erupted with unexpected results. It will be interesting to see how they hold up as the race goes forward.

Fred Thompson January 10th Debate Performance Has Republicans Buzzing
Thompson Gaining Traction?

1/12/2008

Following January 10th's Republican debate in Myrtle Beach, South Carolina, twenty-eight people in Charleston, South Carolina's Fox studios, outfitted with little dial gizmos that have become a staple of the network's hand-selected debate-watchers, were polled by Fox News. Who did the viewers think had done the best in the debate?

Professional pundits like Bill O'Reilly (on January 11th) said,

"I thought Thompson helped himself last night." Political analyst Dick Morris (asked by

O'Reilly) weighed in with, "He was fearsome, but effective."

Three of the gizmo-people raised their hands, to indicate they had come into the room supportive of Fred Thompson, former Senator from Tennessee. By debate's end, however, approximately 12 watchers raised their hands to say that they were new converts to Fred's camp, a fourfold increase. Fox seemed very intent on promoting how well Fred had done, although my husband and I, watching from Florida, thought he had placed third, behind Huckabee and Romney. (So much for inviting US to wear those little dial thingies.)

One gizmo-guy said, "Fred will challenge them." Another, almost speechless with enthusiasm, burbled, "He jumps out there and goes after Huckabee…" Only one lone female participant said, "I thought he was one of the most negative in the debate" and said she found him to be "sarcastic, to some degree."

So what, exactly, did Thompson say during the debate that had these listeners all agog? For that matter, what else has Thompson said (or done) by which he might be judged?

A good Thompson debate line: "This is a battle for the heart and soul of the Republican party." Great line. And it didn't involve the usual critter comparisons Fred is so fond of, such as the "bear" story (see article "Fred Thompson Trots Toward the White House"). Thompson used metaphorical bears when campaigning in Iowa, but switched to alligators for this quote in an article entitled, "The Fred Express" in *News-Max*. (September, 2007 interview with John Fund, columnist for the *Wall Street Journal's OpinionJournal.com* and *The American Spectator*). In that interview Thompson said, "I sometimes say that many Republicans came to Washington determined to drain the swamp and wound up in an alliance with the spending alligators."

Thompson, early on in the January 10th debate, declared, "We'd all be better off if the tax cuts were not scheduled to end in 2010." At a later point, discussing United States border issues, Thompson said, "We need to be a nation of high fences and wide gates. And we get to be the ones who decide when to open the gates and when to close them."

Thompson repeated that he wanted to enforce our borders, crack down on illegal immigration and stop sanctuary cities (an often contentious issue between Thompson and Giuliani; Thompson has accused Giuliani of harboring illegal immigrants in the "sanctuary city" of New York City as its Mayor). The illegal immigration issue seems to consume a disproportionate amount of time in all Republican debates, when compared to Democratic debates. Why is that? There are so many other issues facing the nation and the world: the United States economy, the environment and global warming, the war in Iraq and how to conclude that Administration-created quagmire, the price of gas and the search of alternative sources of energy, universal health care for all citizens, education. The illegal immigration debate deserves time, but should it be the Central Issue of the Republicans, eclipsing every other?

It's interesting that Fred Thompson is now lusting after the Presidency. When he left the Senate in 2003, Thompson said, "After eight years in Washington, I longed for the realism and sincerity of Hollywood." In a previous article on the candidates' net worth ("How Much Are the Candidates Worth?") I reported that Thompson made about $3.6 mill acting in character roles in Hollywood.

Thompson describes himself as a Federalist, saying that he believes in "the proper division of power between the states and federal government that so many politicians forget now, unless it's convenient for them."

Thompson's renewed interest in and return to politics has much to do with his marriage in June of 2002 to Jeri Kehn (Thompson), a 40-year-old former Republican National Committee spokeswoman and former media consultant for a lobbyist firm. Jeri Lynn is a slim pretty blonde, who snagged the playboy-about-town after he had gained that reputation in D.C. in the nineties, by dating celebrities such as country singer Lorrie Morgan (among others).

Dick Morris, political analyst, writing in "On Politics," says that Jeri "appears to be running things and approving all hirings in Thompson's campaign," but Morris added, "She is out of her league and is not helping her husband. You can't have someone running a campaign who can't be fired. Mrs. Thompson needs to find something else to do all day." (Ouch!)

So, what are Thompson's motives for storming the Washington Bastille again? Thompson lost his daughter Elizabeth "Betsy" Panici in January 2002 from a coma caused by an overdose of painkillers. She was 38 years old. He has said that "I just didn't have the heart to run again for the Senate" after her death, but then adds, "I changed my mind after 9/11 and the national security challenges we then faced…I never intended to go back into politics."

With the birth of Thompson's two children with new wife Jeri (he was divorced from his first wife in 1985; they were high school sweethearts who married at 17 when she became pregnant), 4-year-old daughter Hayden and 1-year-old son Samuel, he said, "Within the space of a year and a half, I experienced the ultimate tragedy and the ultimate happiness. I count my blessings, and I have a real focused sense of purpose now."

Thompson also has a son from his first marriage, Daniel, who was paid $176,600 over four years as a "management consultant" to Thompson's PAC, although the PAC has no office, phone, or employees and raised no money.

Some critics do not see the "focused sense of purpose" that Thompson claims to have rediscovered. Jon Stewart (et. al.) made fun of Thompson on a recent *Daily Show* for not liking to have his picture taken with supporters on the campaign trail. Stewart suggested that Thompson should let his "stand in" do that. That "doesn't pose with the locals" accusation is not entirely fair. Former Senator Thompson was most gracious in posing

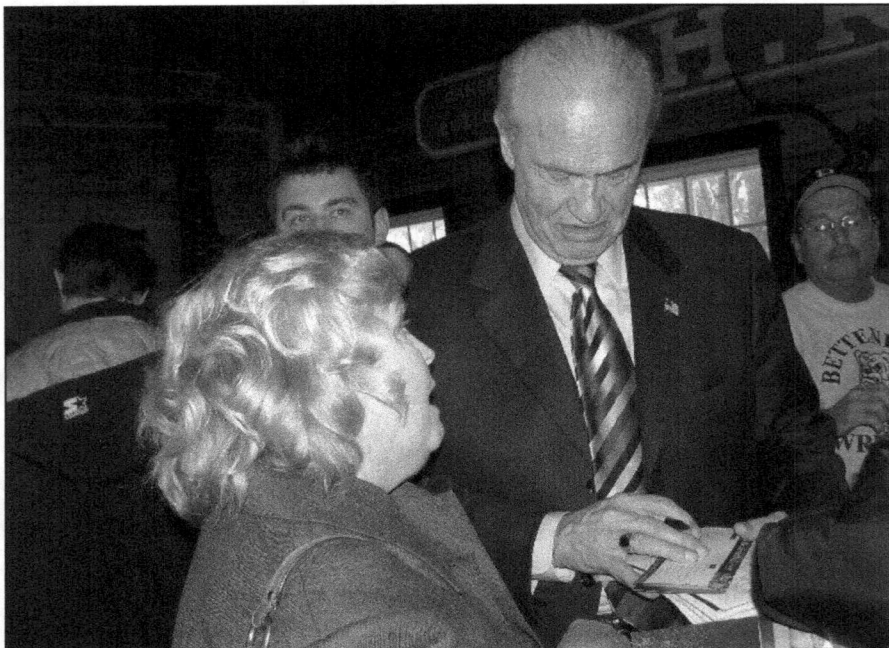

Fred Thompson signing an autograph for me at the Thunder Bay Grill in Davenport, Iowa.

with me in Davenport, Iowa, and the result was a truly hideous picture of the two of us.

Fred was a real trooper posing that day, as was Jeri Thompson, his wife, who told me that "Fred's daughter attended Belmont University" when I remarked that my own daughter is attending Belmont University in Nashville, Tennessee (the school that gave us "American Idol's" Melinda Dolittle). Jeri Thompson's other comment to me that day on the campaign trail: she was wearing a beret because it was "a bad hair day."

Many fault Thompson for being lazy on the campaign trail and acting like his heart just isn't in it. Thompson's response is this: "That's what they said about me before I ran for Senate the first time, and that's what they said about me two years later when I ran for re-election. I won the first time by 21 points, and 25 points the second time. That was in a state that Bill Clinton carried twice. If you can do that while being lazy, I recommend it to everyone."

Fred also said, ironically, "Politics is now one big 24-hour news cycle, but we seem to spend less time than ever on real substance." He reassured his followers this way: "I may not do frenetic campaigning well, but I am purposeful and people seem to appreciate someone who follows a plan rather than engages in perpetual motion. I assure you I have a plan on how to win. And the money to support that plan is coming in quite nicely, thank you."

Senator Thompson, at 65, has a history in Washington, DC, that includes Nixon's assessment of him (from the transcription of Nixon's tapes) as "dumb as hell." This remark was made by Nixon when Senator Howard Baker was urging Nixon to approve Thompson's appointment as Republican investigative counsel for the Senate Watergate Committee in 1973. Having earned the nickname "Moose" in high school probably did nothing to dispel that initial impression of the 6' 5" Senator, back in 1973 and Thompson, was indeed, appointed.

Fred got his moment of revenge during the Watergate hearings when he asked Nixon Assistant Alexander Butterfield, "Are you aware of the installation of any listening devices in the Oval Office of the President?" This bombshell revelation of the existence of the Watergate Tapes led, ultimately, to Nixon's demise. Said Thompson in his book *At That Point in Time*, "I was looking for a reason to believe that Richard M. Nixon, President of the United States, was not a crook."

One of Thompson's best lines in the January 10th Republican debate concerned polls. He said, with sarcasm, "Oh, my goodness! Go against a poll?" This remark was well-received by the appreciative crowd, as it displayed Thompson's folksy sense of humor, just as Huckabee's comment ("If you're not catching flak, you're not over the target...") played well with the audience.

An old story from Thompson's youth has the 6' 5", 225 lb. football player knocked flat on his back on the football field. Coaches come running. Thompson opens one eye and quips, "How's the crowd taking it?"

Another good Thompson remark during the Republican debate (in response to a recent Iranian small boat incident) was: "If they cross the line, they're going to be destroyed." Thompson projected strength without specifics, as he often did on the stump.

There are many "Presidential-sounding" statements, that Thompson convincingly utters with the unmistakable "gravitas" of a man who has played the Commander-in-Chief on film ("The Last Best Chance," 2005 HBO docudrama), as well as Rear Admiral Joshua Painter ("The Hunt for Red October"), and most recently, spent five years depicting prosecutor Arthur Branch on NBC's "Law and Order". (That last fact helps Thompson with voters aged 18 to 34).

So, with "change" the buzz-word of the day, what did political analyst Dick Morris have to say about Fred Thompson in September of 2007 in *NewsMax*: "Fred Thompson is the ultimate insider, a friend of the rich and powerful, and a former corporate lobbyist who worked for whoever was willing to pay the tab… He's definitely one of the boys. And his blatant nepotism is an abuse of the system and the clearest example of a business-as-usual attitude…Thompson is not at all a candidate of change…For the moment, Fred Thompson is still a player. A lot depends on how much money he can raise. In virtually every recent poll, Thompson beats McCain and hovers near 20% of the primary vote. Thompson is a charismatic one-of-a-kind politician. But the reality is that Thompson is the ultimate insider. And, unless he makes some changes, it won't be long before voters understand that."

Michigan Primary: Mitt Romney's Last Stand?

1/14/2008

Michigan Primary: Mitt Romney's Last Stand? When George Romney was the Republican Governor of Michigan 40 years ago, his Lieutenant Governor was a Traverse City, Michigan department store heir by the name of William Milliken.

Milliken backed George Romney when he made a run for the GOP Presidential nomination against Richard Nixon in 1968, giving him his full support. When Romney left the Michigan Governor's position in 1969 to become Nixon's Secretary of Housing and Urban Development, Milliken became his successor. He went on to win re-election 3 times. William Milliken served for 14 years—longer than any other Michigan Governor, and retired in 1983, twenty-five years ago.

When asked by David Broder of the *Washington Post Writers Group* about 2008's two front-runners, John McCain (R, AZ) and Mitt Romney (R, Massachusetts), Milliken said he was "about to jump in. I'm waiting for a phone call from John McCain so I can tell him I'm endorsing him."

This endorsement seems on a par with John Kerry's endorsement of Barack Obama instead of his former Vice Presidential 2004 running-mate John Edwards, but without the self-serving backdrop Kerry's endorsement may reflect in angling for a future position in any winning candidate's Cabinet.

Milliken, long out of politics ("I haven't been involved in the current GOP campaign."), has no such ulterior motive for his views. He's not looking to jump on any bandwagons so that he can snag a position in the administration as the wagons circle in D.C.

So, why does William Milliken support John McCain over native son Mitt Romney?

Said Milliken, "Though I don't agree with him (McCain) on a couple issues (the war and abortion), he is so honest and straightforward, I just respect his integrity. McCain has been steadfast on immigration, even though his legislation was unsuccessful. He has resisted the effort to demagogue the issue. I like him for that. He's been very good on the environment and global warming. He's taken a position on Iraq that I don't happen to agree with, but he's been straightforward and steadfast. There is an overall sense of integrity superior to everyone else in the field, even at the risk of taking positions that are not politically popular."

What about Mitt?

Milliken noted that he had not known Mitt Romney well before this year, saying, "He was quite a young fellow when his dad and I served together, and he left Michigan as a youth. But I met with him at his request a couple months ago when he was campaigning here. He has switched positions quite regularly. He has become much more conservative than his father ever was. I doubt his father would approve of his hard swing to the right."

Milliken and his wife Helen did support George Herbert Bush in 1980's Republican primary, helping him carry Michigan against Ronald Reagan, but Milliken's view of George W. Bush, the son and the current occupant of the Oval Office, is that he has "pandered to the extreme right" and "rushed us into a tragic and unnecessary war that has alienated this nation from much of the world."

Mitt Romney's camp quickly countered that comment by saying that William Milliken has become so alienated from orthodox Republicans, himself, that he endorsed John Kerry over George W. Bush for President in 2004.

With gas prices up ten cents over the past three weeks and Michigan a One-State Depression, the rather unreliable polls show a virtual dead-heat between McCain and Romney, with 27% for McCain and 26.3% for Romney in Michigan (Fox Poll of Monday, Jan. 14, 2008).

Romney is wooing the state's voters with the message that he turned Massachusetts around and has extensive executive experience that will help him to restore Michigan to the prominence it once held, now gone, as documented in Flint, Michigan, native Michael Moore's documentary "Roger and Me" which depicted the fall of the automobile industry in Michigan and the outsourcing of good jobs overseas.

Romney says that Michigan's downward spiral can be reversed and vows to accomplish it, if elected. McCain takes a more pessimistic view, saying that the good jobs will never totally return to the state. After all, during his last run for the Presidency, McCain used a bus called the Straight Talk Express.

With the accelerated nature of the primaries and caucuses this year, polling is much less reliable, so no predictions here, either. Many have wondered if Romney, as a pragmatic wealthy businessman (over $200 million of personal wealth) who has spent upwards of $30 million of his own money in the race, so far, will, at some point, feel it is time to pull the plug on his campaign to cut his losses?

Will Michigan be Mitt's Last Stand?

As a Fox political analyst said on Jan. 14th, "If you can't win in your home state and you can't win in New Hampshire when you're Governor of a nearby state… (complete that thought.)

Words
Connie Wilson

1/14/2008

Words

If fewer words were spoken
If fewer words were said;
If deeds alone were the mark of a man,
Not the "catch" of an eloquent pledge.

If fewer words were spoken,
If fewer words were said.
If, for all the fake forensics,
There were simple words, instead.

And a man stated
Just what he started to state,
Without false fuss
Or further ado.

If you weren't a politician
I'd probably listen to you.

(*Written at age 16, included in "Both Sides Now" by Connie Corcoran Wilson, and just as true today as the day it was composed.)

Rudy Giuliani Rallies Republicans in New Smyrna Beach, Florida, on January 15th, 2008

1/16/2008

As we arrived in New Smyrna Beach, Florida, on January 15th, turning on 3rd Street to reach the Coconut Palm Beach Resort, who was just a couple of hours behind us and a few blocks away at the local Republican Club on Third Avenue? None other than former Mayor of New York City and current Republican Presidential candidate Rudy Giuliani.

Rudy arrived in the "Rudymobile," his own version of the Edwards "Main Street Express." He stood on a wooden box in front of the bus to deliver remarks to a crowd of nearly five hundred supporters.

The Republican Club of Southeast Volusia sends CARE packages to soldiers serving in Iraq and Afghanistan, which influenced Giuliani to stop in this ocean-front resort town. "It's a Republican club doing something for all Americans," he said. Giuliani also told the crowd, "I'm the Republican who can win and then we can have a country with an optimistic future."

A recent poll, released January 14th, shows a tight race here among four Republican front-runners heading into the January 29th Presidential primary, with McCain at 22 % of likely GOP voters and Giuliani at 20%.

A different poll, the second annual Sunshine State Survey, a survey of 1200 Florida residents taken by the Florida Chamber of Commerce, showed that 43% of those who have lived in the state over five years feel that Florida has declined in liveability since 2003. Only 24% of the Florida residents surveyed have confidence that Florida's quality of life will improve, well below the 37% of those surveyed who think life is going to get much worse.

The News Journal (Southeast Volusia Edition) columnist Mark Lane wrote of the concerns of Florida residents this way in his column of January 16th: "We Floridians see a pleasant past, a crummy now and a crummier future. And I suspect anybody who could reasonably assure us otherwise could have a sunny political future."

So, is Rudy Giuliani the candidate who can reasonably assure Floridians of a better tomorrow? Rudy thinks so. He told television reporters from WOFL (Lake Buena Vista, FL) earlier in the week, in an exclusive interview in Orlando, "This is a state where we have tremendous enthusiasm and support...We want their support. We want their vote."

What was Rudy's message in New Smyrna Beach, to reassure Floridians that "the sun'll come out tomorrow," as the "Annie" lyric goes? How did he reassure Mark Lane, the columnist who wrote, "We didn't have all that glorious of a past, are coping with the crummy now, and pretty much discount the beautiful future altogether...We suspect the kids will have to leave town to get a job, but things will look ugly enough that they won't get choked up at the prospect."

How did Rudy respond to the 70% of Floridians in the Sunshine State survey who said they are sick of the growing density marring their once-beautiful state?

Rudy presented a bucket of signed baseballs to the Republican Club of Southeast Volusia and talked about 9/11. His 9/11 remarks brought to mind Senator Joe Biden's debate comment that, when it comes to Rudy, "All he ever says is a noun, a verb, and 9/11."

True to form and right on message on January 15th, Rudy singled out Al Hoehl, a New York City police chief on September 11th in New York City, who now lives in New Smyrna Beach, calling him "a giant" during the 9/11 tragedy. (Mr. Hoel *is* very tall.) Giuliani also made cursory comments about the nation's need to move towards energy independence and the need to cut taxes to stimulate the economy.

Giuliani has had an unusual strategy in this Presidential nominee race so far, skipping Iowa and New Hampshire almost entirely, to focus on Florida's January 29th contest. Most of his remarks have been "All security, all the time," also a good slogan for his post-Mayoral business interests.

In all fairness, Rudy mirrors most of the other Republican contenders, with the possible exception of Ron Paul. Rudy's employees in his campaign organization are also unique in that they haven't been paid lately. Maybe it doesn't matter (except to them, of course) for this reason: he has an extremely active volunteer organization working for him in Florida. Said Mike Scudiero, Volusia County's chairman for Giuliani, charged with getting out the vote, "He's got such a grass-roots operation here (that) nobody else has. I think, in the end, that will be very important." Rudy didn't mind acknowledging that the others will be here soon, though, asking the crowd on Tuesday, "Before the other candidates ever get here to campaign, how about voting for me?"

According to the Sunshine State poll, the most important issues in Florida are taxes and spending, public education, and increasing insurance rates. The residents don't seem as fixated on the Iraq War and/or illegal immigrants, which often seem to be the main themes of most of the Republican candidates, with very few exceptions—one of them being Mitt Romney who picked off Michigan on January 15th by suggesting that he can fix their broken economy. In the state where Romney's father, George, once served as Governor, his son won out with a positive message of turning things around economically. He beat back main challenger John McCain, whose message of executive experience and national security seems to parallel Rudy's.

Should Michigan's voting outcome be a cautionary tale for Rudy in Florida? Maybe any Republican who wants to win here needs to give these prospective voters some nuts-and-bolts concrete specifics about how he is going to ignite their economic hope(s), as the nation teeters on the verge of a potential recession?

I decided to do an informal and highly unscientific political poll of Florida residents I encountered, starting with my waitress at the New Smyrna Steakhouse and ending with a woman standing in the street on January 15th at Rudy's rally.

My waitress at the New Smyrna Steakhouse told me outright that she was a Republican, but that she "hadn't looked into it," yet, in terms of deciding for whom she would cast her vote. The time-share lady in Orlando told me, with great seriousness, that she would move from the country if Barack Obama were elected President, saying that he was "a Muslim." When I reassured her that Obama is definitely not a Muslim, she clammed up. Others asked seemed generally disinterested…perhaps because so few of the candidates have been actively campaigning in this region, as they are forced to divide their time among Michigan, Nevada, South Carolina, and places in between. One other impression (interpret it as you will): Florida is not Iowa or New Hampshire in more ways than one. (Certainly the weather is one way, as it has been in the high sixties and seventies here since January 10th).

The good news, for Rudy? Dotty Parrott, a New Yorker vacationing here, present at his speech on January 15th, said, "We're fans of Rudy's... He's done a great, great deal of good for New York City and New York state and he led us through 9/11." Another bit of "good news" if you're the much-married Giuliani is that the Sunshine State poll showed only 2% of those surveyed thought morals and family values issues should be the nation's Top Priority.

O'Reilly Attacks Edwards, the Forgotten Candidate

1/18/2008

While watching "The O'Reilly Factor" on Fox News on Thursday, January 18th (Fox News Channel), it was jarring to hear host Bill O'Reilly launch into a vitriolic attack on John Edwards, saying, "John Edwards is a charlatan…We deal with facts here on the Factor, not fiction."

What had so enraged Bill O'Reilly?

A clip of Edwards that O'Reilly used was taken from a recent stump speech featured Edwards talking about the 200,000 homeless veterans who served their country bravely, but would sleep under bridge overpasses or on sidewalk gratings that night, a familiar refrain for anyone who has heard Edwards's stump speech in person.

What O'Reilly did not fully disclose was that the comment was part of a much longer Edwards list of those in America who are disenfranchised. If you ever have attended a "live" John Edwards rally, or if you were watching the town hall meeting from the Henderson Convention Center in Henderson, Nevada on January 17th that was broadcast "live" on C-Span on the 17th, O'Reilly should have known that Edwards' remark about veterans was one in a long string. The veterans reference followed a recitation of the many homeless women and children now on the streets, because resources to help them have evaporated (Edwards said that 70 had to be turned away from a local Las Vegas shelter which he had visited that week), and Edwards mentioned other embarrassments to our rich country. Preceding his mention of the homeless veterans was a comment about those who go to bed hungry every night.

On January 17th, in Henderson, Nevada, John Edwards said during that same town meeting in Henderson that there was a "need to focus on what we can do for the people, the Latino community across America," and his recitation of the nearly 200,000 homeless veterans was accurate, according to statistics confirmed by the Veterans Administration.

What was enraging Bill O'Reilly was Edwards' inference that it is the economy that has forced veterans onto the streets, although the candidate has never denied that multiple factors might be at work.

O'Reilly wanted to make the point that most of these homeless veterans have drug, alcohol or mental health problems. O'Reilly seemed to find it disingenuous that Edwards did not bring those factors into play in his speech.

Edwards' speech was not solely focused on homeless veterans, however, as the C-Span live coverage showed, but was enumerating many things that are wrong in our country, the richest nation on the face of the planet.

O'Reilly dismissed Edwards' veteran comment snidely, saying, "It's the class warfare issue, which is all he's got," (Edwards distributes a nearly 70-page booklet of policies he would implement, if elected). O'Reilly trotted out Joseph Califano, author of *High Society*, who confirmed to O'Reilly's satisfaction that 90% of homeless veterans have drug or alcohol or mental health issues, something which Edwards himself would likely not dispute.

Patting himself on the back for his attack on the Democratic candidate lost in the glare of Clinton and Obama publicity, O'Reilly said, "Talk about dishonesty," his voice dripping with sarcasm, and continued, "Everybody else gives him a pass. Nobody but us calls Edwards on his simplification of the issue of homelessness among veterans."

What this tells me is that the O'Reilly element may be doing its best to discount John Edwards as a viable candidate, or, as *Newsweek* magazine front-paged him on their December 24th issue, "The Sleeper." Edwards has often been cited as the one candidate who can win against a Republican in both the red and the blue states, and carries the traditional "white Southern male" mantle of electability worn by winning Democratic candidates of yesteryear like Jimmy Carter and Bill Clinton.

Jonathan Prince, Deputy Campaign Manager of John Edwards for President said, in a news release on January 18th, "The traditional media outlets have their blinders on, narrowly focusing on the two $100 million dollar candidates—trying as hard as they can to keep John Edwards out of the picture."

Citing a "media stampede towards two candidates" Edwards himself acknowledged during the Henderson town hall meeting that he has been largely ignored by the main-stream media, which seems intent on anointing a winner very early in the game.

A woman in the crowd at the Henderson rally (televised live on C-Span) spoke up and said, "Don't let them take your voice away, because you're our voice. This is not a coronation." No less an authority than correspondent Andrea Mitchell is quoted as having said, "Don't count John Edwards out."

The campaign has just begun, the way Edwards sees it. He has said he's in it till the convention, with O'Reilly's attacks or without them. The very fact that O'Reilly would single out the candidate that the national polls are barely even tracking is singular, unless the Republicans fear him the most?

John Edwards is on the record (Dec, 2007, *Newsweek*, Q&A, p. 32) with this statement about his campaign, "I think that what the country is looking for in a president is somebody who has clear, very specific ideas and bold ideas about what needs to be done. I think that's what America needs. It's what I believe, and I think they're looking for somebody to be straight with them about the challenges they face, and very direct."

The question of the hour still remains, for the Democrats, which of the candidates will that be?

True Tales from the Nevada Caucuses

1/20/2008

What follows are true tales from the Nevada caucuses. And, no, I don't mean the group of culinary workers meeting in the Caesar's Palace main ballroom, televised by CNN. And I don't mean me, personally, as I am hunkered down on Florida's I-4 corridor, target of most of the Republicans in the race, now that South Carolina voting is over. You might say I'm waiting to ambush the likes of McCain and Romney, but that would be wrong.

I called up good friend and fellow writer, Dan Decker, Las Vegas resident and founder of the Chicago Screenwriters' Group, to find out what the caucus process in Nevada resembled, up close and personal, from someone actually taking part.

During the phone conversation we had one day after the event, which took place on Saturday, January 19, 2008, Dan confided, "It seemed to me that Obama was outmaneuvered by the local organization." (i.e., the Clinton machine). He noted that Harry Reid's son (D, Nevada) was Hillary's chief Nevada campaign strategist, and referred to "long lines of people standing around."

I asked if Dan had personally observed any problems with the vote, such as the screw-ups noted in South Carolina which caused candidate John McCain to ask a judge to allow for an hour extension of the voting times there. "Sure. All of that. Mostly, people didn't seem to know what to do."

Ah, yes, said the Iowan familiar with the caucus game. The oh-so-familiar unorchestrated chaos of the Iowa caucuses, now transplanted to Las Vegas with a few minor factors tweaked. Nevada even brought in

Iowa caucus veterans, to explain how a candidate remains "viable" only if he (or she) gets 15% of the voters who are there. Then, in Nevada and Iowa alike, the non-viable candidates' people (i.e., those with fewer than 15% of those present) are released to join another group.

But, in Nevada, unlike Iowa, the re-assembling pretty much stops there. In Iowa there is still some possible re-alignment (usually brokered on the floor in a horse-trading fashion), but in Nevada, the second alignment is permanent. And there is the matter of "the ballot" that Dan mentions in this first-person account, which does not appear at an Iowa caucus, unless you are a Republican.

Here's Dan Decker's True Tales of the Nevada Caucuses, generously shared:

Nevada! Nevada! Nevada!

Caucus Precinct 1352

Silvestri High School. (*Charles Silvestri, for whom the school was named, is an education professional and lobbyist.)

Packed and disorganized, but individual heroism is on display everywhere as a sense of urgency directs and motivates the multitude. This is the American form of taking to the streets—such as it is.

The crowd is peppered with people who seem to know what's going on; they are smooth, confident, knowing, but they aren't the ones speaking. The ones speaking aren't too sure about what's going on. The long long line is made up of people in the wrong place. I'm not sure what's to become of them, as I pass them up to go into the school gym.

Nevada's first caucus. One would expect it to be a cluster and it doesn't disappoint. All concerned parties must be in one place at one time for a physical head count in support of his or her candidate of choice. It's a public ritual like a wedding, conducted to resolve all doubt in the eyes of the people of the village as to what transpired. I will see with my own eyes for whom the people voted, without the intercession of the corrupted voting machines. (At least I'll see the choice of Precinct 1352 and three other precincts assembled here in the gym of Silvestri High School in Nevada at noon on January 19th, 2008.)

Blue Hillary signs dominate, held by middle aged white people. The doors lock—we're sealed in—we the band of voting brothers, the few, the otherwise free. Roughly five hundred total, it appears.

There are ballots. There is a show of hands. Many people count heads. I can't hear the people talking to my precinct group. The group next to us in the stands is led by one of the silent, knowing people who has suddenly found his voice. His voice booms out instructions and leads a cheer for Hillary. The same thing happens across the gym in group number 3. One of the knowing ones pops up there, leading Hillary cheers and explaining exactly what is expected of everyone in that group. I wanted to sit in their groups; at least I'd know what's going on.

The chaos continues. How many total voters? How many for whom? Arguments on the floor amongst the leaders of the big groups next to us. That group is twice the size of our 72 voters.

Our group goes 44 for Obama, 26 for Hillary, 2 for Edwards. In terms of delegate count, that equates to 6 delegates for Barack, 3 for Hillary.

Now mark the ballots. They won't be counted, don't matter, but do it anyway so they can see who voted for whom, I guess. You have to put your name on the ballot.

The little section across from us votes 53 for Obama and 47 for Clinton. Five delegates each.

The two big groups (Hillary Clinton's) seem to have been augmented by busloads of people from large apartment complexes. The first one elects 8 Clinton delegates and 5 Obama delegates.

The big group still has infighting amongst its leaders. I hear the Obama guy on the phone. He is unhappy that these "New Yorkers" are muddying things up. The count ends up 76 for Clinton, 58 for Obama, 6 for Edwards. This plays out, delegate-wise, to 8 delegates for Clinton, 6 for Obama.

Total unofficial delegate count in our gym: 24 for Clinton, 22 for Obama.(*It is worth noting that, while Hillary won the popular vote, Obama actually finished ahead in the delegate count from Nevada, those people who will go off to cast their votes for the eventual party nominee in Denver.)

The day's work is done. Off to lunch.

(**Note**: *Thanks, Dan! I think we're all as thoroughly confused as it sounds like the voters in your precinct in Las Vegas, Nevada, were on January 19th, but it's a fascinating slice of Americana. And don't you feel that your vote has made a difference much more than if you hadn't interacted with your neighbors in Precinct 1352? Hmmmmmm?*)

GOP Candidates Have Been Busy Bees in Nevada and South Carolina

1/20/2008

The GOP candidates have been busy bees the past few days. (With the possible exception of Rudy, who is busy only in Florida.)

The January 19th Republican vote in Nevada went to Romney, with 51% of the popular vote. Ron Paul, the only Republican candidate who publicly says he'd bring our troops home from Iraq, ended up in second place with 14%, edging John McCain by one percentage point and Mike Huckabee, of those initially considered Republican front-runners, trailed the field with 8% of the vote. After Huckabee, came Fred Thompson, nearly tied with Huckabee with 8%, Rudy Giuiliani, with 4% and Duncan Hunter with 2%. ("Orlando Sentinel," January 20, 2008, front page).

Hunter dropped out of the race soon after receiving only 890 votes. Romney, scoring 22,649 votes in Nevada, which has a 25% Mormon population, steamed on to South Carolina, where he would place a disappointing fourth in that state.

With 1,797 precincts reporting in Nevada, though, Romney had 22,649 votes; Ron Paul had 6,087 (14%); John McCain had 5,651 votes (13%); Mike Huckabee had 3,616 votes (8%) while Thompson had 3,521 (also 8%), Giuiliani trailed with 1,910 votes or 4%, and Duncan Hunter got only 890 votes, or 2% of the Republican votes cast.

Before this year's contest, the turnout in Nevada had been underwhelming, but 114,000 voters were said to have turned out on January 19, 2008.

One thing that set Nevada apart from the two votes that preceded it (Iowa and New Hampshire) was the ethnic make-up of the voters there, with many more Hispanic voters, (as well as many Mormon voters). One big issue in Nevada, where 5.4% unemployment plagues the state, is the housing crisis, with Nevada having the highest foreclosure rate of any state, according to CNN.

Ali Velshi, commenting on CNN on January 20th, said, "In the Southwest it's different; it's about housing," and then moved on to catalogue the woes of South Carolina, the Republicans next battlefield, where the 94,000 manufacturing jobs lost since 2001 and trade policies in the textile and manufacturing industry are a big issue. (CNN)

Nevada voters anointed Mitt Romney on January 19th, whereas voters in South Carolina, which held its Republican contest the same day (Democrats in South Carolina will vote on January 26th) gave John McCain a big win with 33% of the vote, over Huckabee's 30% of the vote (*Orlando Sentinel*, front page, 1/20/2008).

Trailing McCain and Huckabee were Fred Thompson at 16% and Mitt Romney (winner in Nevada) with 15%. Ron Paul's good showing in Nevada dropped to only 4% of the vote (15,235) in South Carolina and Rudy Giuiliani brought up the rear with 8,518 votes, or 2%. These statistics appeared on almost every news show and newspaper in the country. (Page A20 of the Orlando Sentinel).

It became my mission…and that of most other political junkies… to try to make sense of these widely differing race results. I watched every major Sunday morning (January 20) news talk show until my brain turned to mush.

People like Bill Bennett looked ahead to Florida, saying, "Florida matters huge…Big time," and the uber-Conservative Ann Coulter, when asked to comment on Rudy Giuiliani's strategy of waiting out the primaries hunkered down in Florida, said, "It's either brilliant or completely bone-headed, and we'll know in a few weeks." In her brief and typically controversial statements, Coulter remarked, "I really do not know what Republican voters are thinking if they're voting for John McCain." (*Note: my vote on Giuiliani's All-Florida, All-the-time campaign strategy: bone-headed.)*

Tom Brokaw on "Meet the Press" could have filled Coulter in on that. They told the nation on that show that character matters and people think John McCain is an honorable guy who might, just possibly, be telling the truth (his bus is, after all, called The Straight Talk Express).

The American people want someone who is an honorable candidate with integrity, who is willing to speak the truth, even if it is not politically expedient to do so AND who can do the job. The American people have been told so many half-truths and untruths and cherry-picked outright lies, in order to facilitate the agenda of those at the top opportunistically running the show, that…if they ever *did* trust those at the top of the food chain— they sure don't now.

When nearly 4,000 of our best and brightest die, as a result of half-truths and misrepresentations and bad intelligence, and 1 in 5 of those that come back are likely to suffer from some form of head injury or PTSD (Post Traumatic Stress Disorder), integrity and telling the truth become a scarce but valued commodity. I still remember Senator Joe Biden (D, Delaware) talking on the stump in Iowa about how there have been more amputations in this war than in any war since the Civil War and that the average Iraq veteran will require care for an average of 38 years of his/ her remaining life. The bill, needless to say, will be huge, and it is growing larger with every passing day and every additional tragic death.

This election is coming down to, "Who(m) do you trust in your gut?" And, no, we don't mean who you'd most like to sit down and have a beer with. That voting strategy might be what got us into this mess in the first place.

There are lots of questions facing the candidates today and thrown out there for discussion:

"Can Bill be Dennis Thatcher?" was one of them. "Is Bill an asset or a liability to Hillary as she fights for the White House?" That question was posed on Chris Matthews' Sunday show, as he sat with Richard Stengel, editor of "Time" magazine and Howard Finneman of "Newsweek," and Cynthia Tucker, editorial director of the "Atlanta Journal Conservative" and Kathleen Parker of the "Washington Post's" Writers' Group.

Later, on "Face the Nation" with Bob Schieffer *(*Note: Schieffer, age 78, retired the end of May, 2015),* the questions of the hour for Democratic contender John Edwards were: "Can you keep your campaign going?" (A: yes) "Why can't you get your message out?" (A: not enough money). "What, exactly, is your strategy?" (A: take the long view) and, "Why are you the better choice as President over Barack Obama or Hillary Clinton?" (A: She's too "Old School" and Obama's more academic.)

To his credit, Edwards remarked, "I got my butt kicked in Nevada," (where he ran no ads of any kind) and he laughingly remarked, "I hope that that slogan, 'What happens in Vegas stays in Vegas'…I hope that turns out to be true."

Edwards then said, "It's time for me to get up and fight on," which, for some of us, is what is losing him delegates in the first place: too much talk of fighting; not enough talk about the policies he has laid out, in writing, on the issues that matter most to America's voters.

And what are those issues?

The issue of the economy seems to be rearing its ugly head, and that is characterized as the issue coming to Romney. It is his single biggest source of street credibility. What bothers me about Romney is how quickly he takes over the words-and, sometimes, the positions— of others. In the background of Romney's televised appearance I saw "Change" banners. Obama coined "Stand for Change" and Hillary and Edwards quickly followed in talking about change. The other slogan that Romney has co-opted I first heard used by Christopher Dodd in Iowa, as he referred to "this broken time." Now, with Dodd out of the race, it's Romney's, apparently, from the recent use of it that I have noted. (Isn't Romney rich enough and creative enough to either think up his OWN original slogan, or to pay someone to think one up for him?)

My head is literally swimming with good quotes from one Talking Head or another.

Obama, who gave a sermon at Martin Luther King's Ebenezer Baptist Church in Atlanta employed phrases like, "We can no longer afford to build ourselves up by tearing ourselves down," and,—one that I, personally, thought was apropos—"None of our hands are clean." (*Amen to that!*)

Perhaps the most amusing bit of post-Nevada, post-South Carolina televised discussion came from a young man named Kevin Godlington, a former British Special Forces officer, who was asked about the impression all of the above is having in England (on CNN). He noted that the British have not embraced George W. Bush because "it's not just about the sword being mightier than the pen," hoping that a new President might take the United States into a new era of diplomacy. He correctly noted that the person who was elected President of the world's richest nation was important. "It has a massive effect on global stabilization over the next decade."

After noting that our election process seems "very grand and celebratious," he rattled off a series of comments that brought outright chuckles. Kevin said, "You've got the black guy and the woman and the Mormon and the former Baptist minister and the Hollywood actor" and you next expected him to say it was like a soap opera, but he didn't, because he was asked to predict winners and losers, which is when his humorous remarks turned to reality. He said, instead, "I would have absolutely no idea. I couldn't possibly comment."

And that, my friends, was the best statement I heard all day.

Republican Candidates Appear in Orlando, Florida

1/22/2008

Within seven hours of each other, Rudy Giuliani, Mike Huckabee and Mitt Romney appeared in Orlando, Florida on Monday, January 21st, jockeying for position in the Interstate 4 East/West corridor where many Florida voters reside, and vying for a state that is worth 57 delegates to the national convention and 27 votes in the electoral college.*(And we all remember what happened under Governor Jeb Bush in Florida in 2000, with Al Gore, George W. Bush, the hanging chads and the Supreme Court).*

Only John McCain, of the front-runners, was MIA in Orlando, where I am now, on Monday, (supposedly courting the Cuban vote in Miami), but McCain was expected to arrive as early as Tuesday, January 22nd. Ah, yes! The Sunshine State is awash in candidates painting a rosy picture of Life With Me As President

Huckabee arrived about 4 p.m. at the Orlando International Airport, greeted by an enthusiastic crowd of supporters. He pressed the flesh and flashed that dimpled grin. Although Giuliani and McCain are supposedly the leaders in Florida, Huckabee has one gold medal (Iowa) to his credit, and he'd like to try for two here in Florida.

Rudy Giuliani, who has been campaigning here for over 50 days, ignoring the wintry weather of Iowa and New Hampshire, is banking on transplanted New Yorkers to give him a Florida win. He recently visited The Village, a retirement community in Orlando, and has been watching with dismay as his lead in his home state of New York evaporates. A New Siena College poll showed Rudy trailing John McCain by 12 points in New York state.

Another candidate watching less-than-happily the result of the recent Palmetto State vote must be Fred Thompson, who did not do as well as he had hoped in South Carolina and whose candidacy may, therefore, be doomed. There were rumors that the Fredheads would soon be Deadheads (along with those who were staunch supporters of Biden, Dodd, Richardson, Hunter, et al.). It was rumored that Fred did not board the bus or plane for Florida, but went home.

One does not know how many of the Republican hopefuls will make the cut and stay the course until Super Tuesday (February 5th), when 22 states vote, but it does appear that McCain, once written off as politically dead-in-the-water, and Romney are still alive and kicking.

Some changes were noted in the stump speeches of the front-runners. Giuliani, who once spoke only of terrorism, sealing our borders and national security has been touting his economic plan(s) recently, telling Floridians in ads that are running on television here that he supports a national catastrophic insurance fund to help states that are hit by natural (think New Orleans) or terrorist (think New York City) disasters.

Said Rudy regarding the economy to a group of about 100 supporters recently, "I truly believe that, given the situation the country now faces, the very best thing we can do is a major stimulus package that would lower taxes and lower taxes dramatically...My proposal would put more money back in your pockets, so that you'd be able to spend it, and by spending it, that's how you stimulate the economy." Missing was the key component of Rudy's plan, i.e., "How are you going to pay for those tax cuts?"

After the economy, if you are dealing with Florida's I-4 corridor, be prepared to talk about space, discussing our nation's space program and where it heads after the shuttle is retired in 2010. The Interstate 4 corridor, which runs east-west in the state (and was the location for a recent 70-car pile-up), links the Daytona Beach area and Tampa. It is considered the swing region for the state. The corridor encompasses both those who worship at the altar of Mickey Mouse and the Star Wars crew, i.e., the Space Coast, which is dependent on jobs related to NASA.

In a presentation entitled "The Keys to the Oval Office Are At Kennedy Space Center," its author, Dale Ketchum, a 53-year-old Cocoa Beach native who worked on university programs for NASA and serves as the Director of the University of Central Florida's Space Research and Technology Institute wrote, "This isn't rocket science. It is crude but compelling political arithmetic."

Just as Fred Thompson came to Florida and committed a faux pas, suggesting to environmentally-minded Governor Crist that it might be a good idea to drill for oil in the Everglades, John McCain has been the only front-runner to turn down an invitation by Linda Weatherman, Chief Executive Officer of the Economic Development Commission in Florida, to take part in a "space round table." Giuliani and Romney accepted. Governor Mike Huckabee is expected to attend this week.

On the Democratic side, Hillary jumped into the space debate early with a detailed plan, laid out way last October. She said that she would "capitalize on the expertise of the current shuttle program work force... and prevent a brain drain such as that which occurred between the Apollo and shuttle missions."

Soon after the Clinton campaign threw down the gauntlet, others got into the debate. Amongst the Republicans, Rudy supports President Bush's plan(s) to return to the moon and go to Mars. Rudy says he will spend whatever it takes to insure that the U.S. remains "Number One" in space and spend whatever is necessary to assure that." Again, no specifics, a la the tax cut announcement, as to where the money will come from, given his penchant for cutting taxes, which generally means less money available for projects on Earth, let alone on Mars and the moon.

Huckabee has no specific policy, but "supports more funding for NASA." McCain thinks that a US presence in space "is of major importance to America's future innovation and security," and Romney, alone among the Republican leaders, has a detailed policy.

Ron Paul says he "would like to see more space travel done privately" as well as being "absolutely committed to human space exploration."

And Fred... well, is Fred still a player?

After Hillary weighed in, Obama said that he would delay manned missions to the moon and Mars in order to help fund the $18 billion needed yearly for education reforms; he also opposes weapons in space. Edwards said that he would "support solar system exploration as an important goal for our human and robotic programs."

If you're an engineer working for NASA, you are paying close attention to what the candidates are saying about work in the future. This isn't JFK's day—and we didn't even get to the moon until 6 years after JFK's assassination—but a President who can fix the economy and has plans for NASA other than the scrap heap will be met with enthusiasm here in central Florida.

The Gloves Come Off in South Carolina Democratic Debate

1/22/2008

"We have a woman, a black…and John." So said Barack Obama during the live Democratic debate from the Palace Theater in Myrtle Beach, South Carolina on Monday night, January 21st. The look on John Edwards' face when the camera panned to him was priceless. In fact, Edwards frequently ended up looking like the only one on the stage who wasn't involved in a "he said/she said" face-off, which he characterized as "squabbling," saying, "How many children is this going to get health care for? How much is this going to get children an education?"

The gizmo people, 17 undecided South Carolina voters outfitted with those little dial gadgets, gave John Edwards high marks in the debate, saying that he had won. They followed up that glowing review by saying that they still wouldn't vote for him, because they thought one of the other two more contentious candidates had a better chance of winning the Democratic nomination. Sad, but true, like Rodney Dangerfield, John Edwards doesn't get any respect these days.

It was fun watching the fiery debate for its humorous moments, though.

One of my favorites was the point at which Barack Obama was asked to comment on black writer Toni Morrison's contention that Bill Clinton was our first black President. Obama began with a long drawn-out, "Wellllllllllll," and proceeded to say, " I would have to investigate more fully Bill's dancing ability to see if he was, indeed, a brother."

Touché, Barack!

During the first half of the debate, the charges and counter-charges were flying so fast and furious between Obama and Clinton that Edwards,

151

on the right end of my screen, was the forgotten man I characterized him as in a piece I did about his feud with O'Reilly.

Edwards waited patiently while Hillary Clinton seemed to usurp most of the debate time, and then, since she had attacked Barack Obama, Obama got to respond directly. So there he stood, the forgotten candidate, patient to the end. Even Wolf Blitzer commented on it, saying, "Senator Edwards has been remarkably patient."

Countered Edwards, "I just want people to remember there are three candidates in this race, not two." A recent e-mailing from the Edwards campaign shows any number of pundits completely ignoring his continued presence on the Democratic political scene, acting as though he has dropped out of the race, when, so far, he has not and Edwards has vowed to stay in the race until the end. At one point, acknowledging the inequity in time given the only white male in the Democratic race, Barack Obama said, "I feel bad for John Edwards. He's not getting any time." Edwards retorted, with exaggerated sarcastic emphasis on the word "that," "You don't feel THAT bad (about it)." Edwards said this good humoredly, but, when Edwards was trying to get a straight answer about taking money from lobbyists and PACS, he stuttered, "Is that...is that...is that a no?" seemingly truly puzzled by the lack of a straight answer to his question(s).

I liked the point when Barack patted John Edwards on the shoulder and said, "It's all right, man." This came immediately after Edwards had asked, "Who can compete versus John McCain across the nation?"

There has been much television replay of Obama's charge during the debate that he was on the streets of Chicago, fighting for poor people when Hillary was sitting on the board of Walmart as a corporate attorney. Hillary was actually booed (as was Romney in a debate) when she fired back at Obama with a comment about his work for a "slum lord" (Tony Rezko) in Chicago. "It's just very difficult to get a straight answer," she said to Obama, saying, "You never take responsibility for any vote." She cited his "present" vote 130 times when in the Illinois legislature. Obama attempted to explain the intricacies of voting in the state of Illinois (versus the United States Senate) and seemed, at times, to "hem and haw" in his attempts to clearly articulate his point(s).

Edwards was able to, once again, make some headway when he took Obama to task for not standing up to be counted in the "present" votes that Hillary cited, saying, "I do think it's important on whether you're willing to take hard positions. What you're (Obama) criticizing her for you've done to us. What's fair is fair," noting that he and Senator Clinton had voted for controversial issues and their record was there to be examined.

Obama countered: "It was not smart for me to vote against the war, at that time, but I did because it was the right thing to do. I haven't simply followed; I have led." Later, some of the post-debate analysts felt that was a wise strategy for Obama, who leads in South Carolina. Show the people that you can fight back and hold your ground. The analysts also felt that Clinton was playing to a wider audience than just the Palmetto State, which she is likely to lose, since its voter make-up is half African-American.

After the debate ended, Mark Halperin, "Time" magazine's senior political analyst commented, "A lot of political people I know said they haven't seen a political debate like this in a long time. Obama's comment, "I would be upset if there was too much civility. I'm being given a hard time and that means I'm doing pretty good," reminded me of Huckabee's earlier (Republican) debate "you know you're over the target if you're taking flak."

Of Edwards, the CNN post-debate commentator said, "Edwards clearly came out very well tonight." Then the third-place candidate, who has to fight just to be heard over the din was brought on, "live." He said, "Petty bickering is not going to get health care or help New Orleans. I thought there were moments when it got very 'in the ditch.'" And he added, "I am the underdog, but I'm a serious underdog. Anyone who came to this debate with an open mind, I suspect I did very well with… "

Just as an exercise, I timed the responses where Wolf Blitzer, the moderator, asked the candidate to take only 30 seconds (John Edwards said, sotto voce, "Good luck" to Obama in making his case in such a short time allotted to a complex issue.) Hillary seemed to speak more than the other two and, in the one response I timed near the end, she used 90 seconds, while the others used about a minute. When the question was regarding ending poverty, Obama used 60 seconds and Hillary used 70 seconds to respond.

Refreshingly, there was talk of withdrawing our troops from Iraq, something you don't hear in Republican debates. Citing the cost of $9 to $10 billion dollars a month, Barack Obama said, "It's not just the loss of life. It's also because it's financially unsustainable…and has made Al Qaeda more dangerous." Here's another line you probably won't hear during a Republican debate, "(George W.) Bush has done extraordinary damage to us," commenting on his belligerence and the need for America to "be that light of hope again" (Obama). The African-American candidate also said, "If we just play to the same fear-mongering we're just playing on their battlefield."

Up next, a debate January 30th in Las Vegas and on January 31st in Los Angeles. Bring on the rhetoric.

John McCain in Florida; Bush on TV

1/24/2008

Continuing my unscientific and totally unreliable polling of Florida voters, I asked a gentleman in Orlando whether he lived in Florida. (Down here, a lot of the time, the person asked responds in Italian or Spanish or French that he does not speak English, which tells me that the lure of Mickey is the ultimate reason for their presence here.)

"Not now, but I did," he responded.

"Where did you live?"

"Marco Island."

"What caused you to move from Marco Island?" (to Branson, Missouri, he said).

"We got hit by Hurricane Charlie. My insurance company paid us, but then they up and moved out of state. When I sold the house, we had six months left on our insurance, and the new owner wanted to assume the six months of insurance left on the house, but the carrier wouldn't let him, so the buyer had to get insurance from Citizen's Insurance, which was set up by the state after all the big carriers moved out of here after Katrina and all that. It cost him twice as much (for insurance) as it cost me."

"And how much was that?

"Eight thousand dollar a year."

Wow!

So, the Florida resident…who originally hailed from the snowy state of Michigan before moving to Marco Island and, more recently , back to Branson, Missouri, with time spent in Florida in January…had pinpointed one of the economic issues facing Florida voters in the upcoming election. Insurance. How to get it, how to keep it affordable, and who will provide the most comprehensive plan for same.

Therefore, it probably wasn't too surprising that, when John McCain came to Orlando on Wednesday, January 23, for an economic roundtable in a south Orlando warehouse with executives from Florida Hospital, Fifth Third Bank and the Orlando Utilies Commission, among others, in attendance (an attempt, no doubt, to "tweak" his campaign message more towards economic issues), the executives present, who were generally receptive to McCain's message of cutting corporate income taxes, repealing the alternative minimum tax and making Bush's tax cuts permanent (even though, originally, McCain opposed the Bush cuts), did find fault with McCain's opposition to a national catastrophe fund to reduce insurance rates. Giuliani quickly jumped on the insurance issue with claims that he is "the only candidate who'll fight for a national catastrophe fund to reduce insurance rates." Right about now, the national catastrophe that Giuiliani might think about insuring is his Florida-only strategy.

McCain said the national catastrophe initiative would be "too expensive." He did suggest a regional fund made up of coastal states, or a clamping down on insurance companies by regulators, to keep them from selling policies only in profitable areas, and he has said, on numerous occasions that FEMA "needs to be fixed," but he showed his unwillingness or inability to simply say what the crowd wants to hear when he opposed a national catastrophe fund. Others might criticize by saying that the over-70 candidate showed Twentieth Century solutions to Twenty-first Century problems, and a stubbornness that we have seen too much of over the past 7 years, but he did remain true to his earlier opposition to the idea.

John "Mac" Stipanavoch, a Tallahassee strategist who has been advising the McCain campaign, told newspaper reporters, "He's not your paper-doll cutout of a traditional right-wing, head-banging Republican. But these are troubled times, and my sense of it is the people of America—including Republicans—would like an adult who has some life experiences, knows something about war, is fiscally conservative, and isn't so ideological as to be intolerant."

Those sentiments are very close to what I expressed in a previous article, which answered Ann Coulter's (and Rush Limbaugh's and a host of others) comments as to why Republicans might well vote for McCain, even though he has never completely kow-towed to the Republican party on all issues and has crossed partisan lines, when necessary, to get things done. The days of "my way or the highway" seem to be over. "The Great Decider" is about out of time and, judging from the man on the street, that Bush operating philosophy is viewed in a very dim light these days. People would like someone who will bring us together, keep us in the black, and dig us out of the deep ditch we seem to have dug for ourselves in Iraq (and, indeed, the entire region.)

The problem with McCain is that he is a military man—a bona fide war hero. He has been quoted as saying we might have to stay in Iraq for 100 years or some such unbelievable statement. His ad running on TV here, entitled "Never Surrender" ends with the dubious premise that, "America will never surrender. They will."(That's a paraphrase, but it's very very close. I was in too much shock to write the patently weak assumption down verbatim, and my sole ballpoint pen had just run out of ink, depositing it, instead, on the sleeve of my jacket.)

We've recently occupied a country which appears to have one of the worst standards of living in the world (post-war destruction of necessary infra-structure elements like electricity, etc.). We are unwelcome, just as the British were in India and colonialists historically are when they invade and occupy another country. And yet John McCain thinks that they are going to be the ones surrendering? O… K…

Turn the tables and imagine our land occupied by a foreign nation. Who do you think would fight the hardest and longest for that land? Us or them? Add in the horrible life you're living daily in that foreign land—partially due to the encroachment of the World's Most Powerful Nation—-and you pretty much have to say that the inhabitants of said nation would probably be asking themselves, "What do we have to lose by fighting to the death…every last man, woman and child of us?"

Don't even get me started on "jihad" extremist terrorists from other nations who enter to opportunistically stir the pot, nor religious zealots who do not consider killing of innocents to be morally reprehensible, as we learned all too well on 9/11/01. (*Note: And many times, since then, with ISIS.)*

McCain has this going for him in Florida: there are 21 military installations and (roughly) 1.7 million military personnel in the state, information I gleaned from non-stop watching of CNN and Fox News. And McCain is definitely the winner, hands down, on the issue of military allegiance. Although Rudy (Giuliani), too, has been working that gold mine and citing his 9/11 experiences. Recently, some picketers have appeared who are relatives of fire-fighters who bravely served New York City on September 11th, and they aren't too happy with the non-working walkie-talkies that the Mayor should have replaced, which might have allowed their relatives to get the word about abandoning Tower Two, if they had worked, and, therefore possibly saved their lives. Nor do they think the mask situation at Ground Zero was adequate during and after, so Rudy's basing his entire campaign on 9/11, early on, might not be totally a winning strategy, and certainly, given the recent poll numbers, his strategy of sitting out the early primaries in Florida is looking more and more questionable...possibly outdone in bone-headedness only by Fred Thompson's leisurely Trot Towards the White House.

As I left to write this article, CNN was hosting Scott Rasmussen, who conducts polls at www.Rasmussenreports.com. He was informing the nation that "If McCain wins in Florida, it is very hard to take the nomination away from him." Having said that, Rasmussen went on to tell interested viewers that the economy is now the Number One issue and that Romney is leading in Florida 27%, to McCain's 23%, Giuliani's 20%, Huckabee's 15% and Ron Paul's 14%. (Taken from a phone poll of 675 Florida votes, after Thompson's drop from the race.)

The www.Realclearpolitics people, in their poll, had McCain at 24.5%, Romney at 23.5%, Giuliani at 18.8% and Huckabee at 15.5%. But it was not clear if this poll was taken before or after Fred Thompson dropped out of the race. About the only thing you can say about the polls is that it's too close to call here in the Sunshine State, and the issues in the news do seem to be going Romney's way a bit more than McCain's, as Romney positions himself as better-suited to turn the nation around, economically.

Right after Scott Rasmussen gave the nation the rather startling news that Giuliani has dropped to third in a state where he has been pumping roughly a million bucks a week into advertising and a state (Florida) where he has been encamped for over 50 days, as well, the current President came onscreen, to announce an economic stimulus package.

George W. Bush muttered some platitudes along the lines of, "I know Americans are concerned about our economy," and went on to cite energy and housing as among the nation's problems, before saying, "Our economy is strong, dynamic and resilient. We have led the world for many decades. We have an opportunity to come together and provide the leadership our economy needs."

Then George rather stiffly, sort of like a wind-up doll that has marched out and said its piece and now needs to retreat, marched off, stage left, and left Secretary Paulson standing there alone to carry the heavy water of answering questions and explaining the details of this "plan", although neither of those things happened. My initial reaction was, "I wonder if, once he disappeared through that door, George just came to a complete halt like a wind-up doll or if someone came over and gave the key another twist so that he could make it back to the White House to talk sports?" *(or whatever it is he does seem to mentally engage with, since it does not look like it is the actual running of the nation, most of the time.)*

It seems too bad that McCain's own party seems to be trying to derail the old boy. Party operative Grover Norquist called him "the nut-job from Arizona," Radio Rush has been ranting against him and Huckabee (not "conservative" enough) and no less an august leader than the infamous Tom DeLay once said of McCain, "He has done more to hurt the Republican Party than any elected official I know of." Interesting, coming from the pot (DeLay) who gave the Republicans a bigger black eye than the kettle (McCain) ever could or would.

Stay tuned for the details of that economic stimulus package, while I go to work researching how the Republicans stand on reducing taxes, another story in and of itself.

Republicans Debate Before Florida Primary; Hillary Blind-sided on "Today" Show

1/25/2008

The Republicans debated from Boca Raton, Florida (Florida Atlantic University) on January 24th, shedding little light and almost no heat. It seems that the Republican candidates, themselves, had talked out their party's strategy and decided to lob only "soft-ball" questions at one another. Each candidate was given the opportunity to ask one of the other participating candidates a question, but the questions asked were all tame and the targets were seldom the obvious or expected ones.

By that, I mean, one would have expected Romney and McCain to question one another vigorously on their supposed areas of strength (the economy, for Romney, and national security, for McCain). That didn't happen. Instead, viewers got : a softball question from Romney to Giuliani about China and trade; a question from McCain to Huckabee about his fair tax proposal; a question from Paul to McCain about the tax system; a question from Huckabee to Romney about whether he approves of a ban on assault weapons (and guns, in general); and a question from Giuliani to Romney on his position on a national catastrophic fund (Giuliani supports same; McCain does not).

After the most-watched debate in history, the Democratic front-runners on the eve of South Carolina, which garnered 5 million viewers, the effect of last night's televised spectacle was razzle-fizzle. The razzle went to the Democrats, who seemed to let it all hang out in their debate. The fizzle goes to the Republicans, who, from a small comment Giuliani let slip about how the candidates had talked amongst themselves, backstage, about who would ask what, appear to have "scripted" and orchestrated their debate to best display to the country at large their less-contentious selves. The operating philosophy amongst the Republicans seemed to be to attack Hillary Clinton, not each other; that strategy was on display quite a bit, and it was interesting that no other Democratic candidate's name was even mentioned.

Still Brian Williams and Tim Russert pressed on, asking hard-hitting, provocative questions and getting generally lackluster answers.

Russert, in particular, rattled off a string of bad news facts and figures, from rising gas prices and unemployment to foreclosures plaguing the land, and wanted to know, "Why keep Republicans in charge?"

Russert didn't get very straight or strong answers to that question. Most of the time, the individual asked would tap dance around the bad news facts and spout more of the same old/same old.

There was one provocative question, however, asked by the moderators, where the response elicited the only spontaneous applause of the night. The question dealt with Iraq and asked "whether the price we have paid to remove Saddam Hussein was worth the price we have paid in blood and treasure?"

There were the usual responses supporting the President's decision to take us to war, with a criticism of the follow-up that Rumsfeld supervised. However, alone among the candidates (as usual), Ron Paul said, "It was a very bad idea and it wasn't worth it. AlQaeda wasn't there then. They're there now. This decision on policy was made in 1998. It wasn't worth it, and it's a sad story because we started that war and we should never be a nation that starts wars needlessly." Long-time Iowa Republican Senator James Leach recently praised Ron Paul's prescient opposition to the war when it began, but Leach was beaten in the last election, after a long and distinguished career as "the thinking man's Republican" and now teaches at Princeton.

I pay attention when people are boo-ed (most recently, Hillary Clinton when she attacked Obama on the issue of "slumlord" Tony Rezko); I also pay attention when spontaneous applause breaks out amongst the audience, and only Paul's answer struck that responsive chord. It is true that Ron Paul supporters tend to be very vocal (and young), but national polls have supported Paul's anti-war viewpoint, which he alone among the current crop of Republican Presidential contenders articulates.

McCain, by contrast, kept maintaining that the U.S. can win in Iraq, saying, "I'm proud of the job the military are doing there. They know we can win. Their message to you and to me is: let us win." He likened Hillary Clinton to someone "waving a white flag of surrender." (All the Democratic candidates support getting out of Iraq, but Senator Clinton actually drags her feet on the time-table more than Edwards or Obama). McCain even has an ad running on Florida television entitled "Never Surrender." (Last time I heard that phrase, it was basketball coach Jimmy Valvano saying, "Never give up. Never give in," in regards to his terminal cancer. He died shortly after saying it.) *(*Note: Maybe Kenny Rogers' Know When to Hold Em', Know When to Fold Em' is a better slogan for these troubled times.)*

McCain took to the podium in Miami on Friday, January 25, immediately after the Thursday night debate, attacking Romney with renewed vigor and rancor, as merely a "manager" of economic matters, not a true leader or visionary. But none of that sentiment was expressed during the Thursday night debate. Why didn't we see some of that heated rhetoric on Thursday night? Did someone somewhere decide it would be "bad" to let the American public get a true look at the candidates' real feelings and, instead, orchestrated the mind-numbingly bland television spectacle that we viewers saw? So much for talk of "transparency in government."

If you want to see and hear only what "they" want you to see and hear, look elsewhere than what was billed as a debate. Keep following the candidates post-debate, as they tear one another apart on the stump. You aren't going to get the much-needed "transparency in government" while watching a debate like the Republican one last night. No "warts and all" for this bunch. They left that to the Democrats, hoping that, by staying above the petty bickering, remaining above the fray, the Republicans in the race would appear more statesmanlike and adult. More "Presidential," if you will.

Maybe. Maybe not.

What we got on television last night was a love-fest that reminded me of a previous Democratic seated debate, when all was sweetness and light among the three top candidates. That early accord soon gave way to the South Carolina Democratic debate, however, and the gloves came off, seemingly for good.

Last night, with the Republicans, Romney was heard to say, "I trust these two gentlemen and I respect them greatly" (indicating McCain and Giuliani). McCain joined in, making a special point of telling the crowd what a heroic sweetheart Rudy Giuliani was during 9/11, right on the heels of a *New York Times* endorsement of McCain (and Clinton) for President that specifically singled out Giuliani for criticism, citing the former New York Mayor's "arrogance and bad judgment."

On Friday, as life on the campaign trail returned to business as usual, the Republicans in Florida attempted the Herculean task of covering a state that stretches more than 800 miles from Pensacola to Key West and spans two time zones. This is a state where it is winner-take-all for the Republicans and there are no Democratic delegates in play because of sanctions against Florida levied by the Democratic Party as punishment for moving their primary up. McCain's own mother has said that the voters may have to "hold their noses" and vote for her son John, as divisions within the Republican party (not conservative enough?) emerge.

The Republican candidates still standing are fighting for their very political lives. It looks a lot like Romney could unseat the old war-horse (McCain), merely by being more "up" on the economy and what it would take to "fix" it. Even during the debate on Thursday night, McCain kept referring to his "circle of advisers" (the name Jack Kemp came up a lot). The country has seen, over the past 7 years, what happens when a President relies totally on a "circle of advisers" and doesn't have a handle on the issues himself. Bad for McCain; good for Romney. And Rudy Giuliani just seems like the old restaurant in town when a couple of brand-new ones open. It's perhaps not that the old restaurant wasn't good; it's the novelty of something new and the promise of something better. Let's try it out!

The day began with Matt Lauer blindsiding Hillary Clinton on the morning "Today" show, displaying a picture of Bill and Hillary Clinton posing cozily with Chicago "slumlord" (Hillary's term) Tony Rezko. It was not a Kodak moment. Probably no candidate has regretted being photographed with someone as much since Roslyn Carter's photo with part-time clown turned serial killer John Wayne Gacy surfaced. Kind of an "oops" moment, which the former First Lady tried to shrug off.

You also had Robert Reich, former Labor Secretary under Bill Clinton, blogging that Bill Clinton's tactics in excoriating Hillary's closest contender, Barack Obama, were "not fair—indeed, it's demeaning." Reich found it beneath the dignity of a former President to twist the voting record of the African-American man running against Bill's wife and our former First Lady. Reich insisted that it was Clinton, not Obama, who was "playing the race card."

Meanwhile, back in Chicago, national viewers who had never heard the name Tony Rezko before the heated South Carolina Democratic debates, were reading up. Tim Novak, Editor of the Chicago *Sun Times* newspaper, confirmed that Rezko was "the Jack Abramoff of Chicago politics." Novak's paper ran stories that confirmed that Rezko, always a player in Chicago Democratic politics, got government loans to develop housing, and that, currently, 2/3 of the properties Rezko developed have been foreclosed upon or have become slum properties. Novak stated, in comments on CNN, "seldom have such housing loans gone that bad, that quick, that much."

CNN also reported that Obama, whom Rezko supported early on, upon learning of the charges against Rezko, donated $86,000 of Rezko's early campaign contributions to charity.*(Hillary and Bill were dumping stocks like Walmart with a vengeance to protect her against charges, before the campaign got fully underway, according to "Money" magazine, so there are apparently skeletons in a lot of closets.)*

The fact that Rezko's wife bought a lot next to Obama's house for full price on the same day that the Obamas were able to purchase their house for $300,000 below full market value does not look or sound good. The information that Obama later purchased a sliver of the Rezko lot, was also presented to CNN viewers, with Obama's camp acknowledging it to be a less-than-smart move. As Editor Novak said on CNN, "The problem with Chicago politics is that it's hard to stay 110% perfectly clean."

I try to look for moments of light-heartedness amidst the squabbling, whether intentional or unintentional, so let me end by mentioning one moment that occurred during the Republican debate.

The moment of mirth came when Huckabee disavowed Chuck Norris' claims that McCain is "too old" (at 72) to be President.

Huckabee—always seeking to get political leverage from his droll sense of humor—said that it was Chuck Norris who had made those charges against the white-haired over-70 Arizona Senator, not him, remarking, "I didn't disagree with him at the time because I was standing right next to him." Huckabee went on to gallantly maintain, in the love-fest spirit of the evening, that McCain has "the vigor to run."

When the Norris comments initially hit the air waves, McCain made some comic points of his own, saying that he would "send my 95-year-old mother over there to wash Chuck Norris' mouth out with soap." Last night, the one-time host of "Saturday Night Live" said, "Now that Sylvester Stallone has endorsed me, I am sending him over to take care of Chuck Norris right now."

No predictions here in the Sunshine State, although I suspect that the polls showing Romney and McCain in a dead heat and Giuliani just plain dead in the race are right. In South Carolina, all polls show Obama winning (no surprise there) but be prepared for a possible upset for second place not unlike Iowa's, with a native son in the race who is now able to bill himself as "the adult wing of the Democratic party." Edwards is an underdog, but as he himself has said, 'I'm a serious underdog.'

Here's a good quote from Barack Obama which all candidates would do well to remember: "We can disagree without being disagreeable."

It's "Gone with the Win" in Florida Primary

1/29/2008

It's almost gone with the wind in Florida now. The polls close in roughly an hour and a half. From all indications, Rudy Giuliani will be toast. The thrice-married former Mayor of New York City, during the period of his divorce from his second wife (one of the cast members of "The Vagina Monologues") billed his security expenses for taking his mistress to the Hamptons to the city's loft board.

But Giuliani was still proclaiming on the morning of the Florida primary, Tuesday, January 29th, "I believe I've been the candidate who has been the most relevant to the people of Florida…There are a lot of good, positive reasons to vote for me." Rudy's strategy has been to urge Florida voters to vote for *him* before the other Republican candidates arrived, using absentee ballots and the right to begin voting on January 14th that several states offer.

If Florida's voters took him up on that strategy, they may now be suffering buyers' remorse, as it appears that a vote for Giuliani is going to be blowin' in the wind. If Giuliani finishes third, he'll be doing well, as he could even lose the bronze medal to former Arkansas Governor Mike Huckabee, the winner in Iowa, who is also competing in Florida, playing to very small crowds, often comprised of evangelical Christians and home-schoolers, who follow him from venue to venue.

With an hour and a half to go before the polls close, CNN exit polls showed that an overwhelming majority of all voters, whether Democratic or Republican, felt that the economy was the biggest issue on their minds. The Florida voters are also an older bunch, with 45% of Republicans interviewed in exit polls 60 or older and 44% of the Democrats in the same geriatric age range.

Ninety-one % of the Democrats coming out of the polling places, (and 63% of the Republicans) identified the economy as their most pressing concern, saying that it was "not so good" or "poor." Mitt Romney has been capitalizing on this shift in the issues in his favor saying, "live" on CNN, "One of the candidates out there said the economy is not his strong suit. Well, it's MY strong suit."

This emphasis on the economy might bode well for Mitt Romney, who has been billing himself as the expert on matters economic. An old quote John McCain gave to the *Boston Globe* was even being circulated on this election day, to discredit him. McCain supposedly said that he "didn't even really understand the economy." The old quote was being circulated by Hugh Hewitt, author of the book *A Mormon in the WhiteHouse?*(an author who is anything but impartial about who he'd like to see selected by his party). McCain's camp may well have a few rebuttal comments in response when this hectic last day of Florida campaigning is over.

After maintaining for weeks that he was going to remain neutral in the race, Florida's Republican Governor Charlie Crist changed his mind and endorsed John McCain, an act that gave the old warrior's final push to the polls some of what is termed "the Big Mo." (Mo being short for momentum).

Crist, when asked by Wolf Blitzer (CNN) about why he suddenly changed his mind and endorsed John McCain, answered, (from St. Petersburg), "I think he's a good man. I know he's a good man. And that's what influenced my vote," saying that trust and integrity were key issues and that McCain had proven himself a true patriot. There were some naysayers who privately wondered if Charlie Crist envisions himself as a Vice Presidential running mate with McCain, but Crist deflected such questions, repeating, "I trust this man. He's not going to say things just to appease me. He's going to say what is in his heart."

McCain has a reputation as a maverick, joining the Gang of Fifteen; originally not supporting the Bush tax cuts. McCain's feet are held to the fire over McCain/Feingold, as well as his bi-partisan efforts with Senator Joe Leiberman (once a Democratic Vice Presidential candidate with Al Gore; now an Independent) to establish cap and trade carbon emission standards to positively impact global warming. There is also the issue of Guantanamo Bay, which McCain finds to be a national embarrassment. Most of these McCain positions seem more Democratic than Republican to the conservative wing of the Republican party, and the talking heads like Rush Limbaugh and Hugh Hewitt have crucified McCain on talk radio in the run-up to the Florida primary.

Nearly all of the candidates acknowledge that Florida's 57 "winner-take-all" delegates make the state a pivotal part of the march to the White House, or, at least, to the Republican party's nomination of a candidate who will try to slog to the White House, climbing over the debris left by the "slash-and-burn" Bush politics of the past 8 years.

As Wolf Blitzer was told by the many on-air experts that CNN consults during their political broadcasts, if there is not a clear-cut winner coming out of Florida, a brokered convention is a reality. The absentee ballots also shape up to be a big factor. McCain's camp did not have the money to mobilize the absentee ballot voting strategy, while Romney and Giuliani left no absentee ballot unturned. This use of absentee ballots or early voting to turn the tide for a candidate makes it even more difficult to use traditional methods to predict who will win on the actual day of voting.

I have a little personal experience with absentee ballots and the opportunities for cheating they present, having once run in a small-town city council race where 28 such votes were cast. I, personally, went back and polled all absentee votes (since I had won the popular vote, only to be told that nearly all of the absentee ballots went for the opponent; the count, however, could not possibly be "right," as my entire family had voted for me using absentee ballots, and the tally did not match up with what the "authorities" said I had garnered). I learned that at least 25% of the absentee votes cast were fraudulent... people bussed in from other districts; people who worked for the Democratic County Chairman; people who were in the hospital near death and had no idea what they had signed. Playing fast and loose with absentee ballots is something that can definitely threaten fair elections, as I learned firsthand.

The rule in Illinois politics, anyway, is one called "proportionate reduction," which means that, when such a fraudulent vote is found (and it's not easy to uncover such fraud), the voters who voted for you then have to sign notarized affidavits, and show up in court, in person, (assuming a Judge orders them to do so, as he did in my own case), but you, the plaintiff, have no time allotted to subpoena those voters and some of those voters are probably out of town or near death and physically unable to appear.

Proportionate reduction means that one vote is taken from your total, and one vote is taken from your opponent's total ("proportionate reduction"), which pretty much makes it impossible to "win" fair-and-square if absentee ballots are filled out fraudulently and then used to "turn the tide" against the candidate who actually carried the popular vote at the polls on election day. It's a little like Al Gore in Florida in 2000. The voting system favors the "winner" initially announced and there is no time allotted for the hapless candidate who has been snookered to prove it, as "the vote must go on," in the same way that the show must go on. It was certainly an eye-opening experience in my own case about how dirty politics has become. My dad was an office holder back in the 1940s and warned me that "politics is a dirty business." My biggest regret was not the $8,000 cost of the challenge, but the fact that a news media person standing there during the recount… when it was quite clear that I had "won" more votes cast at the polls than my opponent had garnered…never saw fit to report anything about the incorrect information printed the day after the election in the local newspaper.

I remember vividly my attorney taking me out in the hall and telling me, "You and I are probably the only two people in the room who understand that, because of 'proportionate reduction' you can't possibly win, because there weren't enough absentee votes cast. Even the Republican judge doesn't know, or he wouldn't have ordered the recount. What do you want me to do?"

After that, Rick (the attorney) and I decided to throw in the towel with grace, as it was quite apparent that, when the Democratic County Chairman said to me (during a courtesy call I made to let him know I was running against his hand-picked former Secretary), "You can't possibly win, because you weren't born here and you weren't in a union," he was telling me that he was going to make *sure* that I couldn't win. I actually *had* been in a union; in fact, I organized a teacher's union from scratch, and I had lived in my district for over 40 years.)

But enough crying over spilt milk, as my mother used to say.

To the CNN viewers observing all the action on the national level the past week, it seems as though the vitriolic attack-dog campaign strategy garnering so much attention amongst the Democrats last week (and so much criticism from the public), as Clinton and Obama went head-to-head, is now coming from the Republicans in Florida. Some say the unseemly attacks on Obama by former President Clinton resulted in Senator Edward Kennedy's endorsement of Barack Obama. The worm has now turned and it is the Republicans in Florida who are providing us with the "how low can they go" contest.

With 1% of the vote reported right now, in Florida, McCain is pulling in 29% of the vote and Romney 28%. Talk about close! Giuliani is running a distant third at 18%. For the Democrats—largely a beauty contest, as there are no delegates in play—Clinton has 58%, Obama 21% and Edwards 17%.

Gunfight at the Reagan Library

1/30/2008

Rudy Giuliani found out that it's easy to get burned in Florida, and, from the peeved tone in John McCain's voice as he debated last night from the Ronald Reagan Presidential Library, it might be easy to get burned in Simi Valley, California, if he continues acting and sounding like a peeved, cranky old geezer. The dial people hooked up to those omnipresent measuring devices didn't like his tone at all. Nor did I. Nor did Mitt Romney.

The four Republicans left in the race, starting with Mike Huckabee on the far left of the stage and moving to the right (figuratively speaking) with Ron Paul, John McCain and Mitt Romney seated next to one another answered questions such as, "Are you better off than you were 8 years ago?" To be honest, Romney changed that question to one he preferred answering about his record while Governor of Massachusetts. Finally, with irritation, Anderson Cooper called him on that old political dodge and reined him in, asking, "Are you running for Governor or are you running for President?"

Ron Paul, was the usual voice crying in the wilderness, and answered, "No. No. We're not better off… Republicans were elected in 2004 to have a humble foreign policy and we're trying to police the world." Paul even went so far as to say (horror of horrors), "It's partially this Administration's fault."

One of the worst points in the snarky debate, for me, was when McCain patronizingly pointed out to Romney that the *Boston Globe* had not endorsed Romney, but had endorsed McCain. He said, "I'll guarantee you the *Arizona Republic* will be endorsing me, my friend."

Somehow, given the tone of the comments, I don't think these two are destined to be BFFs. (Best Friends Forever).

171

McCain said that Romney's own Lieutenant Governor had not endorsed Romney (thrust), but had been traveling around with his team, and Romney was quick to parry that Kerry Healey, his Lieutenant Governor had endorsed him, but it was Governor Swift, his predecessor in Massachusetts who was helping helm McCain's campaign.

Peggy Noonan, famed speechwriter, recently wrote that George W. Bush has "destroyed the Republican party" and the candidates were asked about this quote from her article. Romney replied, "He kept us safe these last six years." The audience actually applauded that...although a little bit of reading would suggest that Bush the Younger has helped create a much more fertile breeding ground for terrorist cells than existed before his ascension to the throne. (*Note: Proving truer with every passing day 8 years later.)

Romney was noticeably peeved that John McCain insisted that Romney supported a specific time table for withdrawing from Iraq, saying it was "absolutely wrong" and going further to say that "Raising it a few days before the Florida primary, when I had very little time to rebut it, was the kind of dirty politics that Ronald Reagan would have found reprehensible." Romney also said, with deep exasperation, "How is it that you're the expert on my positions?"

McCain (parry) said, "You did not take a position on this when it was a critical issue."

Ah. Yes. Shades of the Walmart attorney/Rezko slumlord exchange that was so entertaining during the last Democratic debate.

McCain insisted, at one point, that Republicans lost the mid-term elections NOT because of the War in Iraq, but because of overspending.

Wellllllll. Maybe; maybe not.

Ron Paul articulated all of our frustration at the childishness on display when he said, "You're talking about these technicalities of who said what when? ...How many men are you willing to let die. It's unconstitutional. It's time we only go to war with a declaration of war." Hear, hear, oh weird Squirrel-like figure. I'm actually liking what you have to say... for the most part. He quoted Reagan's agreement with his position that, "No great country that ever went off the gold standard ever remained great." Don't know much about gold, other than that, currently, it is at an All-time High.

The shenanigans between Romney and McCain were at an All-time Low and on display for the entire nation last night.

If I were grading them like the children on the playground they seemed to be ("My daddy can beat up YOUR daddy!" "Oh, no he can't."

"Oh, yes he can!"), I'd say that Huckabee and Paul did better than their more contentious opponents on the stage, and that it's a good thing this was the last debate or fists might fly.

Latest news: Arnold Schwarzenegger (aka, "the Terminator") will endorse McCain (aka, the cranky, old war horse.)

Illinois Casts Votes for Barack Obama on Super Tuesday

Voters in Illinois Brave a Blizzard to Vote for Obama

2/05/2008

The traffic at South Moline Township's Precinct One polling place in Rock Island County, Illinois was steady at 3:00 p.m. on Super Tuesday, as it had been all day. Outside, it was snowing big white flakes. When I asked how many people had voted that day, the judges told me that they had helped at least 500 voters.

"But," said one judge, "we've had 900 before in a primary."

I snapped a picture of the judges at their posts, and one male Republican judge asked me if I was a reporter.

"Sort of," I replied. "I write for a blog. You might see yourself on there."

He wrote down the name of the blog and smiled as I snapped his picture and that of the other judges.

I took the magic marker from the female judge nearest me and entered the voting "booth," if you can call it that. There were no curtains. It was really just a tall table with sides.

This is a heavily Democratic county, and it was possible for those who are not registered Democrats to vote Democratic, as my husband, a staunch Republican, illustrates. My husband voted in the Democratic primary on Tuesday, which supports the contention that Obama is attracting disenchanted Republicans and Independents. My husband voting Democratic is like Bill O'Reilly endorsing Hillary Clinton for President: unlikely in the extreme.

There was a proposal to fully fund medical benefits for military veterans on the ballot (it passed 92% to 8%), and there was a proposal to raise funds for our deserving local Niabi Zoo (It also passed). A television spot was even running with Jack Hanna, the zoo guy from "Letterman," explaining that the zoo does not plan to levy the maximum tax increase of up to six cents per $100 assessed property valuation that they are requesting.

One contested race here in this part of Illinois involves the 71st District state legislative seat, currently held by incumbent Mike Boland, but being sought by challenger Jerry Lack. The local Democratic equivalent of a Clinton or Bush dynasty in this county is the third-generation-in-politics Jacobs family. State Senator Denny Jacobs retired mid-term in order to hand the reins over to his son in a brokered deal that many found unseemly. Son Mike Jacobs served out his father's term and faces a challenge from Republican Paul Rumler. The race is tight…52% to 48%…with 40+% of the precincts. There is bad blood between the Jacobs clan and Mike Boland and they are out to get his seat, so the outcome of this small local election will be interesting. As I write this, it appears that Boland will prevail, but the outcome of the Jacobs/Rumler race is still very close. (*Note: Mike Jacobs remained in office until 2014, when the Jacobs political dynasty lost.)*

Depending on where a voter resided in Rock Island County, residents could find as many as five referendum questions on the ballot, and there were several Democratic contests on the ballot. By contrast, there were no contested local races on the Republican Party ballot. Hence, my husband's decision to vote in the Democratic primary.

As I left the polling place, I talked with fellow 1st Ward voters Gerald and Doris McLaughlin about their concerns. Call it my personal exit poll.

Gerald works at Bowlesburg School (physically situated in Silvis, but an elementary school in the East Moline School District) and Doris works at Help at Home, which supplies nursing care for elderly homebound residents of the county. We shared our enthusiasm for Illinois State Senator Barack Obama's candidacy, our native son candidate. Since Gerald and I have both worked around young people, we were concerned that the blizzard swirling around us might cut down on the turnout of young voters.

More than anything else, Obama's candidacy depends on the "passing of the torch" to a younger generation. It is the youthful voters who can make or break Obama's campaign. As Gerald and I both know only too well...when you're young, you are sometimes not as likely to show up during a blizzard, especially if there is something else to distract you that sounds like more fun. Young student voters haven't paid taxes yet, haven't started jobs or families yet; haven't been buffeted by life's storms yet. Yet the youth of America are our future, so I hope they do vote.

Having said that, early returns from Georgia indicated that Obama was doing better than expected with voters between the ages of 40 and 59, garnering 49% of their votes. He swept Georgia, a state with a majority of African American voters, easily. Obama also carried Illinois, his home state, with 66% of the vote, and Minnesota voters gave him the same approximate margin, while Kansas liked him 72% to 28% over Hillary.

However, with 942 delegates at stake, and 2,025 delegates needed to carry the candidate to the Democratic nomination (and 1,191 to win the Republican nomination), the race was far from over at 9 p.m. CDT.

What was certain was that the zoo referendum had passed with 68% favorable yes votes (Thanks, Jack Hanna!) and there would be a new coroner in Rock Island County, as the old one (Sharon Anderson) decided not to run again.

In talking with Gerald and Doris McLaughlin, I learned that we are in agreement with the concerns of much of the nation. Exit polls on MSNBC showed that 45% of voters were most concerned about the economy and 91% of those voters had pronounced the state of the economy "not good" versus only 8% who proclaimed it to be "good." Twenty-nine % of voters in MSNBC exit polls had listed the war as their second most pressing issue, and 18% were concerned about health care. So were we here in Rock Island County, Illinois.

Is Iowa Just Idiots Out
Walking Around?

2/07/2008

Yup. That's what they're calling Iowa in the *New York Daily News*. That particular appellation was bestowed in a blog comment from someone calling himself "wharfrat."

A transplanted Iowan, I felt I should seek a visual for all you readers in other states that would depict an Idiot Out Walking Around…in this case, me! I found the perfect spot in the Iowa/Illinois Quad Cities, complete with teepee and a (more-or-less) covered wagon. And I found this site while we were getting 8 to 12 inches of snow in 30 mph winds. Definitely an idiot out walking around. At night. In a blizzard.

Why did "wharfrat" of the *New York Daily News* "diss" Iowans?

It started with a comment from 74-year-old Senator (and farmer) Charles Grassley (R, IA) of Butler County, who said that he thought Rudy Giuliani failed in the race for the Republican nomination for the Presidency because he was too liberal for the rest of the country. Apparently, Senator Grassley implied that New Yorkers were lacking in basic moral values or decency or politeness or any number of other fine qualities Grassley values, because Rudy was a bit liberal on issues like abortion and gay rights.

Adjectives like "egotistical, bigoted, arrogant, obnoxious, morally bankrupt and moronic" were circulating in regards to the now defunct Presidential candidate, prompting one writer to the February 1st *Daily News (p. 16)* to respond, "Rudy lost because the rest of the country had to see what we knew all along. The man is just plain nasty."

But, while heavy snow and wind were closing Interstates 80 and 74 in Iowa on February 5th and 6th, dooming we idiots out walking around to be doing so in deep snow, another New Yorker took off on Iowans, too.

This time it was Guardian Angel founder Curtis Sliwa, who once came to the Iowa Quad City of Davenport, Iowa, an old river town on the Mississippi, at the request of 5th Ward Alderman Bill Lynn, supposedly to help organize a band of Guardian Angels to patrol the streets. *(Some of the locals weren't too thrilled with the vigilante method of justice Sliwa espouses, but apparently Alderman Lynn is a big fan.)*

Among other things, Sliwa charged that, "We, the suckers in New York, pay their FEMA bills. Grassley loves New York when it comes to subsidizing FEMA." In reality, Iowa has been very low on the list of states receiving Federal Emergency Management Agency aid and protection. Try Louisiana, perhaps, not Iowa.

Then, Sliwa said that there were more hogs than people in Iowa. Well, actually, according to 2002 statistics, he's right on that one: 15 million pigs versus only 3 million people. Does Sliwa eat ham or bacon? If he does, he should thank an Iowan. Pigs are also among the smartest of animals, although Sliwa perhaps has not associated with enough pigs to know that. Get to know pigs, Mr. Sliwa. Pigs are your friends!

Then, Sliwa said that Iowa didn't represent the rest of the United States. Point well taken. Neither does New York City.

However, while we're arguing which is better (if we are), let's not forget that it was the nearly all-white state of Iowa that proudly (and unexpectedly) gave Barack Obama his ticket to ride, hopefully to the Presidency of the United States over New York Senator Hillary Clinton. (More breaking news on that later.) There's a moral lesson in there somewhere. Probably a joke in there, too, if anyone wants to find it. Believe me, if Hillary Clinton (D, NY) does secure the Democratic nomination, the Republicans will find the jokes AND the dirt. Oh, my yes. Republicans are practically salivating at the prospect of Hillary to compete against. They're not so keen to take after the articulate young Senator from Illinois, another large hog-producing state.

Sliwa went on in his rant to talk about "blocking the hogs."

Nobody in Iowa knows what that phrase means. Obviously, neither does Sliwa, as pointed out by Ed Tibbetts of the *Quad City Times* in an editorial in February 6th's newspaper.(p. A15)

Meanwhile, the person who started all this (i.e., Senator Grassley, R, IA) was being criticized for his polyester pants (well deserved) and his comment that New Yorkers had "personality problems." One writer to the *Daily News* (My Nickel's Worth) said, "Rather than dis' Senator Grassley, I sentence him to life in Iowa."

Ouch!

Life in Iowa can be pretty boring, true. Having just visited the Big Apple for five wonderful days, it is definitely an exciting wonderful city and I "heart" New York. Still, let's not forget that it *was* Iowa—a nearly all-white state—that gave Obama his First Big Win over Hillary Clinton. It is New York (her state) that is backing the Old Guard she represents.

Maybe it's just as good to be an Idiot Out Walking Around in Iowa as anything or anywhere else? We have our teepees, our covered wagon (or what's left of it) and our ideals of change and a brighter tomorrow.

What else could your average Midwesterner...or New Yorker... want?

Exit Polls Confirm Obama Momentum – Obama Gains the Big Mo(mentum)

2/09/2008

Exit polls after Wisconsin's voters spoke on February 19th show that Barack Obama has gained ground on Hillary Clinton in critical areas of her previous base. White males preferred Obama 66% to 32% over Hillary Clinton, (and, from what I've heard white males say about Hillary's candidacy, this sounds right.)

Another area where Obama gained ground that surprised some was in response to the question, "Who would be the best Commander-in-Chief?" Previously, Hillary Clinton had held an edge in this area, but now, Wisconsin voters responded that he would make the best Commander-in-Chief, 52% to 48%, according to CNN.

It was no surprise that youth preferred Obama, as they have all along. The percentages in Wisconsin showed youth going for him by 20 full percentage points, 59% to 39%. The surprising thing in the CNN exit polls in Wisconsin is that voters who make LESS than $50,000 are now backing Obama, by 53% to 46%. More affluent voters, earning over $50,000, had always supported Obama, and that remained true by a margin of 59% to 40%.

On the issue of electability, 63% felt that Obama would make a better opponent to oppose (R) John McCain in November, versus only 37% for Clinton. He won over Hillary by 15% or more, which is considered a landslide.

When questioned about the issues (the economy, Iraq, health care, etc.) in exit polls, it didn't really matter what the issue was. The Wisconsin voters preferred Obama's take on the issues 50% to 48% over Clinton's.

Ultimately, 10,916 (54%) wanted Obama to head the ticket, wheras 9,254 (45%) preferred that Hillary Clinton prevail, in early CNN exit polls.

What has become clear to this reporter, who has been following the primaries and caucuses since the beginning, is that—once it became clear that Obama was "the real deal" and had a legitimate shot at winning this nomination... in other words, once he won in Iowa and beat Clinton there, in a nearly all-white state—the prevailing wisdom that we were about to have a coronation and not an election went out the window. With every contest since then, Obama's appeal has broadened and deepened, to the point that he is now threatening to take categories that were once ceded to Mrs. Clinton as indisputably "her" power base.

Hillary is banking on Texas and Ohio, her camp calling Texas her "firewall" against Obama's seizing the nomination from her grasp. When James Carville was asked (on "Larry King Live") whether, after 9 straight losses to Obama, Hillary's wins in Ohio and Texas were absolutely essential, he answered with one word: "Yes." It was refreshing to hear a straight answer from someone working in the Clinton camp, for a change. But the author of the phrase "It's the Economy, Stupid," minced no words. The Latino vote represented by Texas is supposed to remain firmly in Hillary's camp, according to the "experts." (Those are the same experts who said that Obama didn't have a chance in Iowa.)

Several things seem likely, to me. First, we are likely to see HIllary try to cheat by seating Florida and Michigan. Second, John Edwards will emerge as an even more powerful force, and his endorsement will be sought at a critical time, should he provide one (as will those of other also-rans, such as Christopher Dodd and Joseph Biden). Third, those Super-Delegates are going to continue to be Super-important.

I did a little sleuthing here in the state where it all began on January 3rd (Iowa) and learned that the Super Delegates here are Loebsack, rising star Bruce Braley (who previously endorsed John Edwards; he was beaten by the very conservative Republican Joni Ernst in 2014), Boswell, Senator Harkin, Governor Culver, and two citizen delegates, Sand Optsredt and Jerry Crawford. I'll be interested to try to contact some or all of those folks to find out "who's zooming who" or, in this case, "who's courting whom."

As Jessica Yellin said on CNN, "The bottom line is that this is a state where Hillary Clinton should have been able to win... She really needs Barack Obama to stumble if she is going to pull this off." With 627,455 votes (58%) for Barack Obama and 439,134 (41%) for Hillary Clinton in Wisconsin, a nearly all-white blue-collar state, the fact that America wants change and that this generational battle is one where Hillary is "the Old Guard", i.e., the past, and Barack Obama is the future is like watching a fortune-teller read the tea leaves. The more things settle, the clearer it all becomes.

Hillary Clinton (aka "Miss Frigidaire") Losing Popularity Contest

What Are You Gonna Do When the Most Popular Kid in the Class Takes You On?

2/10/2008

So, I'm watching Fox ("Fair and Balanced") Television on Sunday afternoon, February 10th, when Hannity or Colmes (whichever...I pay scant attention to either, so don't know 'em apart) says, to the world, on this "fair and balanced" network, "I'm leading the Stop Hillary Express."

My first thought? Get in line.

Then, Geraldo Rivera, he of the drawing plans of our Iraq invasion in the sand for the enemy to scope out (surely a "d'oh" moment) says, "For the first time in this race, I am beginning to feel that he (Obama) is going to be the Democratic nominee for the President of the U.S." Gee, Geraldo. Where have you been for the past year? Living under a rock? What was your first clue?

Could it have been the fact that Obama swept Iowa, an all-white state way back at the beginning of this campaign season? Naaaah. Apparently not, because, even though some of us predicted his ascension to the throne, I don't remember Fox News suggesting that an upset nationwide was in the wind on their "fair and balanced" newscasts.

Perhaps Geraldo—on top of things as always— got the word after Super Tuesday, when 15,417,521 Democrats turned out to vote (as opposed to only 9,181,297 Republican voters). Do you think that could be because Obama is the only major party candidate who is viewed favorably by a majority of youth in this country? (He has half again as much support as his nearest competitor, regardless of party affiliation.) Did it take Obama's sweep of Louisiana, Nebraska and Washington State to convince Geraldo?

The signs have been there for a long time, Geraldo. I reported on this blog back on January 2nd—the day BEFORE Obama carried a 95% white state— how much the party "regulars" I had been encountering on the ground in Iowa told me they hated Hillary when out and about covering the many Democrats then vying to be the party's nominee.

The woman is just not "likeable," and, like it or not (pun intended), voters today vote for candidates they like. (Didn't they vote for "W" because they liked him and thought he would be the best guy to sit down and have a beer with...despite his supposedly being on the wagon all these years?) In the state of Michigan, nearly 50,000 voters under thirty voted "uncommitted" rather than be forced to put an "X" next to Hillary Clinton's name, which happened to be the *only* Democratic name on the ballot because of the penalties imposed by the Democratic National Committee for moving their race up. That might have given you a clue, Geraldo. Here's another clue from way back on January 26th: in South Carolina, Obama drew more under-30 votes than all Republican candidates combined, an astounding statistic.

So, what's the race looking like, right about now?

Well, Obama added Maine to his list of triumphs. Hillary fired her longtime scheduler in the White House (for 8 years) who had been working as her campaign manager, Patti Solis Doyle, and installed Maggie Williams. Seventy-eight % of AOL voters (48,554 overall) polled on February 10th thought that this firing signified Trouble in Hillary City and that her campaign was in trouble, versus only 22% who said it was sailing right along.

Up ahead for the candidates are the Potomac Primaries of DC, Maryland and Virginia, held this Tuesday (February 12), where Obama should do well, and then Hawaii (D), Washington and Wisconsin will weigh in on the 19th. The contest will continue to drag on into March, with Ohio, Rhode Island, Texas and Vermont up on March 4th, Wyoming on the 8th, and Mississippi on the 11th.

Then comes April 22nd and Pennsylvania.

In May: Indiana and North Carolina vote on the 6th, followed by Nebraska and West Virginia on the 13th and Kentucky and Oregon on the 20th, Idaho on the 27th and, on June 3rd, limping to the finish line, Montana, New Mexico and South Dakota.

So, where are we now?

It's close, folks...very, very close. Clinton has 1,125 delegates; Obama has 1,087. Needed to carry the day: 2,205. There are 796 Super Delegates and supposedly Clinton has 248 in her pocket while Obama has 156. The thing about Super Delegates is they are beholdin' to no one. They can (apparently) change candidates at will, to hear the Talking Heads tell it. (I, by the way, saw one Talking Head of Fox News Sunday, Bill Crystal, trying to hail a cab at 47th and Broadway in New York City's Times Square on February 3rd, and he is short, Folks… REALLY, REALLY short.) I'm 5' 2 and 3/4" and he is at least 2 inches shorter than me.

So Hillary treks down to Chapel Hill and tries to cut a little deal with Edwards to get his endorsement, while both candidates appear on "Sixty Minutes" on Sunday, February 10th.

But, you know, when your nickname in high school has been "Miss FrigidAire" (something Katie Couric sleuthed out) and people just don't like you, what are you gonna' do, really, when the Most Popular Guy in the Class decides to run against you?

Barack Obama and Hillary Clinton Appear on "Sixty Minutes" on February 10, 2008

Hillary Says Obama Isn't Used to Being Attacked with Negativity: She Is

BARACK OBAMA AND HILLARY CLINTON APPEAR ON "SIXTY MINUTES" ON FEBRUARY 10, 2008

2/11/2008

Steve Croft interviewed Barack Obama on "60 Minutes" on Sunday, February 10th, while Katie Couric did the same with Hillary Clinton. How did they fare? What did they sound like? Here is an assessment from a viewer.

I particularly enjoyed this Obama comment, "I feel that the longer we're in this race, the stronger we get." Kroft asked Obama this question:

Q: "Aside from the Harvard Law Review, what have you ever run?"

A: "I've run my Senate Office; I've run this campaign."

While that answer may have been underwhelming, Obama went on to speak clearly and articulately about how he was different from his opponent, Hillary Clinton. He explained that, in regards to Iraq, as a nation, we were going to "have to send a clear message that they (Iraquis) are going to have to solve their sectarian violence themselves." Citing the half a trillion dollars spent on the war so far, Barack stated that staying in Iraq as long as front-running Republican John McCain wants to is not a good idea, saying, "I think that is a recipe for disaster."

Obama also said that, before every primary or caucus, the Obama election team plays basketball, because that's what they did before the first big Iowa win. He cited his "even temperament" and said that he would be the strongest candidate to run against the Republican nominee because, "I don't start off with 47% of the electorate saying they won't vote for me."

Then Hillary had her moments onscreen, with Katie Couric questioning her. I thought that Katie asked questions that were more hard-hitting, but she asked them in her "girlsy" style, as though she really meant no harm. Baba Wawa she is not, however, and I felt that she was letting fly with a few quality zingers, such as:

Q: "Why him (Obama) and not you?" A: Experience, of course.

Next, Couric wanted to know how Hillary keeps at the drudgery of campaigning so long and hard and doesn't lose heart or become ill.

A: "I'm doing this the only way I know how to do it. The only way I know how to do it is to believe in my heart that I'm going to be successful."

Q: What if it's all for naught?

A: "Katie, you can't do that," spoken with a slightly condescending tone, I thought. (My thought: surely you've given *SOME* thought to losing… ? Anyone with normal human emotions would have given it *some* thought. In rehashing that question, however, that last line has just explained Hillary's response.)

Q: "Why did/does she do it?"

A: "I do it because I really believe in what I'm doing."

Then, Hillary revealed her "keeping healthy on the campaign stump" tips. To wit: vitamins. Drink tea rather than coffee. Don't drink so many soft drinks. Drink lots of water. Wash your hands or use germ-killing tissues. Eat hot peppers. (Which she claims she has been doing since 1992; no wonder Bill strayed. I definitely won't be rushing out to stock up on hot peppers any time soon; I'd rather be sick.)

Now came Hillary's "sales" pitch: "I am ready to be Commander-in-Chief on Day One." [IF I HEAR "DAY ONE" ONE MORE TIME FROM

HILLARY, I'M GOING TO HAVE TO SMITE SOMEONE!]

Q: "Is there not one scintilla of bad blood between you and Obama?"

A: "Not from my side," (sweetly). Hillary went on to describe how she had gone to Chicago to campaign for Obama in 2004 and mentioned a photo of Barack and his wife that still remains on her study wall. No mention from Clinton of whether that photo is being used as a dartboard.

Couric asked Clinton if it was true that Obama had sought her out for advice when he entered the Senate. Hillary admitted that it was true. What advice did Hillary give Barack? "Work hard and keep a low profile." I'll bet Hillary wishes she had added, "Work hard, keep a low profile, and don't run against me for President." Hillary. Hillary. Hillary. *(shaking head)* Hindsight is always so much better than foresight.

Hillary rambled on about how Barack has never experienced a barrage of negative attacks…never had a negative campaign ad run against him. "He's never been on the receiving end of negativity." Hillary said she was "Much better prepared and ready" to weather such negative attacks.

Couric countered with, "Are you saying he couldn't handle it?" but Clinton didn't take that bait, although she did say that she thought that the mainstream press had been more unkind to her than to Barack or any other candidate, prompting this question from Katie Couric.

Q: "Why are you seen as polarizing?"

A: "I've been active on behalf of a lot of controversial causes: a woman's right to choose, global warming, " (etc.) At this point, Clinton did not mention the nation's voters who hold a grudge against her husband's shenanigans while in office. All that impeachment unpleasantness was swept under the rug. Be gone, Monica Talk!

Couric repeated for Clinton's benefit an answer that Barack Obama had given Steve Kroft during that part of the interview. Obama had equated Hillary Clinton to the "status quo" and his own candidacy to change. Hillary neatly deflected that charge by saying that the "status quo" meant Bush, McCain and the Republicans, citing Bush's latest budget which would build a $400,000 billion deficit and pointing to the $9 trillion in debt Bush has created for the country after taking over from Bill Clinton when the country actually had a surplus.

Katie went on the attack, asking about Clinton's vote to go to war with Iraq, eliciting, "Most Democrats did it, as I did, on information we had at the time. The real issue now is, how do we get out?" Candidate Clinton spoke of bringing troops home within 60 days and said that staying the 100 years McCain had mentioned "would absolutely enrage me."

Then Couric switched gears and started going back to ancient high school history, i.e., Hillary's demanding father, who was described by Bill Clinton during his funeral eulogy as "tough and gruff." Hillary would come home with straight "A's." Dad would say, "You must be going to an easy school. You can do better."

By this point I was beginning to feel a little bit sorry for the Robo-Candidate in spite of myself. It took me back to Bill's cheating days. Nobody likes her. Her dad sounds like a jerk. Her husband cheated on her and was publicly chastised on national television. And, as the piece de resistance, her nickname in high school was "Miss Frigidaire." Yikes! How did they dig THAT up? I'm thinking about now that Hillary should cross MSNBC and CBS both off her list of channels on which she will appear in the future.

Q: "What if this doesn't work out?" asked Couric.

A: "I'd go back to the Senate and work for the citizens of New York."

Barack Obama Displays Eloquence Before Virginia Vote

The Most Charismatic Speaker in Decades Delivers the Goods in Richmond, VA, on February 10th

2/11/2008

I heard Barack Obama giving a speech (from Richmond, Virginia) on CNN on Sunday, February 10th prior to Virginia's Tuesday primary race on February 12th. I was struck, once again, with how many people he constantly thanks. People like to be thanked. I'm sure Tim Cane and Mark Warner and Doug Wilder and Bobby Scott and Jim Morain and Rich Baucher and Dick Granevald and Amy Rieger and all the others Barack was thanking so profusely were grateful. I remember that, when he appeared in Davenport, Iowa, he brought out all the young campaign workers and thanked each of them personally in front of the crowd. This "niceness" may well be a big part of Barack Obama's appeal.

Said Obama, in the televised speech excerpt, "It has been one year since we began this race to the Presidency on the steps of the Old Capitol in Springfield, Illinois…I knew we wouldn't be the favorite. I knew we would be the underdog from January till June. I knew it wouldn't be easy. But then something started to happen. Across this land, the message is the same: we are tired of being disappointed by our politicians. While Washington is consumed by the same distractions, another father puts up another for sale sign on the lawn…and it goes on and on and on and on and on. We become cynics. We lower our standards."

And then, swinging into full Obama Oratorical mode, Barack said, "Not this time. Not this year. The stakes are too high. People want to turn the page. People want to write a new chapter. Yes we can! We won in (fills in blank with recent states of victory) and I believe we can win in Virginia on Tuesday (February 12) if you're ready to stand with me and fight…"

Obama went on to use the "no more Scooter Libby justice; no more Brownie incompetence; no more Karl Rove politics" line I have heard him use in person. "We are gonna' be unified as Democrats to make sure that we bring it in from the failed politics of George W. Bush. That's how we are gonna' win in Virginia and that's how we are gonna' change this country."

Get this man a church! He is dynamite from the pulpit!

If you have the chance to hear Barack Obama, in person, do not miss it. To wit: "There's a moment in the life of every generation when we must act. Virginia, this is our moment. This is our time. You and I together will transform this country." Chills.

I was instantly reminded of my all-time favorite Shakespeare quote, which I will (roughly) paraphrase for you here:

"There is a tide in the affairs of men which, if taken at the flood, leads on to fame and greater fortune. If omitted, all the voyage of our lives is bound in the shallows of misery and despair." That's not exact quoting, but it reminds of Obama's eloquence and the sentiment is certainly similar.

You gotta' love it! Unless you're a Republican and you're seeing doom in the upcoming November election trying to defeat Barack Obama, should he secure the nomination. The most charismatic speaker in a long time has come down the pike, and he's intelligent, too!

Fifty Ways to Leave Iraq, Now!

February 17th, 2008

(Sung to the tune of "Fifty Ways to Leave Your Lover")

The situation's not as bad as that, they said to us...
The answer's easy if you only learn to trust...
We'd like to help them in their struggle to be free,
And then it's: 50 ways to leave Iraq, now.
Give Iraqis back their land, now.
That said, it's really not our habit to intrude...
I hope our meaning won't be lost or misconstrued...
So let's repeat this phrase, at risk of being rude:
There must be: 50 ways to leave Iraq, now.

Chorus:
We'll never be welcome; it's a problem that's large, boys!
It surely looms large, boys, in the quest to be free.
They said, "It grieves me so to see your country in such pain...
We wish there were things to do to make things seem more sane.
Then, would you please explain, boys, about..
The 50 ways to leave Iraq, now.

Bush said, "Why don't we both just go and sleep on this tonight?
And I believe that some time soon they'll see the light."
And then a bomb exploded, obscuring our plain sight,
Of the 50 ways to leave Iraq, now.

(Chorus repeats)

Barack Obama, Hillary Clinton Debate for the 19th Time in Austin, Texas

Feb 22, 2008

True to my usual practice of listening for either applause or boos, during Thursday night's Democratic debate on CNN televised from Austin, Texas, from on campus at the University of Texas, the only "boo-ing" was directed Hillary Clinton's way, as she took after Barack Obama for (purportedly) plagiarizing a speech by Deval Patrick, the National Co-Chairman of his campaign (and Governor of Massachusetts). Hillary's sharp retort that using Patrick's words is "Not change we can believe in; change we can Xerox" did not go over well with the crowd. This was the only instance of "boo-ing" in the extremely civilized 19th debate the two leading candidates have had.

First, from a woman's perspective, what was up with Hillary's outfit? The neckline of the black outfit reminded me of a costume from an old Star Trek set. It had a high collar that was edged in gold, which then looked as though it connected physically to her gold omega chain. It was not an unattractive look; it just looked like an early sketch of something Michael Jackson would design, with epaulets still to be attached. To be fair, it was fairly slimming and fetching from the waist up— until Hillary stood up. The hemline of the jacket then ballooned unfetchingly, making her look larger through the hips than she actually is (surely not the desired effect?).

Fashion aside, here were some of the "zingers" heard during the largely friendly debate, listed in chronological order:

Obama: "What's lacking now are not good ideas. Washington is a place where ideas go to die."

Obama: "What the American people want is an America as good as its promise."

Obama: (on talking to Cuba's new leadership): "I do think it's important (for a nation) not just to talk to its friends, but also to talk to its enemies." (The gizmo people liked this one.)

Clinton: "The Bush Administration has alienated our friends and emboldened our enemies. I want to send a very strong message that the era of arrogance, pre-emption and unilateralism—those days are over." (I wondered how this pronouncement would dampen the budding friendship between Bill Clinton and his newfound friend George Herbert Walker Bush.)

Obama: "I think the President today needs to take a more active role than 30 or 40 years ago. That's the extra step." (on talking to other nations)

Clinton: "The wealthy and the well-connected have had a President for the last 7 years and I'd like the middle class to have a President now." Clinton followed that up with the phrase, "innovation nation," a nice rhyming phrase. She should have trotted that one out earlier in this campaign.

Clinton: (Talking about how young Latino children might come home to find their parents deported and no one there to take care of them) "That is not the America that I know. That is a stark admission of failure." Pressed further on the immigration issue, Hillary, when asked if she would reconsider the border fence or commit to finishing it, said, "There is a smart and a dumb way to enforce immigration. I would say, 'Wait a minute. We need to review this.' As with so many things, the Bush Administration has gone off the deep end. I would listen to the people who live along the border."

Clinton: "My opponent gives speeches; I offer actions…Actions speak louder than words." (*It was right about here that the offending Xerox comment crept in, surely the biggest faux pas of the night from either candidate*).

Obama: (responding to Hillary's plagiarism charge), retorted that her objections were "silly" and that it had become "silly season." He added, "We shouldn't be spending time tearing the country down; we should be building the nation up."

Obama (on whether he is ready to be President "on Day One," which, lets' face it, Sports Fans, is becoming a really annoying phrase to hear over and over and over): "I wouldn't be running (for President) if I didn't think I was ready (to be Commander-in-Chief)."

Obama: (on the surge in Iraq) "The fact is that the purpose of it has not been fulfilled. We need to send a clear message that the Iraqis no longer have a blank check, like they had under President Bush… It is up to the Iraqis to determine what kind of future they will have." Obama, after praising the efforts of the 1st Cavalry stationed out of Fort Hood, said that the decision to invade Iraq was "a tactical maneuver based on a huge strategic blunder." He proceeded to decry how poorly our returning veterans are being treated and how veterans in Southwest Texas have to drive 250 miles to access health care. Spending $12 million a month in Iraq has kept the nation from attending to building up relations with Latin American nations (among others), and we are only spending about what is spent in one week in Iraq. He added, "Iran is the single biggest beneficiary of our invasion of Iraq."

When asked about "earmarks", the audience learned that there were $91 million in total "earmarks" from Obama, to secure funds for his home state of Illinois, and $342 million in earmarks from Hillary Clinton, for her home state of New York.

Obama: "The people want to know that they have a government that is listening to them again. They want their government back (*echoes of Howard Dean in 2004 here*) and that is what I'm going to provide them with."

The final question each was asked was, "Describe the moment when you were tested the most?" (Oh, oh. I thought. Is there really going to be an instant replay of the "I did not have sex with that woman, Miss Lewinski" days? Democrats can rest assured there will be if Hillary is the nominee.)

Obama gave a bland answer that dealt with his work on the streets as an organizer, early in his career, a task which he committed to out of idealism rather than accepting a high-paying job with a prestigious law firm.

Hillary paused and made a comment about how everyone in the audience knew of some of her difficult moments. After the debate was officially over, some of the analysts considered this final answer—which went waaaaay off on a tangent about returning disfigured Iraq veterans and how hard they have it, compared to anything she ever had to put up with—as a "humanizing" moment for the Robo-candidate. I just found it manipulative and staged. It didn't look or sound "real" to me, at all. I was surprised that all these smart people, these paid analysts, had been "snookered" into letting a candidate twist the "real" question around and answer whatever-the-heck she felt like. I suppose we can give her points for agility and thinking on her feet ("Boy! I sure don't want to talk about Bill's infidelity. Where can I go with *this*?"), but I don't think we can give her too many points for candor in her "stagey" answer. To me, it was as bad as when a job applicant says that his chief failing is that he "cares too much for others." Contrived. Manipulative. Deceitful. Not honest. Not real. Not human. Said for effect.

In the CNN Newsroom, post-debate, some of the prevailing wisdom included this prescient line from Gloria Borger (CNN Political Analyst), "We've heard all the themes we are going to hear. It is what it is." (Bring in Bill to parse the meaning of the word "is," please. I know he can do it. He's done it before.)

Jeffrey Toobin (CNN analyst) said, "Maybe she's going to lose with dignity." (My reaction: not bloody likely).

David Gergen, political analyst, decrying Hillary's inability to "connect" with the voters emotionally said, "If she can't establish that, I think she is going to lose." (Gergen seems to be coming to this realization rather late in the game, but whatever.)

Donna Brasile, who ran Al Gore's campaign and is a Super Delegate to the convention, said, "She (Hillary) needs a message firewall" and declared "Barack Obama tonight was exceptional."

Donna Brasile, in all previous appearances and debates, had seemed to support Hillary Clinton, so this newfound enthusiasm for Obama may be indicative of the erosion of support from amongst the Super Delegates previously pledged to Clinton or previously listed as leaning towards Clinton.

A couple of other good moments for Obama came when he said, "On the single most important decision of our generation (the decision to invade Iraq), I have shown the judgment to lead." He also skewered likely Republican opponent John McCain, saying, "John McCain says he doesn't know much about the economy and he has proven that by embracing the failed policies of George W. Bush."

One CNN analyst said, "It sounded as though Hillary was just reciting her resume."

This was the tamest and most civilized Democratic debate since the last seated debate, when Edwards was still in the race. I found it telling that Hillary Clinton invoked John Edwards' name not once, but twice, in praising various positions he had articulated while still a candidate. It made me wonder if she was, as they say, "sucking up" to Edwards to try to get him to endorse her and/or to try to woo and influence his committed delegates to come over to her side (the Dark Side?). Both Clinton and Obama are known to have been in contact with the North Carolina ex-Senator at his home in Chapel Hill, but no endorsements have been forthcoming so far.

It's now do-or-die for Hillary Clinton. Most analysts expect that she will not be able to pull Texas out of the fire (it's neck-and-neck), but that, if she does, it will be largely on the backs of the Hispanic voters in the state. Even if she does win in Texas, Hillary also has to take Ohio to be viable, according to her husband, the ex-President, and James Carville, who advised Bill Clinton and is advising Hillary.

I don't see wins for Hillary in both Ohio and Texas happening. I've thought since Iowa (January 3rd) that Obama has the charisma and the rock-star aura that Hillary, on her best day, cannot summon. Nor could Bill lend Hillary his charisma. If anything, Bill has managed to tarnish his elder statesman image while bringing home few wins for his ambitious wife. Crowds, yes; wins, no.

Part of Obama's appeal is gender-based. Part of his appeal rests on his mad oratorical skills. Much of his appeal is generational. Most of it is the "gut instinct" that each and every voter in our democracy is allowed to follow through on privately in the voting booth. (What a great country!)

It almost seems that, like Giuliani and Thompson, Hillary Clinton and the Clinton campaign all made huge mistakes (of different sorts) in planning their campaigns. In Hillary Clinton's case, she did not anticipate this upstart Senator from Illinois being the tenacious performer he has proven himself to be. He was well-organized beyond the Clinton campaign's wildest dreams…or nightmares. The carefully scripted plastic appearances in Iowa, prior to the first January caucus, didn't do much to endear Hillary to voters there, and that's where Obamamania began. Keeping Chelsea under wraps and away from the press only reinforced the image that Hillary is remote, in an ivory tower, not "one of the people."

The biggest sticking point of the evening, the biggest debate point (which the candidates almost would not let go) was over health care, with Hillary accusing Obama's plan (as she has on the stump) of leaving 15 million uninsured. Obama fired back that Hillary's plan mandated that everyone have health care, which would prove a hardship. He made the very valid point that people who don't have health care don't have it because they can't afford it, and garnishing their wages and making them have it, through a mandate, is not the way to go. (Obama's plan does, however, mandate health care for children.)

Obama, while saluting Senator Clinton for her previous attempts to head up a health reform bill when Bill was President, pointed out that it was all done in secrecy, behind closed doors, and that he values transparency and would be better suited to bring people together to work to undo the damage of the Bush years. Nowhere has that been clearer than on the campaign trail.

"Meet the Press" and "Face the Nation" Handicap the Presidential Race

March 2nd, 2008

On Sunday, March 3rd's versions of "Face the Nation" and "Meet the Press" expert political commentators filled us in on how this year's race for the Presidential nomination is playing out. A bi-partisan mixture of Republican and Democratic strategists had the opportunity to put in their two cents' worth. This is how it sounded.

Republican strategist Mike Murphy, a guest on "Meet the Press", said, "I'll make a cash money bet right now on Obama." There were no takers. Murphy backed up his bet with the information that, even if Hillary wins in both Texas and Ohio, she would have to win 70% of the votes in the 12 states that remain, which represent 611 delegates. (Most of those states, for the curious, are: Oregon, Montana, West Virginia, South Dakota, Indiana, Kentucky, Pennsylvania, North Carolina, Mississippi, Guam and Puerto Rico, which has 63 delegates.)

Bob Schrum—famous for his soaring speech work for the Democrats—commented, "You cannot go into this convention and not have some moral claim." James Carville, the bald strategist to both Bill and Hillary, who appeared on "Meet the Press" alongside his Republican strategist wife Mary Matalin, said, "Nobody in the world can look at these polls and predict with any accuracy." He did acknowledge, however, that he agreed with Bill Clinton, who told Texas voters during a campaign rally for his wife in Beaumont, Texas, "If you don't deliver for her, I don't think she can (win). It's on your backs." Carville agreed with his former boss, saying, "You gotta' win something."

Mary Matalin, his Republican spouse, laughed at most of the comments made about the continuing Democratic death struggle on "Meet the Press", ultimately commenting, "It's so khumbaya that they (the Democrats) can't pick a nominee."

Countered her Republican counterpart Murphy, "Turnout is his (Obama's) demographic. The thing I'd be watching on Election Day is turnout. He creates a turnout demographic that is very powerful. My gut tells me he's gonna' take 'em both (Ohio and Texas), and that'll be the end."

Democratic strategist and speechwriter "Schrummie" (Bob Schrum) interjected, "What we're really seeing is a generational struggle inside the Democratic party." He went on to liken Hillary to the Beach Boys when the Beatles came to America. The analogies were flying thick and fast. At one point, Obama was even compared to the hula hoop craze! Is it a fad? Will it last? What about staying power?

There was a lot of scrutiny of the latest ads that Hillary and Obama are running. The ads show a phone call coming in to a home with sleeping children in the dead of night. Hillary answers the pre-dawn ringing phone, dressed to the teeth (my husband wondered why she wouldn't be in her nightgown, a valid Republican observation). The implication: a crisis call was coming in. Who is most qualified to answer it?

Obama immediately countered this Mark Penn-designed ad with one that used the same imagery, but underscored his judgment as being sounder, as he had been against the Iraq War since the beginning. Carville categorized both ads as "fair." Then the experts began picking them apart, saying that the origin of such a ringing telephone ad goes all the way back to Walter Mondale in 1984, running against Gary Hart and using an image of a red phone. (Boy! Did that phone look dated!) The problem, the strategists said, is that the "red phone" fear message has become a bit of a cliché. The implication: this cliché charge is also true of Hillary's entire campaign.

Next came some finger pointing. "Mark Penn has called the strategy in this campaign, dominated it." This from Jason Horowitz's *New York Observer* newspaper article titled "Ickes: Blame Penn." As her chief strategist, Penn actually wrote the current phone call ad.

There were moments of mirth. After the phone ad began appearing in Texas and Ohio, someone asked Hillary during a campaign stop to give an example of a time when she had to handle a crisis phone call. There was apparently not a lot of thought given beforehand to this particular question arising. The best answer the campaign spokesman came up with was, "She's on the Armed Services Committee." Said Democrat Schrum, laughing, "You know the only crisis on the Armed Services Committee is when John McCain loses his temper." Republican Murphy, laughing, added, "The only crisis call she (Hillary) might get is from Texas."

Chuck Todd, the NBC News Political Director was quoted ("Meet the Press") this way, "According to our delegate math, Clinton winning both Ohio and Texas by 52% – 48% would net her a combined 5-6 delegates. Yet, toss in a potential Obama landslide in Vermont, and then her next March 4th haul could be as little as 2-5 delegates."

On "Face the Nation" Governor Bill Richardson was interviewed, as was former candidate Senator Chris Dodd (D, Connecticut), who noted that "If experience is the sole criteria, it should be Joe Biden and me," something he said more than once on the campaign trail in Iowa. Democratic Senator Evan Bayh of Indiana, a Clinton supporter, was interviewed onscreen as well, and commented, "We're hiring someone to do the toughest job in the country, and a big part of that job is being Commander-in-Chief. Intelligence people report renewed attacks. It's a risky world. We need someone with the seasoning and the ability to be Commander-in-Chief. It's a dangerous world."

Chris Dodd (D, CT), who has endorsed Obama, countered with, "This is a person (Obama) eminently qualified to lead. It's not, as they say, just about who answers that phone, but about what they say." For those of us who have heard Hillary Clinton's shrill tone of voice, we might add, "and it's about HOW that individual speaks when they answer."

From Santa Fe, New Mexico, Governor Bill Richardson on" Face the Nation", who has endorsed neither candidate, weighed in with, "I am legitimately torn (between the candidates)," saying, "The concern that I have is that the bickering is going on too long. D-Day is Tuesday. I want to see us, after Tuesday, come together and move towards the general election." He added, "McCain cannot be taken for granted." Richardson noted, "We haven't elected a Senator in over 40 years. I guess we're going to this time."

Many charts and graphs were used to reinforce points being made. To share just a few: In Ohio, Clinton attracts just 38% of men under 50, while Obama gets 52%. Hillary gets the vote of 54% of those over 50 in Ohio, while Obama gets only 36% of those over 50. By race (in Ohio) Obama claims the vote of 86% of African-Americans (to Clinton's 6%), while 62% of Hispanics favor Clinton, compared to only 30% for Obama. ("Meet the Press" graphic).

As to Super Delegates, those much-discussed 800, the change since February 5th has seen Obama pick up 38, while Clinton has lost 6, giving Obama a 111-vote lead. In a Pew Foundation Poll shown on "Meet the Press", when asked whether a candidate was "very likable," "somewhat likable" or "not likable," Obama was judged "Very likable" by 50% to Clinton's 26% and McCain's 21%. In the "somewhat" range, the split was 35% for Obama, to 37%

for Clinton, to 55% for McCain. In the dreaded "Not Likable" category, Hillary scored 33%, while McCain was at 18% and Obama at 10%.

Republican strategist Mike Murphy on "Meet the Press," commenting on the general election, said, "We've got the one different kind of Republican this year who can go to the center, and a lot of the Obama stuff—the energy behind his campaign, other than the war—is stuff John McCain built his reputation on and frankly has shown a lot more courage on than Barack Obama ever has. He'll (McCain'll) co-opt that middle space and beat him on experience and leadership."

All agreed that, if Obama were to be elected, it would "set the Conservative movement back 50 years."

In another interesting bit, respondents to a CNBC Current State of the Economy survey ("Meet the Press") were asked to respond with one word to the three remaining candidates in the race. The responses to each candidate and the word used most frequently follows:

McCain:	Old	55
	Honest	32
	Experienced	29
	Patriot	21
	Conservative	14
	Hero	13
	Liberal	12
Obama:	Inexperienced	45
	Charismatic	32
	Intelligent	25
	Change	23
	Inspirational	14
	Young	12
	New	11
Clinton:	Experienced	34
	Strong	16
	Untrustworthy	16
	Intelligent	15
	Smart	14
	Determined	12
	Rhymes with "witch"	11

"Fox News Sunday" and "Meet the Press" Debate Florida and Michigan "Do-Over(s)"

March 9th, 2008

The Sunday morning news programs were focused on the Obama/Clinton face-off…again. It was only a matter of time before Hillary Clinton would begin focusing on trying to seat Florida and Michigan delegates, who were previously denied delegates to punish them for moving their primaries up. Britt Hume, on Fox News Sunday, interviewed 2 Super Delegates, both named Debbie.

One was Debbie Dingell (no, I'm not making that name up), a Super-Delegate from Michigan and a Democratic National Committee member. The other was Debbie Wassermann Schulz, a Super-Delegate from Florida. The conversation focused on "do-overs" and "firehouse primaries" and any number of means by which the Democratic Party can seat the delegates from Florida and Michigan who were supposed to be being punished for their actions by *not* being seated.

Expense of a special election is, of course, at issue. The cost of a special election is estimated to run about $30 million dollars and all kinds of people are stepping up to the plate to make suggestions as to how a special election might now be financed, from James Carville to Governor Ed Rendell (D, PA) to Dr. Howard Dean, Chairman of the Democratic National Committee.

Without Michigan's and Florida's votes factored in, Barack Obama has a popular vote total of 13,318,906 to Hillary Clinton's 12,690,404, but if Florida and Michigan are factored back in, the count becomes 13,895,120 for Obama to 13,889,699 for Hillary, according to Fox News Sunday's poll. Fred Barnes of the Weekly Standard commented, "She's (Clinton's) gonna' have to have a majority of the popular vote, because she's not gonna' have a majority of the delegate vote, even if she wins in these electable contests between now and the convention…They're gonna' do something in Michigan and Florida, and it's up to Hillary Clinton to get ahead in the popular vote, because, otherwise, she's not gonna' be the nominee." The other contributors, Mara Liasson of NPR, Juan Williams, also of NPR, and Bill Kristol of the Weekly Standard agreed that, "These delegates are going to be seated. The only question is, 'How are they gonna' be counted?'"

All the expert commentators noted Obama's difficult position in the matter. Obviously, Hillary is desperately trying to lobby for changing the rules, since she needs an "overtime" to win, but where is the advantage for Obama? There is none, but he runs the risk of being seen as trying to disenfranchise voters in Florida and Michigan if he isn't supportive of these recent efforts asking for a "do-over."

Juan Williams put it this way, "I don't see how he (Obama) can avoid, in essence, giving in to what Hillary Clinton wants."

Fred Barnes, on the other hand, said, "Barack Obama obeyed the rules that the Democratic Party set down. He didn't participate in these primaries. You cannot have an outcome that is fair to Barack Obama. It's gonna' be unfair to him, because, without these two states, he's ahead, he wins the nomination."

Britt Humes asked, "How likely is it that she can still come from behind to beat him (Obama)?" Fred Barnes responded, "Well, I'd say that she's the underdog and, in these 11 states coming up, she is going to have to do well." The graphic displayed showed Obama with 1,578 delegates versus Hillary Clinton's 1,468 delegates.

The talk after that turned to the Super Delegates and how they would behave in the event that Hillary Clinton limps into Denver behind in both popular and delegate count. Said Kristol, "You cannot be behind in both Super Delegates and popular vote and win." This truth seems to be self-evident. Juan Williams commented on the electability issue, with Obama having won 25 states and the District of Columbia while Clinton has won in only 14. There are 9 remaining states.

Later on Sunday morning, on "Meet the Press" with Tim Russert on NBC, commentators Lester Holt and Jenna Wolf discussed the way things have been going, with Obama picking up 45 Super Delegates since Super Tuesday, while Hillary Clinton has lost 6 of them. Current standing as the candidates head into Pennsylvania on April 22nd and move past Mississippi's vote on March 12 show 1374 delegates for Obama, with Clinton at 1232, a 142 lead for Barack Obama. In terms of the popular vote, Obama commands 49% of it, while Hillary Clinton has 47% of the popular vote. There are still 599 delegates to be chosen.

One of the most interesting exchanges of the morning occurred with Tim Russert moderating a lively discussion between Senator Tom Daschle (D, SD) and Governor Ed Rendell (D, PA), about what anointing Hillary Clinton as the nominee might do to the young voters and the ethnic voters who have supported Barack Obama in his quest. If Hillary Clinton is announced as the nominee, despite Obama's having beaten her, fair and square, in almost every way imaginable, what kind of message will that send to America, the youth of America, and the rest of the world?

Russert put the question this way: "Should the candidate who has won the most electoral votes be the nominee?"

Daschle answered, "Absolutely. I don't see how we could possibly do anything else but say that we respect the wishes of the people who have voted. And what would it say to the world and to the country if we overturned the will of those people who have voted? It would be a travesty for the party and for the country."

Daschle referenced a poll that was just taken that showed Barack Obama winning, nationwide. Said Daschle, "It doesn't matter who's at the top of the ticket. The Democratic nominee is gonna' be in a very commanding position in New York and California and I think we can even put Texas into play this year."

Governor Ed Rendell (D, PA), a Hillary Clinton supporter, tried to suggest that Hillary Clinton deserves to be the nominee because she could win in the big states that count, reasoning that was offensive to not only Daschle, but also the residents of all the other states that aren't Pennsylvania, Ohio, Florida or Michigan. Rendell, saying, "She's clearly the strongest candidate in the states we have to take," also offended by suggesting that caucuses were not democratic, because shift workers and older residents couldn't vote by absentee ballot.

Russert seemed incredulous as he asked Rendell, "So, the Iowa caucuses and the Nevada caucuses were undemocratic?" Rendell answered, "Yes," which prompted Tom Daschle, an Obama supporter, to say, "Well, Tim, first of all, I think it will come as a real shock to Iowa and Nevada voters that they don't have a Democratic process. I think it's very democratic. I don't concede that point at all."

As an Iowan, born and bred, I was happy to hear South Dakota's Senator stick up for us. The conversation went on about "do overs" and whether they should be primaries or caucuses or even mail-in ballots.

Daschle said, "There are, as we have to address, a lot of issues with primaries as well, but the bottom line is that we all agreed to play by the rules and one campaign, now, has broken those rules and has decided not to abide by them, and our campaign has decided to abide by those rules. We recognize that these are 2 very important states and we are committed to working something out. We'll be competitive, whatever it is. If there's a fair approach that can be worked out, we're for it, we'll work for it, we'll do it. But it has to be fair and it has to be worked out in concert with the parties and we have to abide, as much as possible, with the rules that everybody worked out six months ago."

Stay tuned for further developments in this very messy situation.

Charlie Crist: Possible Republican Vice Presidential Nominee?

March 14th, 2008

Charlie Crist, current Governor of Florida, is mentioned as a possible Vice Presidential contender on a ticket with Arizona Senator John McCain. The 52-year-old white-haired Governor has the classic good looks of a political candidate. Crist endorsed McCain in Florida at a crucial time, and Crist's support played a key role in McCain's win in Florida and could well prove instrumental in helping McCain secure Florida's 27 electoral votes at the St. Paul, Minnesota, convention in September.

Crist has the resume of a potential VP, also, having served as Attorney General of Florida from 2003 to 2007, where he earned the nickname "Chain Gang Charlie" because of his hard stance on crime and his belief that prisoners should work on chain gangs. He also proposed a program known as STOP (Stop Turning Out Prisoners), a bill to make sure that prisoners in Florida serve at least 85% of their sentences (Phil Lapadula's blog, Friday, October 27, 2006).

Crist's positions, according to Wikipedia online are as follows:

- Abortion: pro-life and pro-family.
- Adoptive parents: $3,000 subsidy to heterosexual adoptive parents and $5,000 to foster parents.
- Education: advocate of parental choice of schools and strict, standardized testing (Crist served as the last State Education Commissioner. He supported a $3.8 billion dollar bill to reduce class size in Florida schools.)

213

- Health care: prescription drug tracking for assurance of safety.
- Homeowners' insurance: advocate of lower rates (*a hot-button issue in Florida.)
- Citizens' insurance: Crist wants to abolish it and have report cards for insurance companies, businesses which have been fleeing many coastal states after Hurricane Katrina or charging outrageous fees for homeowners' insurance.
- Right to die: supports this, including respect for living wills. (*Received criticism for failure to more strongly support her family in Terry Schiavo case, when Governor Bush was on the opposite side.)
- Eminent domain: legal protection in such cases.
- Lawsuit reform: eliminate joint and several liability.
- Property tax flexibility: just campaigned all over Florida in television ads to reduce taxes by 1%, a bill that passed.
- Defense of Marriage Act: supported it (Nov, 2006). (Interesting article by Julia Reischel on Oct. 19, 2006, in the Broward Palm Beach News entitled **"Charlie Crist is NOT gay."**)
- Death penalty: cautious support for death penalty. Known for STOP, "Stop Turning Out Prisoners," which requires prisoners to serve at least 85% of their prison sentences. Crist's website tells us that this earned him appointment as an Honorary Sheriff by the Florida Sheriffs' Association, the 3rd person to receive such an honor.
- Gun rights: Endorsed by the NRA as an "A+" candidate.
- Hate crimes: trying to stop the "clear pattern of growth" in such crimes.
- Immigration: supports closed borders.
- Legalized gambling: opposes further statewide expansion of legalized gambling.
- Environmental protection: strong advocate of a ban on oil drilling near Florida's coastline. Supported $100 million to protect the Everglades.
- Identity theft: worked with the legislature to pass new laws that dramatically toughened the penalties for identity theft and counterfeiting or dealing in prescription drugs.
- Civil rights: worked to pass Florida's landmark civil rights legislation, the Marvin Davies Civil Rights Act of 2003.
- Internet: worked to target those who distribute illegal spam on the Internet.

- Utility rates: worked to freeze utility rates and telecom deception.
- Emission controls: July 2007, announced plans to sign executive orders imposing strict air pollution standards in the state, with aims to reduce greenhouse gas emissions by 80% of 1990 levels by the year 2050. Wants state to go green.
- Creation of Research Flagship Universities: signed into law SB-1710, which allowed the Board of Governors to allow Tuition Differential only for the University of Florida, Florida State University, and the University of South Florida. Supported a $3.8 billion bill to reduce class size.
- Insurance companies: has been embroiled in public disputes with property insurers over homeowners' insurance rates. He had expected insurers to lower their rates, with new reinsurance coverage, available from the Florida Hurricane Catastrophe Fund. Doubts exist in the marketplace whether the FHCF can really offer coverage. Moody's, Standard & Poor's, and A.M. Best have warned insurers that, if they accept too much reinsurance from FHCF, they risk being downgraded. Therefore, insurers have gone to the private reinsurance market and the rates are significantly higher.

So, what else is there to know about this potential candidate for Vice President of the United States?

Governor Crist signed a petition for an anti-gay marriage amendment and opposes repealing the law that prevents gay or lesbian couples from adopting. Having said that, the rumors that Charlie Crist is gay have circulated in political circles for years. Don Jacobsen, a Palm Beach lawyer, was heard to say (at a Donald Trump fund-raiser), "Well, first Crist needs to admit that he's gay," according to a *Broward Palm Beach News* article by Julia Reischel (10/18/06, "Charlie Crist is NOT Gay"). The man who ran against Crist claims they discussed Charlie's sexuality, and he is bi-sexual, but this individual made these charges on a radio show at the time he was running against Crist, creating a healthy dose of skepticism as to the validity of the charges.

A blog devoted to gay issues (the name of which cannot be printed in a family blog) by Phil Lapadula, reported the issue this way: "I'm not surprised that the daily newspapers aren't covering it. If someone comes forward and says I worked with him and he gave me perks because I was having an affair with him, or he molested me, or he abused me in a relationship, that's a different story. But the mere accusation that someone is gay is a non-story." Another individual (McBride) pointed out that in the cases of former Congressman Mark Foley, former New Jersey Governor Jim McGreevey and former Spokane Mayor Jim West, "It was not the fact that they were gay that brought them down. It was the fact that they abused their power. If they had done that in a heterosexual relationship, it would still be a story." (Eliot Spitzer, anyone?)

What can factually be determined regarding Crist's personal life? He was married for 7 months in 1979-80 to a woman named Amanda Marrow. They had no children. Since their 1980 divorce, he has lived in a rented one-bedroom apartment in St. Petersburg, has only a single VISA card on which he carries no balance, seldom tips more than 20%, and remains a bachelor. He went from $0 to $400,000 in 20 years, by letting Charlie Crist, Sr., manage his money, which put him ahead of roughly half of Florida's 160 lawmakers and most of his contemporaries, according to Caryn Baird and Mary Mellstrom, who reported on Crist, along with Scott Barancik, in a July 9, 2006, article in the *St. Petersburg Times*.

Other facts we might note about Charlie Crist, before reciting his sterling academic credentials: he owns no property or corporate stock. He has zero debt and says it "helps me sleep better at night." He does not itemize, but uses the standard deduction. He donated $1,000 to 3 charities in 2006. His net worth in 2006 was $422,000. He leases a yellow 2006 Mustang V6 convertible and also drives a yellow 97 Jaguar XK8. He also purchased a 25-foot fishing boat, one of his few indulgences.

Famous supporters include John Walsh ("America's Most Wanted"), Donald Trump, and the Reverend O'Neal Dozier, who once called Islam a "cult" and "a dangerous religion" and was forced from the Broward Judicial Nomination Commission as a result of other anti-Islam statements.

Governor Crist's web-site says that his life "illustrates the American dream," and cites his Grandfather Adam, who came to America from Cyprus, penniless, nearly 100 years ago, and worked shining shoes. Grandpa Crist owned a small business, raised 7 children, and saw Charles, (the Governor's father), go on to school to become a doctor. Although Charlie Crist, the Governor, was born in Altoona, Pennsylvania, the son of Charlie Crist, Sr. and Nancy Lee Crist, the family soon relocated to St. Petersburg, where young Charlie attended Riviera Middle School.

Upon graduating from high school, where he was the starting quarterback on the football team and class president, he played at Wake Forest

University, but transferred to Florida State in 1978, where he was named Mr. Seminole and served as Vice President of the Florida State University student body. Charlie then earned a law degree from Cumberland School of Law in Birmingham, Alabama.

After working in the State Attorney's Office, he took a position as General Counsel for the minor league division of the Baseball Commissioner's Office. He worked in this position for five years. In 1986, Charlie took a run at a popular incumbent for the 1986 state Senate, and lost by 20-some points. He then worked for Connie Mack as State Director in 1988. By 1992, he was ready. He ran again and won a position as State Senator.

In 1999, then-Governor Jeb Bush appointed Crist Deputy Secretary of the Department of Business and Professional Regulation. Despite this tie to the Bush family, Crist did not utilize President Bush in his last run for office, a time when the incumbent President had historically low approval ratings.

Crist campaigned long and hard for John McCain in the Florida primary, and it was a big boost to the Arizona Senator's campaign. He is also the first Republican governor to accept the state's NAACP invitation to a convention, and was referred to by Terry Fields, Democratic Representative of Jacksonville, Florida, as the state's "first black governor," a post similar to Bill Clinton's honorary title as the nation's "first black President."

Crist categorizes himself as "a moderate Populist conservative." His strong support of the 2nd amendment ("A well-regulated Militia being necessary to the security of a free state, the right of the people to keep and bear arms shall not be infringed." 1791) may put him at odds with the 57% of citizens who feel that major restrictions or outright bans on guns are necessary, or the 91% who feel that at least minor restrictions on gun ownership are mandated. Eighty-one percent of those polled (Phil Lapadula, Friday, Oct. 27, 2006), said it was "an important issue;" Forty % of Americans own guns.

Ever since seeing the photogenic Governor on Florida television ads, while in Florida in January, I have said that I think he could well be the Vice Presidential nominee, (if McCain secured the Republican nomination.) Crist has been a tireless advocate for citizens, never forgetting his humble roots, and, from all accounts, has devoted himself to the citizens of Florida. Lower taxes, less government, more freedom are hallmarks of Crist's stands, and coincide nicely with McCain's.

On all the issues above, McCain and Crist seem to fit together logically. The open animosity that could be seen and felt between McCain and former opponent Mitt Romney were totally absent during the McCain/Crist Florida campaign. Certainly Crist's positions on the important issues of the day seem more in line with science and the 21st Century than those of one other candidate who doesn't believe in evolution and seems to blur the line between church and state quite frequently.

McCain/Crist seem to be very similar in their views. I, for one, think Charlie Crist's selection as the Vice Presidential nominee by Senator John McCain could be a realistic possibility. (*Note: Charlie Crist would have been a more logical choice than the actual choice, Sarah Palin.)*

West Virginia Win for Clinton on 5/13: A Foregone Conclusion

May 10th, 2008

West Virginia is Clinton country. It is such a foregone conclusion that Hillary Clinton will carry the state on May 13th, that "Election Inspection", online, put it this way: "Clinton will win West Virginia by more than 25%. There's no point in nailing it down further, because it's nearly impossible to be exact when there's a blowout…"

The polls dating from 4/20 through 5/4 show this:

ARG – 5/2-5/4	Obama 45	Clinton 53
SUSA-5/2-5/4	Obama 42	Clinton 54
Suffolk U-5/3-5/4	Obama 43	Clinton 49
Zogby – 5/3-5/4	Obama 44	Clinton 42
Zogby – 5/2-5/3	Obama 43	Clinton 41
Zogby – 5/1-5/2	Obama 43	Clinton 42
ARG – 4/30 – 5/1	Obama 44	Clinton 53
Insider Advantage 4/30-5/1	Obama 42	Clinton 42
Zogby 4/30 – 5/1	Obama 40	Clinton 47
Down C Ctr. 4/29-4/30	Obama 45	Clinton 52
TeleSySA Research 4/25-4/29	Obama 38	Clinton 48
Rasmussen 4/29	Obama 41	Clinton 46
SUSA – 4/25-4/27	Obama 43	Clinton 52
Howey/Gauge- 4/23 – 4/24	Obama 47	Clinton 45

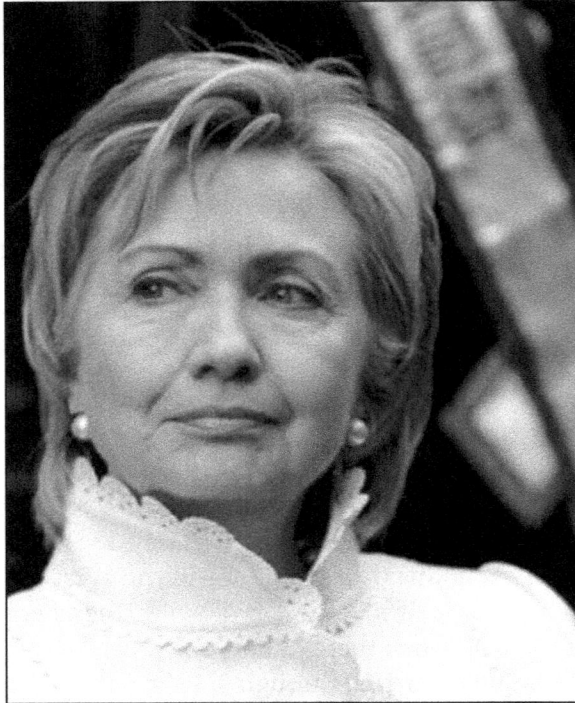

ARG 4/23-4/34	Obama 45	Clinton 50
Reserved TOVO		
4/21 – 4/24	Obama 48	Clinton 47
Selzer & Co/Indiana-polis STAR/WTHR		
4/20-4/23	Obama 41	Clinton 38

Chadwick Martin, writing online on "At the Foot of the Mountaineers" on 5/9/08 reported, "Less than 25% of likely Democratic primary voters are planning to vote for Obama." Martin gave a 43 point lead to Clinton and said that less than 20% of whites would vote for Barack Obama, and even the youth demographic would go to Clinton by 35 points.

This year's vote in West Virginia is noteworthy because it is the first time that the state is having an "open" primary, where voters need only declare their preference to vote, according to Jennifer O'Shea. Back on Super Tuesday, 18 of 30 Republican delegates were committed to Mike Huckabee, but all of the Democratic delegates will be awarded on May 13th, according to *U.S. News & World Report* online on 5/10/08.

Obama has not been campaigning actively in West Virginia, ceding the state to Hillary Clinton. Since 1968, the state has voted Democratic in 6 of 9 contests. It was a pivotal state for John Fitzgerald Kennedy in overcoming Hubert Humphrey's challenge in 1960, and he won it 60.8 to Humphrey's 39.2.

RealClearPolitics online also gives West Virginia to Hillary Clinton by large margins, reporting that, on 5/07-5/08, the ARG poll of 600 likely voters gave Clinton a +43 point lead. Other polls on RealClearPolitics show the lead as +29 (Rasmussen), +40 (TSG Consulting), +15 (ARG on 3/29 to 4/02 and +28 for Rasmussen back on 3/13, all giving the race to Clinton.

"The Fire Society," online, reports that, in a survey taken on May 4th of 840 likely voters, Hillary Clinton had a +43 point lead. She was viewed favorably by 72% of the West Virginia voters, versus 48% who viewed Obama favorably. In fact, Obama's numbers had actually dropped by 5.7 points. The Jeremiah Wright pastor flap had been followed by 78% of polled voters and 57% said that they thought that Obama would "share Pastor Wright's views." (These were ALL voters; not just Democratic voters.)

In a general election, West Virginia voters say they would vote for Hillary over John McCain (72%), but if the nominee is Obama vs. McCain, only 56% of West Virginia voters respond affirmatively that they would vote for Barack Obama over John McCain.

Republican Party Treasurer Accused of Embezzling Millions

Christopher J. Ward, Ex-treasurer of the Republican National Congressional Committee is Fired in Scandal

Mar 17, 2008

One of the big stories making the rounds in Republican circles these days is the alleged theft, through illegal wire transfers, of money donated to the Republican National Committee, by the man in charge, Christopher J. Ward. The matter was turned over to the FBI six weeks ago, according to an article by Paul Kane in the *Washington Post*, (March 14, 2008) and it appears that Ward may have diverted as much as one million dollars to defunct campaign accounts or his own private bank account(s), through the use of wire transfers.

Ward had been on the job as chairman of the National Republican Congressional Committee as audit committee chairman for at least five years, which now seems a bit akin to having a fox watching the hen-house.

Ward had authority to wire transfer funds, the only such NRCC official so empowered without a second approval needed. After he transferred the money into accounts he controlled, which often went into a fundraising committee that was no longer active, Ward would move the money into accounts that represented his political consulting company, or into his own personal bank accounts.

Ward was fired January 28th, after his successor, Representative Mike Conaway (R, TX), a CPA, forced the issue and turned evidence over to the FBI for investigation. Conaway had realized that the audit submitted for 2006 was bogus. It was Ward's practice to submit audits on gerrymandered letterhead from real outside accounting firms, but none of the audits were legitimate.

For five years, Ward forged audits. Not a single member of Congress, nor a single NRCC staffer ever actually met with or talked to any of the outside firms' accountants that were supposedly conducting these "audits."

Walden expressed concerns long before the whistle was blown on Ward's duplicity, but Ward would always offer excuses about why the outside auditors could not meet: a different firm was doing the audit; we're waiting for the newest audit; the auditors are too busy, etc.

Walden is quoted as saying, "It frustrated me that I could not get it done." It should be noted that Walden is not a CPA.

After the 2006 election, Tom Cole (R, Okla.) took over the job and things began to spin out of control. Conaway, who is a certified public accountant, saw through the bogus faked audits and the house of cards began to fall.

Cole, in an article in the Friday, March 14th *Washington Post,* written by Paul Kane, said, "The evidence we have today indicates we have been deceived and betrayed for a number of years by a highly respected and trusted individual." Cole also commented, in an article written by Ben Pershing for the *Washington Post* online that Cole said, "If you remember when I first got there (the NRCC), I was accused of being a micro-manager. You don't hear that much any more."

Cole reported the bright side of this embezzlement scandal this way, "Our team found it, our team reported it, and our team fixed it." The committee has already spent at least $360,000 on legal and accounting fees to "fix" it. The National Republican Congressional Committee collected $49 million in donations in 2007. It had not acknowledged that any money was missing until March 13th, 2008, when it announced that it had discovered "irregularities" and the axe fell on Ward. The year-end report filed by the Federal Election Commission (FEC) in 2006 overstated the NRCC's cash on hand by $990,000.

What Will the Iraq War Cost?

3/24/2008

With the recent news that America's casualties in Iraq have reached 4,000 dead soldiers, we should be asking ourselves, "What is this war costing us, not only in the tragic deaths of our brave soldiers, but in (borrowed) dollars and cents?"

The April, 2008, issue of *Vanity Fair* ("The $3 Trillion War" by Joseph E. Stiglitz and Linda J. Bilmes, p. 147) lays it out for us. Before the war, President Bush's economic adviser suggested that the war might cost $200 billion. Then Secretary of Defense Donald Rumsfeld called that "baloney." Deputy Defense Secretary Paul Wolfowitz suggested that increased oil revenues would allow Iraq to pay for its own post-war reconstruction (also "baloney"). The team of Rumsfeld and Office of Management and Budget Director Mitch Douglas pegged the war in the $50 to $60 billion range then, back five full years ago as of March 19, 2008.

So, how much is this war *really* costing American taxpayers?

A lot. At least close to $800 billion and rising. The Administration has already asked for $200 billion to pay for wars in Iraq and Afghanistan in fiscal year 2008. And it's not going to get better, Folks; it's going to get worse: much, much worse.

According to the *Vanity Fair* article (p. 148), "But even the $600 billion number is disingenuous, which is to say false. The true cost of the war in Iraq, according to our calculations, will, by the time America has extricated itself, exceed $3 trillion."

First, there are issues with the "accrual" versus "cash" accounting system used to explain costs. Another relevant quote: "In the case of the Iraq war, the future obligations are huge. They include the cost of replacing military equipment, which is being used up at 6 to 10 times the peacetime rate. They also include the cost of providing health care and disability payments for our returning troops."

Almost every Democratic candidate campaigning in Iowa before the Iowa caucuses in January (especially Senator Joe Biden) pointed out the huge cost of caring for our wounded young men and women, who are being saved, because of advancements in medicine, at rates that far outstrip anything seen in any previous war. If you look back at my previous Joe Biden article, there are some specifics there.

The problem is, these brave soldiers' lives are being saved, but many are horribly wounded and many that are "whole" will suffer from Post Traumatic Stress Disorder. The already over-burdened Veterans' Administration system is just not equipped to handle the wave of returning soldiers with major problems, both physical and psychological. Problems with V.A. coverage have forced many soldiers to purchase their own health insurance. In 2000, the Veterans' Administration had a backlog of 228,000 pending compensation claims; today, the number is over 400,000. It takes an average of six months to process an initial claim and, if a veteran appeals, as 14% do, it takes another 2 years to process the appeal, while the veteran waits in limbo for needed health care. The V.A. has run out of money and it takes more than 30 days for a seriously wounded veteran even to be seen by a doctor. (Figures from *Vanity Fair*, April, 2008, p. 148).

We have relied on the National Guard in this war, and that has taken workers from the civilian labor force and imposed burdens on many families whose loved ones have been called to serve. This is a hidden cost of the war. Another "hidden" cost of the war comes about because the Administration has requested nearly all the money to fight the war in the form of "emergency" funding, which then makes the money given free from standard budgetary caps or vigorous scrutiny. When we read stories of pallets of cash being flown to Iraq and then disappearing (and we have), we have the "emergency" nature of the funding to thank...or blame...for that. The *Vanity Fair* piece ("The $3 Trillion War") calls this entire method of paying for the war "budgetary sleight of hand that makes a mockery of the democratic budget process." (p. 148).

Casualties: The Pentagon has its own peculiar method of counting casualties. It classified more than half of those who had to be evacuated from Iraq as non-combat casualties (p. 150), because the Pentagon splits hairs when deciding who was killed in the war and who was merely killed in a tank accident on their way to the war, for example.

At least 2.1 million individuals will have been sent to Iraq before the war ends. When we consider that 44% of the Gulf War Veterans (a war that only lasted a few weeks) have applied for disability compensation and almost 90% of their claims were approved, we can see that this is going to be an expensive post-war. Today, we spend $4.3 billion per year paying disability compensations for Gulf War Veterans. (*Vanity Fair*, page 150, as are the figures in the previous two sentences).

The Vietnam War cost the United States an estimated $560 to $805 billion (in 2006 dollars) and 58,000 Americans died there, as did one million Vietnamese. (*Mother Jones*, "Apocalypse Then, November/December 2007, p. 47). Twenty years after Vietnam, 15% of those Vietnam veterans still suffer from Post Traumatic Stress Disorder. (*Mother Jones*, "Apocalypse Then," November/December 2007, page 47).

Here's another Big Eye-Opener: we have borrowed the money to finance this war, primarily from countries like China, and we will have to pay the money back with interest. The interest, over only 10 years, will add $615 billion to the cost of the war, pushing the cost into the $2.8 trillion ballpark. (*Vanity Fair*, p. 150). As the authors of the *Vanity Fair* piece (Joseph E. Stiglitz and Linda J. Bilmes) conclude (p. 153), "The price in blood has been paid by members of the volunteer military. The price in treasure has been financed entirely by borrowing…Deficit spending gives the illusion that the laws of economics can be repealed. They cannot."

Another Big News Flash, for me, regarded how much "the surge" cost. McCain is very "high" on the surge while on the campaign trail, telling us how well he says it has worked, but he fails to mention that the cost quoted to the American taxpayer footing the bill was **for only four months of expenses**, while the surge has and will go on for far longer than that. The surge was supposed to cost $5.6 billion in January of 2007 when we deployed another 21,500 troops. (*Vanity Fair*, April 2008, "The $3 Trillion War"). However, that cost was for deploying combat troops alone. The cost will be closer to $11 billion (also for only four months) when the other 15,000 combat-support troops are factored in, with the surge continuing for 12 to 24 months. (p. 153, *VanityFair* article). Since we are now entering April, obviously the price tag we were given for only four months of "the surge" is going to be much higher.

When you consider how many bridges won't get repaired in this country and how many roads and schools and other infra-structure improvements will not be able to be made in this country because of the cost of this war, you have to factor in a figure that is a "realistic but conservative estimate (for the war's macro-economic impact) of roughly $1.9 trillion." (*Vanity Fair*, p. 153).

To sum up, using the words of Joseph E. Stiglitz and Linda J. Bilmes who did such a good job of laying it all out for us this month:"Thus, the total cost of the war ranged from $2.8 trillion in strictly budgetary costs, to $4.5 trillion if one adds in the economic costs…The President and his advisers wanted a quick and inexpensive conflict. Instead, the Iraq War is costing more than anyone could have imagined." The article goes on to say that these costs will most likely end up being half again as much as Vietnam, two times that of Korea, and four times the cost of World War I.

United States Economic Mismanagement

4/04/2008

An article entitled "Mismanagement 101" by Daniel Gross in the March 24, 2008 issue of *Newsweek* magazine (p. 22) agrees with dire predictions regarding the United States economy that come from almost all knowledgeable economic experts.

In a recent CBS News *New York Times* poll (AOL main page, Friday, April 4th, 2008), 81% of respondents say our nation is heading in the wrong direction. The poll has existed since 1990 and this is the highest number ever of respondents saying that the ship of state is floundering,—due to mismanagement, according to Daniel Gross' article.

Gross points out, "The greenback last week hit new lows against foreign currencies. The dollar is so sad, we should consider renaming it the dolor." (p. 22 of "Mismanagement 101"). He goes on to say that the dollar's declining value reflects poorly on us, as a nation.

Other countries think we are incapable of managing what was once viewed as the World's Super Power. "At some level, the dollar's woes reflect the world's collective verdict on the ability of the United States—businesses, individuals, the government, the Federal Reserve—to manage the global financial system and the world's largest economy. Lately, the verdict has been two thumbs down."

With thanks to Gross for pointing out the obvious, what did we think would happen when we elected a rather dim-minded sort whose crowning achievement in life had been fortunate parentage and cheerleading for Yale and Andover? George W. Bush was a failure even in the eyes of Ronald Reagan, who wrote scathingly in his diary of young "W's" visit to meet him, shepherded there by his father, the Vice President. Reagan was right on the money in viewing "W" as a ne'er-do-well who had "never held a real job" (Ronald Reagan's Presidential Diary). In those fields that he attempted (oil, the Texas Rangers), "W" had failed at every turn or been bailed out by "friends of the family." Drug use. Draft-dodging. Sudden embrace of religion. All good credentials for having a beer with the guy, perhaps, but not-so-good credentials for running a complex economy, or, more accurately, letting his stooges (Cheney, Rumfseld, Wolfowitz, Libby, et al) run the country and the economy into the ground.

So, today, as Gross says, "Thanks to widespread incompetence, American management is on its way to becoming an international laughingstock." (p. 22 of Gross article) On its way? Methinks Daniel Gross doth under-estimate the journey. We are not "on our way" to becoming an international laughingstock. We are there! That ship has sailed! And George W. Bush was the captain of the Bad Ship Lollypop who has (more-or-less guided) us on this ill-fated experiment in electing a not-very-bright-or-hardworking guy to be the leader of the Free World.

A few countries had the great good sense to stay out of President Bush's unfortunate, ill-timed, ill-conceived, expensive, immoral and mismanaged Iraq War (the much maligned France, for one), but the Coalition of the Willing followed like sheep to the slaughter. I'm pretty sure that, today, Tony Blair regrets standing by his man.

Where to begin in listing the nation's woes? The sub-prime mess? Food costs rising? Pollution aplenty? The housing crisis? $4 a gallon gasoline? OPEC President Chakib Khelil responded recently that the price of gas "had nothing to do with the reluctance of the Persian Gulf nations to pump oil, and everything to do with the 'mismanagement of the U.S. economy.'" (Gross article, p. 22) Paul O'Neill, former Secretary of the Treasury and, prior to that, the CEO of Alcoa, wrote an entire book about Bush's incompetent bungling and his desire to hear only what he wanted to hear. It's now running on PBS as "Bush's War." Watch it and you'll soon understand why we're in this mess. Or try Richard Clarke and "In Defense of Liberty." Richard Clarke was the man "on call" when 9/11 occurred and he has some scathing criticism for this President—-one of many presidents he served. The one thing you don't want to do in this Administration is "speak truth to power." Do so and your career is over.

How about our aviation system?

I'm writing this on Friday, April 4th, and the airline—ATA— that was to carry me to Cancun tomorrow just went under, taking with it the jobs of 2,200 employees and my ticket to ride. When I reach Cancun and snake through the security line at the airport, I will be asked to sing this refrain along with the security people there: "Please. Do not. Remove. Your shoes." American management has come down to stupid rules made by stupid men with stupid consequences. Removing my shoes when I board the airliner (the result of the French "shoe-bomber" incident) has made all my fellow passengers feel much, much safer as they sit on the tarmac hoping that this airline, too, won't go belly-up before we get to our destination. Or, worse yet, fail and go bust *after* depositing us all on the shores of some country where we don't speak the language and will have to cope with the fall-out. In my own case, my $500 ticket is now a $1700 ticket on American Airlines—and I was lucky to get it! I've been going to Cancun in the spring for fifteen years and the highest ticket I ever bought cost me $800. This year's will set a new record, and something tells me I'm in for more of the same, largely due to the PTB.

On a "Sixty Minutes" segment recently (NBC's "Sixty Minutes"), Carl Icahn, the 1980s corporate raider who has reinvented himself as a comedian and activist investor told Lesley Stahl, regarding American incompetence in management, "I see our country going off a cliff, and I feel bad about it."

The bail-out that the U.S. government just provided to Baer Sterns was given, I have read, because Baer-Sterns was the lynchpin of a house of cards that, if not supported, would come tumbling down with horrific ramifications, nationwide and system-wide. I think we've all heard Michael Moore's assertions, made in his Oscar-nominated film "Fahrenheit/911" about what would happen if all the banks we owe money to called in the debt on the same day. China has largely funded our misguided war efforts, and the Saudis certainly have their fingers in our national pie.

The same government that bailed out a firm that was floundering, is *not* rushing to bail out all the homeowners losing their houses. Forget the Ninth Ward in New Orleans. Good luck with that, Brad (Pitt). The government can't be bothered.

The "ARMS" that people without enough money took out to purchase housing they should have known they couldn't afford, (which are now rising faster than the Iraq War debt), have come home to roost. The financial "safeguards" in banking and finance, put in place years ago after the Depression-era crash, were tampered with or removed, and we are now reaping as we have sown. My father, a long-time banker, predicted another Great Depression for years, and—even though he is long dead—I fear he is about to get his wish.

The Administration "experts" say it is just a "recession" that will "self-correct" and that we are merely teetering on the edge of it, but those of us filling our tanks and paying more at the grocery store see things a little bit differently than George W. Bush in the White House. And your pension?: You may as well kiss it good-bye if we don't elect a smart candidate to be our next President who understands how to pull our economy out of the mess it's in,(which pretty much excludes the Republican nominee, who has publicly said that he "doesn't understand" the economy much, which makes him fit in nicely with the current crop of White House Republicans. But bombing a country back to the Stone Age? McCain's your man for that!)

As Daniel Gross put it, "But those of us who aren't billionaire corporate raiders—which is to say pretty much all of us—must manage through this management crisis on our own." (*Newsweek*, March 24, 2008, "Mismanagement 101", Daniel Gross in "The Money Culture", p. 22).

Amen, and please say a prayer for the United States of America. If you're an atheist, simply observe a moment of silence. No matter what your religious persuasion(s) (or lack of same), it seems pretty clear that we need to NOT vote for more of the same. The *Titanic*, despite the myth of invincibility, did sink (a lesson in mismanagement) and so can we.

Pennsylvania Primary on April 22: Will It Be Decisive?

4/21/2008

Editor's note: Connie Wilson, a Yahoo writer based in East Moline, Illinois, is blogging about the Pennsylvania primary starting Monday and continuing through Tuesday night from Chicago, Illinois. She'll be posting analysis and news periodically. Also blogging are Robert Dougherty from Philadelphia, Pennsylvania, Mark Whittington from Houston, Texas, and Lami Eyer from King of Prussia, Pennsylvania.

The question I posed at the top of my Pennsylvania Primary blog entries was "The Pennsylvania Primary on April 22nd: Will It Be Decisive?" The Keystone State vote is now in. The answer to that question is no.

Indiana's vote lies ahead. Twenty-five per cent of Indiana voters are in the Chicago media mart. It's similar to Ohio and Pennsylvania in its make-up and it will be a crucial state. While North Carolina, which has a large African American population and some affluent areas, looks good for Obama, Indiana shapes up to be much more like Pennsylvania or Ohio, so Hillary might well win in Indiana, but it, too, will be a close race. Just as Pennsylvania was expected to go for Clinton, North Carolina is expected to go for Obama.

Barack Obama did not receive a death blow in Pennsylvania, but Jeffrey Toobin and other analysts have said (on CNN Election Eve coverage), "This victory may convince Super Delegates that he has problems with blue-collar voters, Catholic voters. They're asking themselves, "Do we have a damaged candidate here?"' Indiana is becoming a pivotal state, as Obama himself acknowledged.

Barack Obama needs to stay ahead in the Super Delegate counts. He needs to keep his momentum going. Having two-thirds of Catholic voters in Pennsylvania vote for Hillary (69% to 31%, specifically), as well as

234 • *Obama's Odyssey*

white male voters voting for Hillary 55% to 45% for Obama, is not good news.

What happened on April 21st, however, was what was expected. In Philadelphia, the Obama supporters came out, including black voters and he won big in the city, 65% to Clinton's 35%. The southeast did well for Obama, as did Delaware and Chester County. Clinton's big victory came in Bucks County (a suburb of Philadelphia), and in rural areas like Allentown and Erie and "the T," (discussed in my original article.) She won the senior vote, the white male vote, the Catholic vote and 57% of the Jewish vote. (Only 7% of the state's voters are Jewish.) All this courtesy of John King's blue map (The Magic Touch or the "wonder wall" as they call it) on CNN Election Coverage.

The thing to remember about Hillary Clinton, as one analyst on CNN said, is that "She's in it to spin it." Hillary and Bill have a well-known reputation for going to almost any lengths to win. She went negative on Barack Big Time in Pennsylvania, and, distasteful as that seems to much of the country, we're bound to see more of it. In fact, those inside Barack Obama's campaign are urging him to become more negative in defending his lead. Keep in mind, if Hillary "spins" the need to "seat" Florida's voters (she's the Mother Theresa of Florida, worrying overtime about their disenfranchisement), where both names appeared on the ballot, at least, (which they did not in Michigan), and, if you add in Pennsylvania's popular vote, the popular vote margin becomes closer: 15,117,521 for Clinton, or 47%, with 15,390,196 for Obama, or 48%. (4% go to "other"). Is pulling within range by changing the rules in the middle of the game fair? Isn't this cheating?

Of course it's not fair, and 6 of 10 voters polled have said that they think Hillary Clinton is "untrustworthy" in CNN polls. It's not fair to suddenly become so concerned about the poor disenfranchised Florida (or Michigan) voters that both candidates agreed to punish early on. But "she's in it to spin it," and, now that she's behind, why not change the rules so that she can seize the nomination from the grasp of the rightful winner

After Pennsylvania was called for Hillary, she made a plea for donations and raised $2 and ½ million dollars from new donors. The money will help Hillary to spread her new message that she's better with blue collar voters, white folks, Latinos, old people, and Catholics than Obama is and help her to put forth the doubt that Obama can win nationally. In fact, she has *already* done this, asking why Obama couldn't "close the deal" before Pennsylvania was over.

No one has been able to explain why the Catholic vote went 2/3 for Hillary Clinton. Thirty-seven % of the voters in Pennsylvania are Catholic, but neither Hillary nor Bill is Catholic. Pennsylvania voted much like Ohio before it. Here are the theories for this I've heard: 1) the Nun theory. Nuns are (generally) mature, white women. Those are Hillary's supporters, so perhaps nuns convinced their charges to vote for the first woman with a real shot at becoming her party's Presidential nominee. Let us not forget that Roman Catholic nuns have been in the forefront of many national movements that require women to stand up and be counted. If you're able to remember the Vietnam War, you will know that both priests and nuns demonstrated, at times, to stop the slaughter (Father Daniel Berrigan, et. al.), and there have been other issues of conscience that have brought forth either outright or tacit support from this group of independent women

(2) Catholics are big on forgiveness, confession and guilt and strongly disapprove of divorce (I know; I'm a Catholic). When her philandering husband publicly humiliated Hillary, she didn't bail on him, but "stood by her man." Some felt she should have served him with divorce papers ASAP, but she did not. She held her head high, bit her lip, and suffered in silence. This period was perhaps the peak of Hillary's personal popularity, as even those who had castigated her previously felt sorry for the poor "wronged and humiliated" wife. While we can all speculate on whether the Clinton liaison is a "marriage" in the traditional sense of the word, or more of a business partnership, we may be seeing the traditional Catholic virtues emerging in response to Hillary Clinton's campaign. It's just a theory; add yours, if you have one.

Over 320,000 new Democrats, up 8% in Pennsylvania have spoken. What they said did not really surprise pollsters, who were already anticipating a Clinton win there. The Clinton side "spins" the win as huge for her, because of the Big State argument (I can carry the Big States like Pennsylvania, and you, Barack Obama, cannot. Nyaaah. Nyaaah, nyaaah, nyaaah!)

The Obama campaign has run a fairer and cleaner campaign, to date. No negative attack ads. No attempt to change rules that were agreed upon by all in advance, like the Vegas voters voting in casinos or the seating of Michigan and Florida delegations, who are being punished for moving their caucuses and primaries up in defiance of the national Democratic Party. (I have to ask: Dr, Dean… you're a smart man? How did you and/or yours come up with that bonehead idea? Surely you could see something like this coming?) No pious mouthing(s) about the poor disenfranchised Michigan and Florida voters, made in order to seize their votes, by the Obama camp.

Obama, himself, said that Clinton would win Pennsylvania *before* the votes were in, but also said, "We'll do better than people expect." Narrowing the gap from 20 or 30% to 10% qualifies and is exactly what he predicted.

As Obama closed a 20-point polling gap. David Gergen, political analyst for CNN said, "He was closing in on her and as he was closing, not only did he stall, but he actually got hurt."

The entire Democratic Party is going to have a "stalling" problem and get hurt if they can't get their candidate picked by June. Representative Patrick Murphy (D, PA), said, "We need to all come together. I hope it's not a brokered convention." There will only be 8 weeks between the end of the conventions and the actual election, so it would be to the advantage of the Democratic party to know who is going to be their pick by June, as John McCain is sitting pretty in that department right now, watching the Democratic fight with great amusement, no doubt. (*Note: The Democrats did not really know till the end of their August, 2008, convention who would emerge victorious, which made the 2008 Democratic National Convention a far more exciting election than that of 2012.)*

The 300 Super Delegates are looking pretty important right about now, as they have for months. I'm wondering if John Edwards will come into play somehow in the North Carolina contest that looms? And what about Florida and Michigan? Remember, Folks: "she's in it to spin it."

Clinton and Obama Speak to Supporters Following 93% of Vote in from Pennsylvania

4/22, 11:30 p.m., Eastern Time

"I'm in this race to fight for you, to fight for everyone who's ever been counted out, for everyone fighting to pay the grocery bills, the medical bills, the credit card bills and the outrageous price of gas at the pumps today… You know you can count on me to stand up strong for you every single day in the White House. This is a historic race, and I commend Senator Obama and his supporters tonight."

From this opening, Hillary Clinton went on to talk about women's suffrage ("See, you can be anything you want.") to the journey we all are on.

"Tonight, more than ever, I need your help to continue this journey. This is your campaign, and this is your victory tonight. Your support has meant the difference between winning and losing. Now, we can only keep winning if we can keep competing with an opponent who outspends us so massively." (And, with those words, she asked for money from the cheering crowd). "The future of this campaign is in your hands."

"Some people counted us out and said to drop out, but the American people don't quit and they deserve a President who doesn't quit, either."

Obama said, "We already know John McCain offers more of the same. …The question we face in this election is, will we?" (Chants of "Yes we can!" in the background). "The truth is the challenges we face are not just the fault of one man or one party. How many Presidents have promised to end our dependence on foreign oil?" He then talked about politicians coming to your town making big promises and going back to Washington and the campaign zone. "The status quo sets in, and, instead of fighting for jobs, they end up going back to the status quo… this is our chance to say, not this year, not this time. We have a choice in this election: we can be a party that says there's no problem with taking money from Washington lobbyists. We can pretend they represent real Americans or, this time, we can recognize that you can't be the champion of working Americans if you're funded by lobbyists who drown out their voices.

Hillary Clinton Victory Speech Imminent Post Pennsylvania Vote

4/22, 10:30 p.m. Eastern Time

It is moments away from Clinton's victory speech. With 55% of the precincts in, Hillary has 54% (628,745 votes) while Barack Obama has 46% with 534,274 votes.

Hillary voters are "hardening" for Hillary, saying that they won't vote for anyone but her. They are the staunch blue collar, less-well-educated, often Catholic voters who own guns and are proud of it.

Obama voters, traditionally, are better-educated and more open-minded when it comes to voting for whoever comes out of the process as the party's nominee.

There is an eight-week window from the end of the GOP convention until the general election.

Many analysts said that Hillary had to win by at least 10% points. Currently, she holds a 10% lead. Is this enough ?

I feel that, even if she had lost, Hillary, like RoboCop or the Terminator would still be chugging along. As one CNN analyst said, "If Clinton's got a shot, she's going to stick with it. She's going to exhaust every opportunity." Stay tuned for further developments on that front.

Spinnsylvania on MSNBC

4/22, 9:30 p.m. Eastern Time

Harold "Bud" Ford on MSNBC, noting that Barack Obama won eleven in a row in February, defended Barack Obama's ability to win "the Big Ones." Chairman of the DLC (Democratic Leadership Council) Ford said, "She shouldn't over-read or overstate this (Pennsylvania) victory tonight." This was at 8:15 p.m. CDT, and the polls still hadn't closed!

On every channel, people were talking about Barack Obama's financial war-chest ($40 million now, it was said). Ford said, "There's no doubt about it, money is critical. This is not a cryptic or even dark message for him. He's up against the most formidable challengers in a Democratic party in Bill and Hillary Clinton. There's no need to complain about it; get out there and gird for battle."

Both of the two debating on MSNBC agreed that the debate in the Democratic party was good.

The pledged delegate count is basically over. It appears that it is impossible for Obama to lose his lead. At her best, Hillary will garner 14 to 16 delegates. His pledged delegate lead is 160 some, and, going in to May 6th, he (Obama) will have 500. She will have to make up 150 pledged delegates. If the delegates are a wash on May 6th in North Carolina and Indiana, there will only be 251 delegates remaining, and she would have to make up 150 delegates, or 80% of the remaining states (WV, Kentucky, Montana, SD, Oregon). Impossible in this proportionate system.

So far, at 8:30 p.m., Hillary is leading Pennsylvania at 52% while Obama has 48%.

Exit Polls Show White Men Went for Hillary

4/22, 7:30 p.m. Eastern Time

Exit poll results continuing to come in from Pennsylvania show that white males voted for Clinton 55% to 45% for Barack Obama. No surprise that 92% of African American voters went for Obama, versus only 8% for Hillary Clinton (a drop from her showing in Ohio.)

The exit polls also show that, on the issue of the economy, 56% of the exit poll voters voted for Clinton, while only 43% voted for Obama. If Iraq is your Number One issue, 57% are for Obama, while 43% are for Clinton.

Interestingly enough, when asked who will get the Democratic Presidential nomination, 54% said Obama, while only 43% said Clinton.

Meanwhile, our current Administration officially has taken the position that we are only in "a slowdown." A Gallup Poll today showed that George W. Bush has the lowest approval rating in the history of the Gallup Poll. With foreclosures in California up 350%, with 63,000 jobs lost last month (the Cafferty Report on CNN), Bush still thinks we are "only in a slowdown."

The presumptive Republican nominee wants to make tax cuts permanent. He seems to have forgotten that his Republican incumbent President has increased our national debt by more than ALL other Presidents combined (from $5 trillion to $9 trillion). One blogging young person retorted (The Cafferty Report) that "responsible parents don't steal from their children" while articulating the angst those young voters feel, knowing that they will be the ones saddled with this huge debt.

Meanwhile, gun-toting oldsters are trotting out to the Pennsylvania polls to vote for Hillary. Sixty-one % of seniors voted for Hillary Clinton, versus 38% for Obama, and gun-toting Pennsylvanians (37% own firearms) voted for Clinton 58% to 42% for Obama, possibly as a result of her Annie Oakley moments, where she spoke of killing a duck with her Grandfather in good old Scranton. (Just once, I would like to hear a candidate say they "smothered a duck" rather than "shot" the poor helpless fowl.)

Stay tuned for further breaking news. Exit polls say that Clinton's people say, if she does not get the nomination, only 50% will vote for Obama. Twenty-six% would vote for the Republican candidate, McCain, and 19% would not vote at all!

First Exit Polls in Pennsylvania

4/22, 7 p.m. Eastern Time

CNN has the first exit poll information available from the Pennsylvania primary, and their analyst Bill Schneider told us this: 42% of voters polled say we are in "a serious recession." Forty-seven % say it is a "moderate recession," ten per cent characterize the highest crude oil prices of all time as a "slow down." That slow down means that gas prices average $3.51 a gallon, nationwide.

When asked "Who would handle it best?" in regards to the economic slow-down/recession/meltdown/catastrophe question the exit poll responses were:

Only Clinton - 27%
Only Obama - 19%
Both - 45%
Neither - 6%

Meanwhile, John McCain has proposed a three-month tax cut for motorists at the pump. This would mean, according to Roger Diwan, Energy Analyst for CNN, 18 and one-half cents off between Memorial Day and Labor Day. Problem is, says Diwan, that if you are a family with 2 cars that fill up 10 times a month, you'd only save about $30.

Obama weighed in, saying, "I think John McCain's proposal for a tax holiday is a bad idea." He went on to cite the need for long-term efforts to stem the rising tide of sky-high gasoline prices.

Barack Obama on Jon Stewart's *Daily Show*

4/22, 5:03 p.m. Eastern Time

Jon Stewart had Senator Barack Obama as a guest on his Comedy Central show "The Daily Show with Jon Stewart" on April 21, 2008, and asked Barack Obama this question:

"Do you have any concern that you could win the nomination at the convention, and defeat John McCain in the general election, and go to your inauguration and Hillary would still be running? (*Big smile from Obama*)

Stewart, in New York City, introduced Obama, in Pittsburgh with scenes of Obama boarding a train: "Barack Obama all-aboarded the train to hopedom, because nothing says look to the future like rail travel." (Actually, railroad stocks *are* climbing in response to increasing gas prices, so that joke may be on Stewart.)

Stewart, in New York, then asked Obama, "How is the sojourn through Pennsylvania going?"

Obama: "It is a mad dash, but the people of Pennsylvania have been great and the weather has been good. We've been seeing the high turnout and energy and enthusiasm we've been seeing all across the country. We started out down 20 and we're now down about 8. People are concerned with the economy and they see a connection between us spending billions of dollars in Iraq and the crisis here at home."

Stewart: "When you leave Pennsylvania, can you leave their concerns behind?"

Obama: "The folks in Pennsylvania have gotten a lot of attention. They deserve the attention just like the people in Iowa deserve the attention." (*Six weeks spent in Pennsylvania*).

Stewart: "As a people, are we nice?"

Obama: "There's a core decency and generosity in the American people that actually makes you feel optimistic. Sometimes, you feel less optimistic about the political process..."

Stewart: "That's interesting, because Senator Clinton says you have not been vetted the way she has, and in a political election, the Republican attack machine will just go crazy on you."

Obama: "There's no doubt that Senator Clinton has done me a favor, so, should I get the nomination, I'll be ready."

Stewart: "So, we are concerned that, ultimately, at the end of the day, will you pull a bait-and-switch, Sir, and enslave the white race? If that is your plan, tell us now." (*Tongue-in-cheek.*)

Obama: "That is not our plan, Jon, but I think your paranoia might make you suitable as a debate moderator." (*Laughter here*)

Stewart: "Do you think that process of running for President correlates in any way with the job of being President? Is this like Donald Trump's 'The Apprentice'? Is there any bearing on the job of being President?"

Obama: "I've campaigned in 47 states now, and I think that being on the ground does put you in better touch with the problems of the people (**Note: my point to Yahoo in its new direction.*) and makes you more optimistic about the country...One of the striking things about the country is that people basically have the same hopes and dreams and attitudes about what they want for their kids and their lives. That makes you optimistic. The second thing is, it is true that you have to put up with a lot of stuff when you're President, and I think it does test how people handle stress, how they manage a big organization. In that sense, the American people probably get a pretty good sense of whether this is someone who gets flustered in a crisis and they can see if you stay steady in a crisis."

Stewart: "Is this too much change for the American people? Are we able to digest this much change?"

Obama: "We've been seeing higher registration rates in every state and more enthusiasm in every state…I'm confident that, when they take a look at John McCain's agenda, that will serve us well in the general election."

AOL's main page on April 21st noted that registration of new voters in Pennsylvania is up 8% and some previously Republican counties in the southeast, in particular, are now Democratic counties.

As the 4 million voters of Pennsylvania perform their civic duty and troop to the polls on Tuesday, April 22nd, an interesting fact emerged. One of the contributors to Barack Obama's Presidential campaign was Julie Nixon Eisenhower, who contributed $2,300, close to or at the legal limit.

Analysis of what the Pennsylvania vote may mean continued in sound bites. Candy Kroehler of CNN said, "This is yet another in a long line of do-or-die states. But she *does* have to do it." That was followed by a clip of Hillary Clinton, herself, on CNN, saying, "I have to win."

Jessica Yellin from the central city of Philadelphia reported for CNN viewers that the people on the streets were "excited and energized." Hillary Clinton followed in another CNN clip, "Maybe the question ought to be, with his extraordinary financial advantage, why can't he close the deal? Why can't he win a state like this one? Obviously, we have a long way to go…"

Final word, from Barack Obama himself, "Going into this, six weeks ago, the Clinton campaign suggested that they were unbeatable, and I think that the strategy they were talking about was that they could overcome our delegate lead and overcome our popular vote lead and overcome the number of states we have won, by winning big in Pennsylvania and winning future contests."

Yes, Barack. That does seem to be Hillary's strategy…that and seating delegates from Michigan and Florida that were not supposed to be seated, as punishment for moving their caucuses and primaries ahead of the sanctioned schedule. Now, Hillary needs those votes, and, even though they weren't voted to her (or anyone else), she wishes to claim them, to catch up. Next up on her radar: the Super Delegates.

Alert: watch your back, Barack. Hillary, quit that muttering! The microphone is picking it up.

Undecideds Will Make Difference in Tight Race

4/21/2008, 11:57 p.m. Eastern Time

It's roughly eight hours before the polls open in Pennsylvania, and it is now the land where "money talks and b - -s - - - - walks." One hundred and fifty-eight delegates are at stake, the most of any of the remaining ten contested states.

Hillary Clinton is blathering on about her Grandfather from Scranton who went to work in the lace mills at age eleven (*shades of John Edwards*) and Obama actually went bowling (scored only a 37, but didn't finish the game), while Hillary did whiskey shots with blue-collar workers.

Right now, Obama is hitting Blue Bell, McKeesport and Pittsburgh. Heavily blue collar. White. Catholic. Struggling. Those adjectives describe Pennsylvania, and the "bitter" debate (a phrase used by Obama while in San Francisco) was one of the non-issues that quickly became an issue. Should that be the case?

Does everyone think that the use of the word "bitter" (paired with guns and religion), uttered by Obama, should be the biggest thing on everyone's mind and lips while gas is soaring towards $4 a gallon and 51% of economists in a National Association for Registered Economists' poll, on Friday said that the economic growth for the first half of the year would be only 0 to 1%? [In fairness, 16% thought the first half of the year would yield 1 to 2%, but only 3% predicted growth of 2 to 3%.]Two-thirds of people in an AP/Yahoo poll say that the economy is "extremely important" as a campaign issue, and 60% of those polled specifically mention the rising cost of gasoline. So, semantics are the Big Story? "Elitist' is the big charge made against a Senator born of a black servant to the British and a white woman from Kansas, by a privileged white female Senator from Illinois who was once First Lady, who filed documents showing millions of dollars ($109) made since 2000. Who's the "elitest" again? I think I'm becoming confused by the ridiculous nature of these non-issues, charges and background campaign noise.

Obama would like to end the race in Pennsylvania. Candy Kroehler of "Raw Politics" (CNN) said, on April 21st, "A Pennsylvania loss (for Clinton) would be not only unexpected, but catastrophic." It could be tough for Obama to end this kind of silliness here, as the voters who are Hillary's base are more blue-collar than Obama's, Catholic, and less well educated, and those three phrases aptly sum up the Pennsylvanians who will go to the polls tomorrow. Some interesting facts about Pennsylvania, as provided by William Schneider on "Anderson Cooper's " April 21st show: Pennsylvania is the second-oldest state in the Union (after Florida) and it has the highest percentage of people who have lived there all their lives. Using Ohio statistics, Schneider drew a picture of Catholic support for Clinton (the Nun factor?), but he also noted that there has been a surge of new voters, up 8% in Pennsylvania, with 61% of voters under 30 in Ohio having supported Obama versus only 35% for Clinton. It was the youth of Iowa who gave Obama his ticket out of the Iowa caucuses, and it is youth and the well-educated and more affluent Philadelphia voters who *could* give him a win on Tuesday, against what seem to be stiff odds favoring Clinton.

Obama has poured $3 million dollars into television spots this past week. He has spent $12 million on television spots, compared to $4 million for the former First Lady. Slowly but surely the Obama war chest, said to be $235 million, overall, and adding up to $55 million collected in just February, alone (AOL main page, April 21st, 2008), is erasing Hillary Clinton's lead.

But is there enough time?

Meanwhile, Hillary Clinton's campaign—despite her personal loan to it of $5 million dollars—, according to financial reports filed on Sunday, April 20th, show that Clinton has $9 million dollars to spend but is $10.3 in debt. It is a remarkable fact that Obama has outspent Hillary Clinton $5 to $1 (some say only $2 or $3 to $1), and much of Obama's support comes in online donations of less than $100…in $25, $50 or less increments. (Definitely does not sound "elitist" when compared to the "bundling" method well-known in Bill and Hillary Clinton's world and the recent Elton John fund-raiser for her.)

On the eve of the Keystone state's vote on Tuesday, April 22, 2008, Nedra Pickler of the Associated Press, under a byline that read "Obama Predicts Clinton Win on Tuesday" quoted him as telling radio station KDKA in Pittsburgh, "We are going to do a lot better than people expect." Originally, Clinton led Pennsylvania polls by 20 points. All that has changed in the run-down to the vote on Tuesday, April 22nd, as Clinton's lead has eroded.

As a former CEO of two small companies, I can relate to the problems that Hillary Clinton must now be facing, as suppliers hesitate to fill her orders because they know she is having cash flow problems. The entire Clinton campaign seems riddled with crises, as chief strategist Mark Penn was the most recent and most prominent casualty. Penn met with Colombian officials to discuss his private work on behalf of a Colombian Free Trade agreement, which is something Hillary Clinton opposes. Exit Penn as Chief Strategist (and…to hear others tell it… Chief Egotist) of Hillary's campaign staff. That doesn't change the fact that the firm for which Mark Penn worked, Schoen and Barland Associates, has already been paid $14 million and is still owed $4.6 million for its services. Nearly half of that debt is due Mark Penn, personally. (AOL main page, April 21st, 2008).

The hits just keep on coming: five of Bill Clinton's former cabinet members have endorsed Barack Obama. The endorsement of Obama by Bill Richardson, former Hispanic candidate for President, must have been a bitter pill. Amidst Hillary's shrinking lead, which could well go the way of the dodo bird, a little levity is much needed. And so I share the following with you, in case you missed it:

All three of the former front-runners (yes, John Edwards appeared, too) showed up on Steven Colbert's "Colbert Report." on April 20th. First, Hillary appeared, in person, to fix Colbert's broken big screen.

Then, John Edwards appeared in person, speaking for the male, white working class voter. He continued to gently tongue-in-cheek rib his own public image for well-groomed hair using "EdWords" and saying that he represented the "white male vote" that many analysts see as essential to a Pennsylvania win. (Edwards, who withdrew back in January, still commands at least 56 delegates, although there has been an erosion of the 70 odd that he originally won.)

Said Edwards, "The white male votes are being courted as a demographic tie-breaker in this election and there is no white male voter's vote that is being courted more vigorously than this one," with an aside on-screen that read "Sorry, Al Gore." He said, "It is no secret that both campaigns have sought my support. On the one hand, I don't want to appear to be anti-hope. On the other hand, I don't want James Carville to bite me." (Onscreen joke: "Carville hasn't had shots"). (Big laugh here). Edwards continued, "So who am I going to vote for in the next last primary?"

He said he'd vote for someone who was for Universal Haircare, which got a laugh, and, "also, I'd like a jet ski. They are so much fun. I don't really care which kind (Kawasaki 800 SXR onscreen), but those are pretty sweet. Elizabeth and I love to go to the lake house in the summer, and those jet skiis are really sweet, so I guess we'll have to have TWO jet skiis."

Edwards then repeated his familiar refrain about there being "two Americas," one that does the work and one that reaps the reward, and Colbert's staff, of course, couldn't resist the joke onscreen: "And a third one that gets rich suing the second on behalf of the first." To which Edwards said, "Hey! Hey!" while the screen said, "Sorry. Had to do it."

Edwards: "I understand what working folk go through. I don't know if I've ever mentioned this before, but my father was a mill-worker." (Onscreen: "1,000,000th mention", with balloons coming down from the top of the screen.) "So, you know what, let's get HIM a jet ski! Now, before anyone goes out there saying that all John Edwards cares about is jet skis, it is a fact that I care about universal health care coverage, so that every single man, woman and child in America is covered goes without saying." (Onscreen: "especially by McCain"). "But what does need to be said is that I will only support the candidate who promises to make me a spy. That would be so cool. I'd get all those hot high-tech gadgets ("Pen that launches child-care tax credits" onscreen). "I want to go on at least one mission a month, but it should be some place awesome like Prague or a moon base, although I'm willing to settle for someplace like Hawaii or Tahiti...anywhere there's a chance for a jet ski chase. But America should never settle for allowing so many to live in economic hardship. If we put our minds to it, we could end poverty in 30 years." (Onscreen: "Bush ended Middle Class in eight."). "I want my grand-kids to be born in a country where true economic equality is no longer a goal for the future, but a reality of the present. Oh, and I want my face on money, Secret Service protection for my dogs, and 3 new national holidays: Kate Day, Jack Day, and Emma Claire Day. OK, Kids, you can go to bed now." (Onscreen, "Or else Daddy won't get you a jet ski.") "So, Barack...Hillary... if you want this white male's vote, you're going to have to show you care just as much about the things that really matter to me as I do. And that is the EdWord."

For a grand finale, Barack Obama appeared on the "fixed" big screen television, but Edwards got the good stuff.

Even more humorous in these grim times, candidates (including Mc-Cain) were all appearing on WWE Raw "Smackdown Your Vote." McCain got the best of the lines: "If you want to be the man, you have to beat the man. Come November, it'll be game over., and whatcha' gonna' do when John McCain and all his McCainiacs run wild on you?" Hillary Clinton invited viewers to call her HillRod and "King of the Ring," ultimately stating that the last man standing might be a woman.

Tonight, as the hours tick down to a "must win" state for Hillary Clinton, "Larry King Live" interviewed her. She seemed to be hedging her bets when she said, in response to King's question about whether a win of 5% or less might mean her exit from the race, that "a win is a win." No sign of conceding the electoral process here. Talk, instead, of "seating the delegates from Michigan and Florida," and how "the path to Pennsylvania Avenue goes through Pennsylvania state…"

A clip of Obama was shown, where he succinctly summed up Hillary Clinton's arguments for her election as follows, "Her argument is you can't really change Washington. Because you can't, you might as well pick someone who can play the game better because they've been at it longer." This comment, made by Obama on the stump, was met with jeers from the audience.

Tony Snow, former Bush White House Press Secretary and now a CNN Political Contributor, noted that Obama has figured out that people want optimism and a sense of national unity. He commented that, "It comes down to personality." He added, "Some feel that Obama is not quite ready for prime time. Inconsistent. Half-baked. Who is this guy?" These were some of the themes that Snow, the Republican onscreen, laid out. Of course, as long as we're talking funny here (*or were*), being someone's wife and in the room when they, as President, conducted official business, does not really give you much of an edge in experience, as Michael Reagan noted, when he said that, if that were the criteria, HE should be running for President on the Republican ticket, as he ticked off various official state visits he made with his late father, Ronald Reagan.

Dee Dee Myers, a former Clinton Press Secretary, was correct in saying that most of what Clinton repeated on "Larry King Live" had been heard before. Perhaps some of us not living in Pennsylvania got our first (and perhaps only) glimpse of the ad that Obama said showed Clinton had "gone negative." It was pretty graphic, with Khruschev, war images, and other negative fear-producing tactics right out of Karl Rove's playbook. In addition to those visuals, Osama Bin Laden was a key player onscreen, with the words "You need to be ready for anything." Obama has said that the ad harkens back to the "the politics of fear."

Tony Snow emphasized that Hillary Clinton is going to have to make the point that "I'm better than this guy." On Anderson Cooper's show, Snow and Gloria Borger discussed Howard Dean's heartburn (Dean is Chairman of the Democratic Committee) over the infighting, and an astute analysis of the Keystone state's political make-up told us that, if Barack Obama wins, he would have to win in the state's southeast corridor where 30% of the population resides. Philadelphia is composed of 15% African American voters, and they must turn out. The point was made that Bucks County and Montgomery County started out as Republican counties, but, thanks to Barack Obama's herculean voter registration efforts, those counties now have more registered Democrats. Chester County still remains more Republican, as it has more affluent voters, as does Delaware County. Also, single unmarried women, who are three times more likely to have no medical coverage and make $30,000 or less, may make a difference in tomorrow's vote. They are being courted by both sides.

The Blue Collar Belt in Pennsylvania may have a "bitter" backlash, with Allentown among those towns, which would be sad when there are so many important issues that should better define the race. From Erie to Pittsburgh, there are many Catholics. Obama is having trouble connecting with the Catholic vote. Let's not forget, as previously mentioned, that Pennsylvania is the second-oldest state after Florida. My first thought was that Iowa, too, where all this began, is a very old state, as well, and yet Iowa gave Obama the win over Clinton. In Florida, we'll never know how Obama would have done there, as he played by the previously established rules against campaigning, while Hillary Clinton did not, something that kept Obama's name from even appearing on the Michigan ballot, while Clinton's was there. Now, Hillary seeks to change the rules to favor her last-ditch efforts to secure the nomination of her party, despite winning fewer states and fewer votes. If Hillary's ploy works, it will be shades of Al Gore in Florida and young voters will be disenchanted for generations. (*Note: The ploy failed, but I remember a Texas delegation in Denver threatening to walk out if Hillary did not prevail in seating the disenfranchised Super Delegates.)

Last, but not necessarily least, there is a section of Pennsylvania called "the T" which contains, rural white conservatives. This area is normally thought to be Republican, but any Democrats living there would probably vote for Clinton

My last sight before posting this Night Before the Vote entry was of Theresa Heinz Kerry stumping for Obama. Ketchup heiress. Foreign-born. Annoying woman who won't give up the microphone: "good" or "bad" for the Obama effort?

Only time will tell.

North Carolina, Indiana Primary Results and What's Happening with Hillary Now

Hillary Wins in Indiana—or Does She? Can She Be Stopped, or Will This Campaign for the Nomination Go On Forever?

5/07/2008

It's 3 a.m. in the Midwest, and it's still not clear that Hillary Clinton has won in Indiana, although CBS called the state of Indiana for her at 8 p.m. That seems a tad premature, especially since they hadn't even started counting the votes in Gary, Indiana, (Lake County) until 11 p.m. Apparently, no one had mentioned to Katie Couric and the other CBS correspondents that this Chicago media stronghold also contains a large African-American population, which turned out in droves to give Obama a comeback finish that, even now, at 3 a.m., could result in a Truman/Dewey moment on the morrow. After all, there were still 16,000 uncounted ballots out there in Indiana, and Hillary's lead was only somewhere in the 20,000 range as late as...well, now.

The news that Clinton was canceling her morning news appearances had all the pundits and political analysts abuzz. However, she was still soliciting donations, and one commentator on MSNBC felt it was less-than-sporting to ask for donations when you might be in the process of withdrawing from the race. All the rest said, "Au contraire, mon frere," pointing out how expensive it is to run for office, these days, nationally. A contributor mused on John Glenn's bid for president, which Glenn was paying off for the next 20 years.

I don't know if that anecdote is true or not, but, when you consider that, as one of the original astronauts, Glenn got in on the ground floor in buying land in and around Orlando that was subsequently sold to Disney to develop Disneyland, (thereby pocketing a pretty penny,) you definitely get the impression that money is on everyone's mind right about now. Success breeds success, and failure breeds failure. Hillary's campaign was running on fumes until she pulled the rabbit out of the political hat in Pennsylvania and got some new fuel with a win. Will those sources now wither and dry up in the wake of a very unconvincing "win"…(if, indeed, it remains a "win")…for the former First Lady in the Hoosier state?

Andrea Mitchell, traveling with the Clinton team, said that the Clinton team had acknowledged that they did not do well in North Carolina, which she lost big, but that they did not expect to do well there, with its 40,000 early voters and its large African-American voting bloc. Indiana was supposed to be closer, and it certainly can't get much closer than the 1 a.m. (ET) reports of 1.2 million total votes, 638,275 to 615,862, or 51% to 49%, with Clinton, at this point, ostensibly the winner over Obama—but just barely.

How does Hillary overcome the math now? The Talking Heads say she doesn't. Super Delegates are now being discussed as Super Important (which is not a new topic these days).

The political analysts think that Oregon is competitive for Clinton, that she has a shot in Montana and Puerto Rico on June 1 (with more than a million voters there supposedly in her camp), that she will do well in West Virginia on May 13 and Kentucky on May 20.

"This is clearly a long shot," said Mitchell. "I think if she had lost Indiana, she would be out of it within days, but having won Indiana, I think she'll go on and continue to campaign."

I agree with Jon Stewart who famously asked Obama on "The Daily Show" if he thought that he might get the nomination, run, beat McCain and still find Hillary waiting for him in the Oval Office on his first day in office. The woman just does not quit.

I agree with those who have written that Hillary is now plotting her departure in such a way that she can gracefully exit, preserving her political future, but I also think that Hillary Clinton is now and always has been "in it to spin it." Evan Bayh said that, if she were to lose Indiana, she would "do the responsible thing." He inferred that a loss would finally drive a stake through Clinton's vampiric political heart. But, when night falls, would she emerge, revitalized, seeking new blood?

Is Hillary really sincere in saying that she will work with Barack Obama to help him become president? Andrea Mitchell thinks the New York Senator is sincere, and that she doesn't have the hidden agenda of watching Obama be torn limb-from-limb by McCain in the national election, so that she could come back, Phoenix-like, four years from now and become president in 2012. That's "just a theory" (the coming back in 2012), said Andrea Mitchell. She thinks that Hillary wants to be a good and dutiful Democrat and help the candidate—even if it is archrival Obama—to seize the day and become president. I guess we'll find out.

Is Hillary Clinton going to know when to quit? Stephanie Miller on MSNBC quoted another as saying, "She'll get out of the race when monkeys fly out of my butt." Clinton supporters (somewhat) are in control of the Rules and Bylaws Committee of the Democratic Committee. Harold Ickes is a senior advisor to Senator Clinton and is on the committee. At this time the focus should be on that committee's meeting more than on the upcoming contests, which involve elections going on all the way through early June.

Howard Dean, Chairman of the Democratic Committee, has said that someone has to step down by June. It was under Dean that the bonehead plan to not seat the Florida/Michigan delegates came to fruition as punishment for moving their primaries up, so I'm not sure that the candidates are listening to his words that urgently, at this point.

The Reverend Wright issue was not Barack Obama's best thing to have happen while running for president, (an understatement of the past three or four weeks). Voters going to the polls indicated that the Wright issue was disturbing to them, saying it was "important," but it was not "important" enough to derail the Obama magic. He still pulled it out in North Carolina, big-time, and the percentage as of now is 51 to 49 percent, with Clinton on top at this moment, but all of us waiting for the other shoe to fall. It is fervently hoped by his campaign that Wright won't toddle off to any more NAACP Legal Defense Fund meetings in places like Detroit, or, for that matter, make any more incendiary appearances at the National Press Club meetings. *(With friends like this, who needs enemies? comes to mind as the appropriate cliché).*

Indiana was supposed to be a "tie-breaker" state. Clinton stood before her cheering supporters, saying, "Thanks to you, it's full speed, on to the White House." *(Them's fighting words, and perhaps not sincere ones, at this point.)*

Oh, boy. Here we go again!

When all is said and done, only 2 delegates were at stake on this night. Clinton's win(s) in Pennsylvania and Ohio have been negated by Obama's picking up either a 50/50 split of 36/36 (delegates) in the May 6 contests in North Carolina and Indiana, or a 37/36 split favoring Clinton. Either way, Hillary Clinton does not have the numbers to claim victory, *unless* the committee scheduled to meet on May 31 plays dirty pool, and she continues to play the role of the Robo-Candidate, who cannot be stopped, no matter how many times she is put down.

I agree with the pollsters on MSNBC: "It's over. There's just no way that Hillary Clinton can do this. It's now just a question of how she can do this gracefully. It's over." But… .isn't that what everyone said just before Arnold (Schwarzenegger) rose, again, as "The Terminator." *[I'm thinking of calling Hillary "The Clintonator" in future posts.]*

Obama's campaign official late-breaking campaign comment: "Clinton needed big wins in both states to cut into Obama's overall delegate lead, and she didn't get them. She missed her last chance…and tonight's results have fundamentally changed this race." My final word on that: Well, we'll all see, won't we?

The Fog of War: A Review with Relevance to Today

In"The Fog of War," the 2003 Oscar-winning documentary produced and directed by Errol Morris which seems very apropos for these war-torn times, interview subject Robert McNamara, former Secretary of Defense under Presidents Kennedy and Johnson during the Viet Nam war, offers eleven lessons:

1. Empathize with your enemy.
2. Rationality will not save us.
3. There's something beyond one's self.
4. Maximize efficiency.
5. Proportionality should be a lesson in war.
6. Get the data.
7. Belief and seeing are both often wrong.
8. Be prepared to re-examine your reasoning.
9. In order to do good, you may have to engage in evil.
10. Never say never.
11. You can't change human nature.

McNamara: "Learn from your mistakes. Try to learn. Try to understand what happened. If people do not display wisdom, they will clash like blind moles, and then mutual annihilation will commence."

McNamara asked Castro, post Bay of Pigs, "Would you have recommended that Khruschev use the missiles?"

Castro responded forcefully, that he HAD told Khruschev to use them, admitting that Cuba would have been destroyed.

McNamara shook his head in incredulity, stunned to learn that this was Castro's position.

"Pull the temple down on our heads? My God!"

John Fitzgerald Kennedy (United Nations, September 25, 1961) "Unconditional war can no longer lead to unconditional victory. It can no longer serve to settle our disputes…Mankind must put an end to war, or war will put an end to mankind."

McNamara: "The human race needs to think more about killing… about conflict. Is that what we want in the 21st century… I was part of a mechanism that, in a sense, recommended it." Ninety-nine per cent of the city of Toyama was destroyed on McNamara's watch. Omuta, a city the size of Miami, was 31% destroyed.

McNamara asks whether killing 50 to 90% of the population of 67 Japanese cities and then dropping two nuclear bombs on two Japanese cities was "proportionate." (Lesson 5). He noted there is "no chance to learn from nuclear war…there is no learning power from such an experience. If we'd lost the war (WWII), we all would have been prosecuted as war criminals. What makes it immoral if you lose and NOT immoral if you win?"

Senator Scott called Vietnam, "The war which we can neither win, nor lose, nor drop…Like "W's" "Bring 'em on!", LBJ is heard, in tapes made in the Oval Office, saying that he wants to "whoop the hell out of 'em…kill some of 'em."

LBJ, after John Kennedy's assassination, said, "You can have more war or more appeasement. I always thought it was bad to make any statements about withdrawing."

McNamara: "We were wrong, but we had in our mind a mindset that led to that action. And it led to such heavy costs…we see what we want to believe."

(Rule #1). McNamara related a heated conversation with the man who had once been President of North Vietnam, which occurred many years after the conflict. "We (the North Vietnamese) were fighting for our independence. You were fighting to enslave us. We weren't the pawns of the Chinese or the Russians. We would have fought to the last man," said the North Vietnamese leader. (Point #1).

LBJ: "We're not getting out, but we're trying to hold on to what we have. This is a nasty little war that has turned into a nasty middle-sized war. But America wins the wars she declares. Make no mistake about that!"

McNamara (Lesson #8, "Be prepared to re-examine your reasoning,"): "What makes us omniscient? Do we have a record of omniscience?

None of our allies supported us. If we can't persuade nations with comparable values of the rightness of our cause, we had better re-examine our reasons."

When asked why he continued to support LBJ as he escalated the war, McNamara answered: "It was my responsibility to try to help LBJ carry out the office he thought was in the interests of our people." McNamara won't answer the question of whether he feels guilt at his involvement in sending 58,000 American soldiers to their deaths. When he left office, the nation had experienced 25,000 deaths in Vietnam, half the ultimate toll.

Robert Strange McNamara says, "What I'm doing is thinking it through in hindsight. We all make mistakes. We all know we make mistakes."

Lesson #9 "("In order to do good, you may have to engage in evil.") McNamara: "Human beings must stop killing other human beings. How much evil must we do to do good?"

McNamara (November 1, 1967):"The course we're on is totally wrong. We've got to change it. I love this man. I respect him, but he's totally wrong. At the end, Johnson and I found ourselves poles apart. Something had to give."

McNamara was dismissed as Secretary of Defense and LBJ, on March 31, 1968, announced that his political career was over.

Why Hillary Lost to Barack Obama, or, "How did he beat her; let me count the ways..."

June 4th, 2008

Barack Obama seems to have (finally) clinched the Democratic nomination for President. The path to this Holy Grail has been long and arduous, no less on him than on the public! I think that most of the Democrats, Republicans, Independents, Green Party and all other factions are happy to see the campaign end before the next campaign begins. I know I am. It's been like the Bataan Death March, and I'm sure the candidates couldn't agree more.

Now, the question has been posed: "Why did Hillary lose?' There are many pundits weighing in on this weighty question, and I keep wanting to tell them to read the "Rolling Stone" article that brilliantly described Obama's "bottom-up" campaign strategy, versus Hillary Clinton's old-style "Top down" campaign strategy. Indeed, that article even went so far as to say that, if the Clinton's much-vaunted political machine could lose to that upstart Obama, this will be the last time you will even see the "Top Down" model used in a national campaign.

I don't want to bore readers with all the details of how Obama's people got the cell phone numbers of transient populations like college students and turned them into votes, or how the voter registration drives cranked up record number of eligible voters for the fall general election, or any of the nuts-and-bolts in that "Rolling Stone" article, but let's just say, as someone invited to become an Obama Organizer and attend a two-day training session to learn all the above, the man's organizational know-how was and is amazing.

And, while we're at it, let's look at some of the other factors being cited in the loss of one of the most well-known, (if not well-oiled), political machines that still exists, that of Billary (Bill and Hillary Clinton).

The reasons I have seen cited most prominently for Hillary's loss of the nomination to Barack Obama are as follows:

1) She represents the "Old" school (and certainly this goes double for McCain). Obama represented "change."

2) They were basically the same on the main issues.

3) Hillary Clinton (aka 'Miss Frigidaire') never had the likeability factor going for her, while Obama did, in a phenomenal way.

4) Did race trump gender as a reason to vote? Obama, after all, is the candidate who best represents how the world will look by 2050: multiracial, polyglot, a white mother and a black father producing a child who grew up in many areas of the world and has ties to them and is intellectually aware.

5) Everyman versus Ms. Entitlement. Need I say more?

6) Bill. Need I say more?

7) Obama the phenomenon. (See Point 3 above)

8) Tactical Errors: I would add that there are those that feel Hillary thought she'd have it all wrapped up by Super Tuesday, and the campaign had not been too well thought out past that date. Thus, they were playing catch-up from the beginning, when things did not play out quite the way the Clinton people thought they would.

9) The 8 Years Under Bush, the Younger. Hillary voted for the war. Obama was against the war. Hillary, much more than Obama, is tied to the failed policies of George "W" Bush, even though she was of the opposition party while a Senator from New York. Is there anyone in this country at this time who wants 8 more years of Bush's incompetence, corruption and mismanagement? If so, raise your hand, and we'll send you somewhere to read a book on why that's a very bad idea.

You might start with "In Defense of Liberty" (Richard Clarke, former White House Security Chief under both Clinton and "W"), or you might move on to Clarke's newest one, "Your Government Failed You." I recommend Paul O'Neill's (Former Secretary of the Treasury) "Against All Enemies" and, failing that, try Scott McClellan's (former White House Press Secretary under "W") "What Happened" now hitting the bookstores. There are just so many books out there that give you chapter and verse on an amazingly bad run of Republican government under George W. Bush that, hopefully, will soon give way to something better. (See point #1).

Even staunch conservative Republican (and former Presidential candidate) Pat Buchanan said, in his column yesterday, that Bush, the Younger, while a better campaigner than his father, was not qualified to carry the old man's loafers, in terms of governing. There are too many facts to support that statement, and some have even wondered if, in an amazing display of hubris, the younger Bush simply wanted to whale away at everything his father had stood for, as the CIA took hits under "W", the "I'll finish the war in Iraq, which you should have done" factor (Desert Storm vs. Operation Shock and Awe and Awesome Horribleness), and all the rest of those Bush 2 vs. Bush 1 comparisons. Books have been written about how George W. Bush viewed Reagan as his hero, and brushed aside his father's accomplishments, because dear old Dad was just playing second fiddle to the former film star. The result was "W's" Churchillian attempt to make bold strokes, even if the bold strokes were all wrong. Don't blame me for that analysis. Read the books.

Now, all we have to do is sit back and wait to see if Hillary Clinton is successful in lobbying for a spot on the ticket as the Vice President. If she gets that, and Obama is elected, she'd be "next in line" for the Presidency after he serves out his one or two terms, assuming election. That could be 16 to24 years of Clintons in or around the Oval Office, if Hillary is granted her wish. [You are either rejoicing or groaning as I write that.]

I am assuming election of Barack Obama. I have to. Otherwise, I have to give up all hope that we will get our troops out of Iraq safely and in a way that will both guarantee national security and save (national) face. It is impossible to occupy a country, long-term; the British proved that in India. We must leave. We must leave in a well-thought-out manner (which means that we don't want Bush, Jr., organizing the withdrawal).

We must use the money being wasted on a senseless, useless war (*Vietnam, anyone?*) to build up our country here at home, and the new national leader of our country must turn his attention to "fixing" the many things that George W. Bush broke, both here and abroad. For openers, that individual needs to turn his or her attention to Al Gore's pet issue, the environment and alternative energy sources, and, beyond that, it would be nice to have the tons of money wasted on this useless war to shore up our nation's infrastructure, fix New Orleans, help make our schools better, get gas costs down or find a better solution to using gasoline to running our country at all, and a host of other worthy projects.

Lots of work to do. Let's get cracking!

There are so many things that need fixing now that we almost need a new Department of What "W" Broke to figure out how to prioritize all the many mistakes. But it goes without saying that any "project" of George W. Bush's that is costing thousands of American lives, snuffing out the lifeblood of our American youth (and our country's future) and sending them home to inadequate V.A. facilities with horrific injuries from which they will (probably) never recover, is Number One on my list. And I suspect it is high on Obama's list, as well.

www.ingramcontent.com/pod-product-compliance
Lightning Source LLC
Chambersburg PA
CBHW060838280326
41934CB00007B/832